Fundamentals of Food Preparation

First Edition

Marcy Gaston

Montana State University—Bozeman

SAN DIEGO

Bassim Hamadeh, CEO and Publisher
Kristina Stolte, Senior Field Acquisitions Editor
Alisa Munoz, Project Editor
Casey Hands, Production Editor
Emely Villavicencio, Senior Graphic Designer
Greg Isales, Licensing Associate
Kim Scott/Bumpy Design, Interior Designer
Natalie Piccotti, Senior Marketing Manager
Kassie Graves, Vice President of Editorial
Jamie Giganti, Director of Academic Publishing

3970 Sorrento Valley Blvd., Ste. 500, San Diego, CA 92121

Brief Contents

Detailed Contents

Culinary Basics

OBJECTIVES

- Demonstrate basic knife skills
- Demonstrate principles of making stock
- Demonstrate understanding of professional kitchen practices
- Explain basics of food safety and sanitation

INTRODUCTION

Professional kitchens utilize a variety of equipment and tools for food production. Essential equipment includes knives, pots, pans, ovens, ranges, and other large pieces of equipment. Small equipment includes mixers, and food processors among many others.

In addition to equipment, understanding basic cooking techniques from sautéing to boiling stock to simmering soup is a major part of culinary basics. Each unit in this book provides you with the opportunity to practice not only your knife skills but also many different cooking techniques.

TOOLS AND EQUIPMENT

Knives

Knives come in a variety of shapes and sizes. When using knives, it is important to keep them sharp and the edge straight. Professional knives should be hand-washed.

Here is a list of some classic knife varieties:

Chef's Knife

A chef's knife is an all-purpose, versatile knife used for chopping and slicing. Chef knives have a wide blade and range in length from 6–14 inches.

Cleaver (or Butcher's Knife)

A cleaver is a heavy, wide knife used for splitting meat from the bone. A cleaver can also be used to split large fruit and vegetables like winter squash and watermelon. Cleavers range in size from 6–12 inches.

Utility Knife (or Sandwich Knife)

A utility knife is shorter than a chef's knife but longer than a paring knife. It is used for chopping fruits and vegetables and for cutting sandwiches. The knife's length ranges from 4–7 inches.

Boning Knife

A boning knife has a flexible blade that is used to separate meat from bone.

Paring Knife

A paring knife is a short-bladed knife used for detail cuts. It is best for peeling fruits and vegetables. The length ranges from 3–4 inches.

Slicer

A slicer is a long, thin-bladed knife ranging in length from 8–14 inches. It is used for slicing meat, poultry, and fish.

Serrated or Bread Knife

A serrated knife (or bread knife) has "teeth" for cutting bread or dough.

Straightening Steel

A straightening steel is a steel rod used to hone or straighten the blade of a knife between sharpening.

Pots and Pans

Every kitchen uses a variety of pots and pans for cooking food. Each piece has a specific purpose.

Pots and pans are made with a multitude of metals: cast iron, stainless steel, copper, and aluminum. Choose pots and pans with a heavy bottom.

Cast Iron

Cast iron pans are heavy and made of iron. These pans have been used for decades because they withstand heat well. Due to the iron, these are considered reactive pans: When cooking acidic substances in the pans, a reaction will occur. Also, when exposed to water, the pan will rust. The more the pan is used, the more seasoned it gets. Avoid using soap to wash the pans, as it will wash away the seasoning.

Stainless Steel

Stainless steel is a popular material used in kitchens because it is nonreactive. Depending on the manufacturer, some stainless-steel pots and pans are made with an aluminum or copper core to ensure more even cooking temperatures.

Copper

Copper is an excellent thermal conductor and makes great cookware. However, copper reacts with acidic ingredients like tomato sauce, which leaches copper metals into the food. To prevent this some copper cookware is lined with stainless steel.

Aluminum

Aluminum is a soft metal that is a good thermal conductor. Like copper, it also reacts with acidic ingredients, giving them a metallic flavor.

Nonstick

Teflon is a common nonstick pan. Nonstick pans are good for cooking eggs and other items that have a tendency to stick. Do not heat nonstick pans above 600°F and avoid using metal utensils in the pan, which can scratch the surface.

Types of Pots and Pans

Sauté Pan

A sauté pan has straight sides. It ranges in size from 3 to 6 quarts.

Skillet

A skillet has sloped sides and ranges in size up to 14 inches.

Stock Pot

A stock pot is a large pot ranging in size from 6 to 12 quarts. Used for cooking stocks, stews, and soups.

Saucepan/Saucepot

Small pots and pans ranging in size from 1 to 5 quarts. Used for a variety of things from making sauces to cooking rice.

Dutch Oven

A dutch oven is a thick-walled cooking pot traditionally made from cast iron but can be stainless steel or ceramic. Generally used for soups and stews as well as braising.

Additional Equipment

Stove

A stove is a direct heat source for cooking food. Heat is produced via gas flame or electric element. Some electric stoves have an induction cooktop that uses magnetic induction to heat cookware. For the induction to work, the cookware needs to be made from ferromagnetic metal such as cast iron or stainless steel.

Oven

An oven is a thermally insulated chamber for heating, roasting, and baking. Fuel source is either gas or electric.

Broiler/Salamander

A broiler or salamander is used to brown or caramelize the top surface of food using gas or electric heat.

Mixer

A mixer can be hand-held or on a stand. They are used for mixing batters and doughs, whipping egg whites and heavy cream, and kneading yeast bread dough.

Food Processor

A food processor contains a sharp steel blade for chopping, grinding, and pureeing food.

Blender

A blender uses a sharp steel blade for emulsifying or pureeing liquids or soups.

Steam Kettle

A steam kettle is a large piece of equipment in commercial kitchens used to cook large batches of soups and stocks.

Grill

A grill is a direct heat source where food is cooked on a metal grate over an open flame fueled by wood, charcoal, or gas.

Tilt Skillet

A tilt skillet is a large piece of equipment in commercial kitchens used to sauté large batches of food.

FOOD SAFETY AND SANITATION[1]

Part of working in a kitchen is utilizing basic food safety and sanitation principles. These principles help reduce incidences of foodborne illness outbreaks.

Good Personal Hygiene

Wash your hands before starting to cook and continually wash your hands as you change tasks, work with raw meat, poultry, and seafood, and after eating, drinking, smoking, and using the restroom.

Cleaning and Sanitation

Clean and sanitize all work surfaces prior to and after cooking.

Prevent Cross Contamination

Keep raw foods separate from ready-to-eat foods by using separate equipment and cutting boards, prepping foods at different times, and/or washing and sanitizing equipment between uses.

Keep Cold Foods Cold, Hot Foods Hot

Keep foods out of the temperature danger zone of 40–140ºF. Cold foods should be kept at 40ºF or below, and hot foods should be kept at 140ºF or higher.

Cooling and Thawing Properly

Cool hot food to 70ºF within two hours after cooking if storing under refrigeration. To thaw frozen foods, use proper methods for thawing food safely.

Food can be thawed in the following ways:

- Under refrigeration
- Under cool running water
- In a microwave (must be cooked immediately after)
- Thaw as part of the cooking process

Cooking to Correct Temperatures

Foods need to be cooked to proper temperatures to ensure food safety. Please refer to the temperatures listed in this book for specific temperatures.

Storing Basics

Leftover food should be kept for up to seven days under refrigeration. Store ready-to-eat foods on the top shelf of the refrigerator and store poultry on the bottom shelf of the cooler to prevent risk of cross contamination.

Food and equipment should be stored 6 inches above the floor. Food and equipment should also be kept away from bathrooms, sewer lines, and locker rooms.

Store chemicals away from food. Keep chemicals in their containers. Do not repurpose chemical containers for food storage.

COOKING METHODS

When cooking food, different cooking methods are used: dry heat, moist heat, or a combination.

Dry heat cooking methods use air or fat to cook foods. These cooking methods include baking, broiling, frying, grilling, pan frying, roasting, and sautéing.

Moist heat cooking methods use water or steam to cook foods and include boiling, poaching, simmering, and steaming.

Braising and stewing use a combination of the dry and moist heat cooking methods.

BASIC COOKING TERMS

Baking—food is cooked in hot oven using hot air

Boiling—cooking food in a liquid that is at its boiling point

Braising—combines moist and dry heat cooking methods. Food is sautéed or seared in a small amount of fat. Liquid is added and the food is simmered slowly until tender

Broiling—food is cooked directly under heat source to achieve browning or caramelization of the food's surface

Caramelization—oxidation of sugar in the presence of protein. Non-enzymatic browning reaction

Deep frying—submerging and cooking food in a vat of hot oil

Deglazing—pouring liquid (water, stock, or alcohol) into the bottom on a pan to dissolve and release food residue

Grilling—food cooked directly above an open flame fueled by gas, charcoal, or wood

Mise en place—put everything in its place. Before cooking, gather and prep all ingredients

Pan frying—cooking foods in a skillet or sauté pan with hot oil or fat

Poaching—cooking food in a liquid, such as water, milk, stock, or wine. Food is cooked at a low temperature to ensure gentle cooking

Roasting—similar to baking where food is cooked in a hot oven

Sauté—French word meaning, "to jump." Cooking food quickly in a small amount of fat in a sauté pan or skillet

Stewing—similar to braising except that the food is covered with a lid during cooking

KNIFE SKILLS

Professional chefs spend many hours perfecting their knife skills. Being able to chop food in a quick and efficient manger is the basis for developing knife skills.

Basic Knife Cuts

Chiffonade—ribbon cut. Great for dark leafy greens or herbs like basil. Stack the leaves of the herb or vegetable and roll up like a cigar. Rock the knife through the rolled-up leaves to produce ribbons.

Mincing—finely chop vegetables like garlic, ginger, and onions

Dicing—cutting food into uniform sizes that can be small, medium, or large cubes

Julienne—cutting food into thin strips that look like matchsticks

FIGURE 1.1 Knife Cuts Labeled

STOCK

Stock is flavored liquid used as the base for many soups, stews, and sauces. Basic ingredients include bones, mirepoix, aromatics, and water. Vegetable and mushroom stocks omit the bones and increase the amount of vegetables used.

Bones

Meat and poultry bones are used to make stock, adding flavor and color. Beef and veal bones contain collagen, making the stock richer in flavor. Bones from other animals can be used to make stock: fish, shellfish, shells, lamb, turkey, and pigs or hogs.

> Collagen: group of proteins formed in connective tissues of animals—mostly mammals. In the presence of heat (140–160°F) the proteins denature and the individual molecules form into gelatin.

Mirepoix

Mirepoix is a mixture of onions, carrots, and celery to enhance the flavor and aroma of stock. Usually measured by weight of 50% onions, 25% carrots, and 25% celery; the amount of mirepoix used is based on the number of bones used. A typical stock recipe yielding in 1 gallon of stock will call for 8 pounds bones and 1 pound mirepoix.

Aromatics

A set of aromatics is added to the stock, lending additional flavor. Peppercorns, parsley stems, thyme, garlic, bay leaves are typical aromatics used.

RECIPES

Vegetable Stock

Yield: 1/2 gallon

- 1 medium onion, diced small
- 3 medium carrots, diced small
- 3 ribs celery, diced small
- 1 leek, rinsed and diced
- 2 broccoli stems, roughly chopped
- 1 bay leaf
- 4 parsley stems
- 2 sprigs fresh thyme
- 1 teaspoon peppercorns
- 1 garlic clove, smashed
- 8 cups water

Add all ingredients to a stock pot. Bring to a boil. Reduce heat to low. Simmer for one hour. Strain and reserve liquid. Cool liquid in an ice bath to 70°F. Refrigerate for up to three days or freeze up to twelve months.

Mushroom Stock

Yield: 1/2 gallon

- 1 pound mushrooms, rinsed and cut into quarters
- 2 leeks, rinsed and diced
- 1/2 medium onion, diced small
- 2 medium carrots, diced small
- 2 ribs celery, diced small
- 1 parsnip, peeled and diced small
- 1–2 tablespoons canola oil
- 1 teaspoon salt
- 1 teaspoon ground pepper
- 1 bay leaf
- 4 parsley stems
- 2 sprigs fresh thyme
- 1/2 teaspoon peppercorns
- 1 garlic clove, smashed
- 8 cups water

Preheat oven to 425°F.

On a baking sheet, toss together the mushrooms, leeks, onions, carrots, celery, and parsnips. Drizzle with oil and season with salt and pepper. Bake for 20–30 minutes or until lightly golden brown.

Scrape the roasted vegetables into a stock pot. Add the bay leaf, parsley stems, thyme, peppercorns, and garlic. Pour in 8 cups water. Bring to a boil. Reduce heat to low. Simmer for 45 minutes. Strain and reserve liquid. Cool liquid in an ice bath to 70ºF. Refrigerate for up to three days or freeze up to twelve months.

Brown Chicken Stock
Yield: 1/2 gallon

- 2 pounds chicken bones
- 8 cups water
- 1 large onion, diced
- 4 ribs celery, large dice
- 3 carrots, diced large
- 2 tablespoons tomato paste
- 6 parsley stems
- 4 sprigs fresh thyme
- 2 garlic cloves
- 1 bay leaf
- 1 teaspoon peppercorns

Preheat oven to 375ºF.

Place the chicken bones in a roasting pan. Bake the chicken until the bones are golden brown. Remove from the oven and place the chicken bones in a large stock pot. Pour 7 cups water over the bones and place over medium heat.

Place the roasting pan over medium heat. Add the onion, celery, and carrots to the pan. Cook until the vegetables begin to brown. Scrape up chicken bits if necessary. Add the tomato paste. Cook for 2 minutes longer. Deglaze with 1 cup of water.

Scrape vegetables into the stock pot with the chicken and add the parsley, thyme, garlic cloves, bay leaf, and peppercorns. Bring to a boil. Reduce heat to simmer. Simmer for 4–5 hours. Strain and reserve liquid. Cool liquid in an ice bath to 70ºF. Refrigerate for up to three days or freeze up to twelve months.

White Chicken Stock
Yield: 1/2 gallon

- 2 pounds chicken bones
- 1 large onion, diced
- 4 ribs celery, diced large
- 3 carrots, diced large
- 6 parsley stems
- 4 sprigs fresh thyme
- 2 garlic cloves
- 1 bay leaf
- 1 teaspoon peppercorns
- 8 cups water

Add all ingredients to a stock pot. Bring to a boil. Reduce heat to low. Simmer for 4 hours. Strain and reserve liquid. Cool liquid in an ice bath to 70ºF. Refrigerate for up to three days or freeze up to twelve months.

Beef Stock

Yield: 1/2 gallon

- 3 pounds beef bones
- 8 cups water
- 1 large onion, diced
- 4 ribs celery, diced large
- 3 carrots, diced large
- 2 tablespoons tomato paste

- 6 parsley stems
- 4 sprigs fresh thyme
- 2 garlic cloves
- 1 bay leaf
- 1 teaspoon peppercorns

Preheat oven to 375°F.

Place the beef bones in a roasting pan. Bake until the bones are golden brown. Remove from the oven and place the bones in a large stock pot. Pour 7 cups water over the bones and place over medium heat.

Place the roasting pan over medium heat. Add the onion, celery, and carrots in the pan. Cook until the vegetables begin to brown. Scrape up bits if necessary. Add the tomato paste. Cook for 2 minutes longer. Deglaze with 1 cup of water.

Scrape vegetables into the stock pot with the chicken and add the parsley, thyme, garlic cloves, bay leaf, and peppercorns. Bring to a boil. Reduce heat to simmer. Simmer for 4–5 hours. Strain and reserve liquid. Cool liquid in an ice bath to 70°F. Refrigerate for up to three days or freeze up to twelve months.

Unit 1 Questions

1. Why is stock cooled down in an ice bath before placing it in the refrigerator or freezer?
2. What are the benefits of chopping vegetables in uniform shapes and sizes?
3. Why are the bones and vegetables in the brown chicken and beef stock recipes roasted prior to cooking in water?
4. What is important to make a flavorful stock?
5. What causes beef stock to gelatinize when it cools?

NOTE

1. "Basics for Handling Food Safely," USDA, modified March 24, 2015, accessed March 27, 2020, https://www.fsis.usda.gov/wps/portal/fsis/topics/food-safety-education/get-answers/food-safety-fact-sheets/safe-food-handling/basics-for-handling-food-safely/ct_index.

BIBLIOGRAPHY

USDA. "Basics for Handling Food Safely," modified March 24, 2015, accessed March 27, 2020, https://www.fsis.usda.gov/wps/portal/fsis/topics/food-safety-education/get-answers/food-safety-fact-sheets/safe-food-handling/basics-for-handling-food-safely/ct_index.

Measurements, Conversions, and Sensory Evaluation

- Evaluate food using sensory evaluation
- Demonstrate proper measurement techniques
- Demonstrate ability to convert recipes
- Evaluate and describe differences in salt and spices

MEASUREMENTS AND CONVERSIONS

Utilizing proper measuring techniques, especially in baking, is important to achieve high quality products with optimal results.

Volume and weight are the two ways to measure food. Weight is the preferred method of measurement because it leaves little room for error, especially if using digital scales. When converting recipes for mass production and for purchasing large quantities of food, using weighted measurements is ideal for ease and accuracy. For weights, the United States uses the imperial system, which includes pounds and ounces. Other countries around the world use the metric system, which consists of kilograms and grams.

In contrast, volume measurement, is the technique most home cooks in the United States use and as a result, it is how most American recipes are written. This method uses standard cups and measuring spoons (both liquid and dry). Gallons, quarts, pints, cups, and measuring spoons are measured in fluid ounces. Volume measurement in the metric system consists of liters and milliliters.

Most recipes that are written with *volume measurements* will typically write the ingredient list as:

- 1 cup flour
- ¾ cup sugar
- 1 cup milk (or 8 fluid ounces)

If a recipe is written using *weight* measurements, the ingredient list will look like this:

- 8 ounces flour
- 4 ounces sugar
- 8 fluid ounces milk

Most ingredients do not have the same weight and volume measurement. For instance, 8 ounces of flour by weight is not the same as 8 ounces (1 cup) of flour by volume.

However, two products have the same weight and volume measurement – water and butter. Eight ounces of butter weighed equals 8 ounces of butter melted.

MEASURING TOOLS

Volume

Liquid measuring cups—used for liquids, not dry ingredients. Most liquid measuring cups have marking for fluid ounces, milliliters, and cups

Dry measuring cups—used for dry ingredients (including peanut butter, yogurt, sour cream, and other ingredients that are between dry and wet)

Measuring spoons—used for measuring small amounts of ingredients both dry and liquid

Weight

Digital scale—offers digital readout along with the ability to change units according to the needs of the recipe

Dial scale—typically specific to one or two units (like ounces and/or pounds)

Balance scales—sometimes called "baker's scale," these use a set of weights for precise measurement

Here is a list of commonly used measurements and their standard abbreviations.

TABLE 2.1

Commonly used measurements	Standard Abbreviation(s)
Teaspoon	t, tsp
Tablespoon	T, tbsp
Cup	c
Ounces	oz.
Pound	lb. or #
Fluid ounce	fl. oz.
Pint	pt.
Quart	qt.

Gallon	gal.
Kilogram	kg
Gram	g
Milliliter	ml
Liter	l

CONVERSIONS

Converting recipes is an important skill for anyone working in foodservice.

The following table lists common conversions for both volume and weight that are used in cooking.

TABLE 2.2

Common Conversions	
Measurement	**Equivalent**
3 teaspoons	1 tablespoon
4 tablespoons	1/4 cup
5 1/3 tablespoons	1/3 cup
16 tablespoons	1 cup
1 cup	8 fl. oz.
2 cups	1 pint
2 pints	1 quart
4 cups	1 quart
4 quarts	1 gallon
16 ounces	1 pound
1 kilogram	2.2 pounds
28 grams	1 ounce
454 grams	1 pound
240 ml	8 fl. oz.
30 ml	1 fl. oz.
15 ml	1 tablespoon
1000 ml	1 liter
1000 g	1 kilogram
1 stick of butter	4 ounces
1 stick of butter	8 tablespoons
1 tablespoon butter	1/2 ounce

Temperature Conversions

Occasionally, you may come across a recipe using Celsius as the temperature. In that case, use the following formula for converting Celsius to Fahrenheit and vice versa.

$$°C = (°F - 32) / 1.8$$
$$°F = 1.8(°C) + 32$$

Recipe Conversions

Converting recipes to serve more or less than the yield of the recipe is important to know for anyone working in foodservice. To convert recipes, you need to first find the *conversion factor*.

$$\text{Conversion Factor} = \frac{\text{desired \# of serving}}{\text{original serving}}$$

After you find the conversion factor, multiply this by the quantity of each ingredient of the recipe.

Example

Recipe yields 8 servings, but you want it to either make 2 or 20 servings.

<u>Two people:</u>

2 servings / 8 servings = 0.25 (conversion factor)
Multiply 0.25 × quantity of each ingredient: 2 quarts of milk × 0.25 = 0.5 quarts of milk

<u>Twenty people:</u>

20 servings / 8 servings = 2.5 (conversion factor)
Multiply 2.5 × quantity of each ingredient: 2 quarts of milk × 2.5 = 5 quarts of milk

Efficiency

Sometimes when you convert recipes, you may need to find a more efficient way to write the quantity.

For instance, in the recipe conversion example above, it would be more efficient to write 1 pint milk instead of 0.5 quarts of milk.

When you convert recipes for bigger yields, you may have an ingredient amount increase from 1 tablespoon to 16 tablespoons. In this case, it would be more efficient to write 1 cup instead of 16 tablespoons.

Volume Measuring Techniques

Flour and Sugar

Flour and sugar should be measured using the spoon and knife method. Spoon unsifted flour or sugar into a dry measuring cup. Level the flour with the back of a knife (the straight edge).

Brown Sugar

Unless otherwise specified in the recipe, brown sugar should be packed into dry measuring cups and leveled off.

Shortening

To measure shortening, use either of these methods:

- Dry measuring method: Spoon shortening into the cup and press down to remove any air pockets. Level the top with the back of a knife.
- Water displacement method: Pour 1 cup cold water into a 2-cup liquid measuring cup. Add the shortening to the desired amount (1/2 cup, 1 cup, etc.). The weight of the shortening displaces the water.

SENSORY EVALUATION

Take a moment and close your eyes. Think of your favorite food. When you think of eating this food, what are you concentrating on? Flavor? Appearance? Texture? Aroma? Are you thinking of all these things?

When we eat food, we use all of our senses to evaluate food. Working together, the four basic senses—taste, smell, touch, sound, and sight—help us determine which foods we prefer.

To evaluate food properly, familiarize yourself with the following terms.

Quality

Degree of excellence. When pertaining to food, quality encompasses many factors such as appearance, taste, flavor, aroma, and texture. It is a subjective form of evaluation.

Appearance

How the food looks, appears, and/or is presented. For appearance, you can evaluate the shape, size, and color of the food.

Taste

Taste uses primary taste buds: bitter, sweet, salty, sour, umami.

Aroma

Smell of the food. The temperature affects the aroma. Higher temperatures create better flavor perception.

Flavor

This is the overall impression of food. It is a combination of taste and aroma.

Texture

Physical characteristics of the food.

Mouthfeel

Physical sensation of the food in the mouth.

When learning to evaluate food, it is helpful to have a list of adjectives used to describe food. Once you gain more practice in tasting and evaluating food, you will add to this list.

TABLE 2.3

Adjectives Used to Describe Food				
Appearance	**Flavor**	**Texture**	**Aroma**	**Mouthfeel**
Wilted	Juicy	Spongy	Ambrosial	Bubbly
Sizzling	Intense	Soupy	Anosmic	Chewy
Shiny	Rich	Soft	Balmy	Creamy/milky
Shape	Stale	Slimy	Comforting	Coating
Moist	Tangy	Crunchy	Fetid	Effervescent
Grainy	Zesty	Rubbery	Foul	Gelatinous
Curdled	Savory	Tough	Fragrant	Gummy
Creamy	Smokey	Lumpy	Floral	Slimy
Puffy	Yeasty	Fibrous	Fresh	Tender
Fluffy	Nutty	Limp	Heady	Velvety
Caramelized	Decadent	Crusty	Malodorous	
Brackish	Luscious	Flaky	Odorless	
Smooth	Peppery	Creamy	Piquant	
Color (brown, black, etc.)	Salty	Chewy	Pungent	
Dry	Metallic	Tender	Rank	
Greasy	Putrid	Gooey	Savory	
Sticky	Minty	Gummy	Sweet	
Rounded	Acidic	Thin		
Sunken	Sharp	Thick		
Blackened	Sweet	Firm		
Appetizing	Bland	Hard		
	Fruity	Rough		
	Milky	Smooth		
	Mild	Crispy		
	Sour	Crumbly		
	Spicy	Gritty		
	Soapy			
	Rancid			
	Eggy			
	Burnt			

Salt/Sodium[1]

Sodium plays many vital roles in cooking. For centuries, salt was used primarily as a preservative to keep food from spoiling due to lack of refrigeration. However, over the years, salt has come to be understood for its many roles, from being a flavoring agent to helping bind food together to improving texture of baked goods.

Sodium versus Salt

Basically speaking, sodium is a mineral (Na), and salt is a chemical compound (NaCl). Sodium is found naturally in foods such as beets, celery, and Swiss chard; salt is a crystallized structure found in oceans and comprised of 40% sodium molecules and 60% chloride. Sodium is found in many preservatives: sodium bicarbonate (baking soda), sodium nitrate, and sodium nitrites. In cooking, however, chefs and food manufacturers typically use salt to season and cure food.

Salt's role in Flavor Perception

When added to foods, salt not only increases the "saltiness" flavor of the food, it also has been found to enhance the perception of a food's thickness and sweetness, mask metallic flavors, and improve the overall flavor balance.

This may be due to several factors, including salt's role in decreasing the water activity of food, which may increase the concentration of other flavors. No matter the avenue salt takes in affecting the flavor of food, it is a major part of cooking and eating.

Herbs and Spices

Herbs and spices are used to enhance the flavor of a particular dish. Even though they are often paired together, herbs and spices are different categories of flavoring agents. Spices are comprised of the seed, fruit, or bark of certain plants. Not only are spices used for flavoring dishes, but they can provide color or be used to preserve food. Spices are generally used in dried form, but a few can be used fresh, such as ginger or turmeric. If using dried spices, the most flavor comes from using whole spices and grinding them just before using. Spices can also be toasted slightly to enhance their flavor or bring a hint of nuttiness to the flavor profile.

Herbs consist of the leaves, flowers, or stems of herbaceous plants and are primarily used for flavoring. Herbs can be purchased fresh or dried. Dried herbs have a more potent flavor than fresh counterparts. If substituting fresh herbs for dried (or vice versa), use the following ratio: 1 part dried herbs to 3 parts fresh herbs.

Dried herbs can be added early in the cooking process, but fresh herbs should be added towards the end of the cooking process to preserve their flavor. One notable exception is fresh rosemary, which can be added at the start of the cooking process to help release its flavor.

Tasting Food

Tasting food for proper levels of salt, spice, or overall flavor is an important step in the cooking process. Some recipes call for a specific amount of salt, spices, or herbs to be added while other recipes may state, "salt and pepper, to taste." Either way, you should train yourself to taste food as it cooks, adjusting the flavors accordingly.

TASTING EVALUATIONS

Evaluation 1: Ranking Test

Ranking tests two or more samples and ranks them according to flavor or odor intensity. Three items of similar flavor profile are chosen. Rank the items in order of intensity and in order of preference.

Food Item	Intensity	Preference
#1 – Most		
#2		
#3 – Least		

Evaluation 2: Describing Food Based on Textures, Appearance, Aroma, Flavor, and Taste

When presented with several varying types of food, practice describing the food based on texture, appearance, aroma, flavor, and taste.

Taste should be limited to describing the food based on the five taste buds: salty, sour, bitter, sweet, and umami.

Use the adjectives provided earlier in the chapter to help you describe the foods.

Food Item	Texture	Appearance	Aroma	Flavor

EXPERIMENTS

Experiment 1: Fat and Sodium

Evaluate the flavor of reduced-sodium soup. Does fat content affect sodium flavor?

Basic Cream of Mushroom Soup (control)

- 1 tablespoon olive oil
- 1 tablespoon unsalted butter
- 8 ounces cremini or white mushrooms, cleaned and roughly chopped
- 1 ounce shiitake mushrooms, chopped
- 2 tablespoons minced shallots
- 1 clove garlic, minced
- 1/2 teaspoon Kosher salt
- 1/4 teaspoon dried tarragon
- 1 cup vegetable stock (regular sodium content)
- 2 tablespoons heavy cream
- 1/4 teaspoon black pepper

Heat the oil and butter in a saucepan placed over medium high heat. Add the mushrooms when the butter is melted. Sauté for 8–10 minutes or until they are lightly brown.

Reduce heat to medium and add the shallots and garlic; cook for 1 minute.

Add the salt, tarragon, and stock to the pot. Increase heat to medium high to bring to a boil; reduce heat to medium low and simmer for 10 minutes. Remove from heat.

Puree the soup using an immersion blender (or regular blender); puree until smooth.

Return soup back to the pot and stir in the cream and black pepper. Cook for 5 minutes on low heat. Serve.

Variations:

1. Regular sodium + regular fat content (control)
   - No change to the recipe
2. Reduced sodium + regular fat content
   - Reduce salt to 1/4 teaspoon
   - Substitute no sodium vegetable stock for the vegetable stock
3. High sodium + regular fat content
   - Increase salt to 1 teaspoon
4. Regular sodium + reduced fat content
   - Substitute 2 tablespoons fat free greek yogurt for the cream
5. Reduced sodium + reduced fat content
   - Substitute 2 tablespoons fat-free greek yogurt for the cream
   - Reduce salt to 1/4 teaspoon
   - Substitute no-sodium vegetable stock for the vegetable stock
6. High sodium + reduced fat content
   - Substitute 2 tablespoons fat free greek yogurt for the cream
   - Increase salt to 1 teaspoon

Variation	Flavor (overall)	Degree of "saltiness"	Additional Notes
Control—Reg. sodium; Reg. fat			
Reduced sodium; Reg. fat			
High sodium; Reg. fat			
Regular sodium; Reduced fat			
Reduced sodium; Reduced fat			
High sodium; Reduced fat			

Experiment 2: Low Sodium

Sodium-free seasonings: Which one is the best?

Basic Chicken Recipe (control):

- 1 chicken breast
- 2 teaspoons canola oil
- 1/4 teaspoon Kosher salt
- 1/4 teaspoon black pepper

Preheat oven to 350°F. Rub chicken breast with the canola oil. Place on a small baking sheet. Sprinkle the chicken with the salt and pepper. Bake chicken until cooked to an internal temperature of 165°F, about 10–15 minutes. Slice into pieces and serve.

Variations:

In place of the salt and pepper, use:

- 1/2 teaspoon Mrs. Dash sodium-free seasoning (any flavor)
- 1/2 teaspoon sodium-free Herbes de Provence
- 1/2 teaspoon lemon zest mixed with 1/4 teaspoon black pepper
- 1/4 teaspoon each of sodium-free chili powder (ancho, chipotle, etc.), ground cumin, and garlic powder
- 1 teaspoon finely chopped fresh rosemary mixed with 1/2 teaspoon minced fresh garlic
- 1 teaspoon finely chopped fresh rosemary mixed with 1/2 teaspoon minced fresh garlic and 1/2 teaspoon lemon zest

Variation	Flavor (overall)	Degree of "saltiness"	Additional Notes
Control: Basic recipe			
Mrs. Dash			
Herbes de Provence			
Lemon zest and black pepper			
Chili powder			
Rosemary and garlic			
Rosemary, garlic, and lemon			

Experiment 3: Measurement

This experiment explores measuring basic baking ingredients (flour and sugar) to determine the difference between volume and weighed measurements.

Method 1: Dry Volume to Weighed

1. Measure 1 cup (in dry measuring cup) of AP flour, granulated sugar, and firmly packed brown sugar. The flour and granulated sugar should be measured via the spoon and knife method.
2. Using a digital scale, weigh ingredients individually. Record results in the table below.

Ingredient	Dry Measure Amount	Weight in Ounces
AP Flour	1 cup	
Granulated sugar	1 cup	
Brown sugar	1 cup	

Method 2: Weighed ingredient to Volume

1. Using a digital scale, individually weigh 8 ounces of AP flour, granulated sugar, and brown sugar.
2. Measure each of the 8 ounces of the flour, sugar, and brown sugar, using dry measuring cups and measuring spoons. Try to get an exact volume measurement. Record results below.

Ingredient	Weight in Ounces	Dry Measure Amount
AP flour	8 ounces	
Granulated sugar	8 ounces	
Brown sugar	8 ounces	

RECIPES

The recipes in this unit all use different spices. When tasting and evaluating the recipes, note the flavor of each spice.

Roasted Carrots with Allspice
Serves 3–4

- 1 pound carrots, cut into 1- to 2-inch chunks
- 1 tablespoon canola or olive oil
- 1/2 teaspoon ground allspice
- salt and pepper, to taste
- 1 large garlic clove, minced

Preheat oven to 425°F.

Place the carrots in a bowl. Toss with the oil, allspice, salt, and pepper. Spread carrots onto a baking sheet. Bake until the carrots are tender, about 20–25 minutes.

Remove from oven and add the garlic. Toss to coat the carrots well with the garlic. Adjust seasonings to taste.

Fennel Spiced Potatoes
Serves 3–4

- 1 teaspoon ground fennel
- 1/4 teaspoon ground coriander
- 1/2 teaspoon salt
- 1/2 teaspoon pepper
- 3 russet potatoes, cut into steak fries
- 2 tablespoons canola oil

Preheat oven to 475°F.

In a small bowl, mix together the fennel, coriander, salt, and pepper. Place the potatoes in a bowl and toss with the oil and spices.

Spread onto a baking sheet. Bake until lightly golden brown and tender, about 25–30 minutes.

Roasted Carrot Coriander Soup

Yield: 1 1/2 quarts

Serves 4–5

- 1 pound carrots, cut into 1/2-inch pieces
- 1 medium russet potato, peeled and diced
- 2 tablespoons canola or olive oil
- 1 medium white or yellow onion, diced
- 1 clove garlic, minced
- 1 tablespoon grated fresh ginger
- 1 tablespoon ground coriander
- 1 quart low-sodium vegetable stock
- 1/2 cup fresh orange juice
- 1/2 cup half and half OR full fat coconut milk
- salt and pepper, to taste

Preheat oven to 375ºF. Place the carrots and potatoes on a baking sheet and toss with 1 tablespoon oil. Bake in oven for 20–25 minutes or until the vegetables are fork tender.

Heat the remaining 1 tablespoon olive oil in a soup pot set over medium heat. Add the onions, garlic, and ginger. Sauté until onions are soft, about 5–7 minutes. Add the coriander and sauté for 1 minute. Season lightly with salt and pepper. Add the vegetable stock, orange juice, carrots, and potatoes. Cook for 15 minutes.

Puree in a blender or with an immersion blend until smooth. Add the half-and-half; blend to combine. Adjust seasonings to taste. Serve hot.

Spicy Black Bean Salsa

Yield: 2 cups

- 1 (15 ounce) container black beans, drained and rinsed
- 1/4 cup red onion, diced small
- 1/2 cup red bell pepper, diced small
- 1 (15 ounce) can diced tomatoes
- 1 cup frozen corn, thawed
- 1 clove garlic, minced
- 2–3 tablespoons fresh lime juice
- 1 teaspoon ground cayenne
- 1 tablespoon finely chopped fresh cilantro
- salt and pepper, to taste

In a large bowl, mix together all ingredients. Let sit for 30 minutes before serving. Serve with tortilla chips.

Roast Chickpeas
Yield: 2 cups

- 2 (15-ounce) cans chickpeas, drained and rinsed
- 2 tablespoons olive oil
- 1 to 1 1/2 teaspoons kosher salt
- 2 to 4 teaspoons spices or finely chopped fresh herbs, such as chili powder, curry powder, garam masala, cumin, smoked paprika, rosemary, thyme, or other favorite spices and herbs

Preheat the oven to 400°F.

Pat the chickpeas very dry with a clean dishtowel or paper towels. They should look matte and feel dry to the touch; if you have time, leave them to air-dry for a few minutes.

Place the chickpeas in a bowl and drizzle with the oil and sprinkle with the salt. Spread onto a baking sheet.

Roast, stirring the chickpeas or shaking the pan every 10 minutes. The chickpeas are done when golden and slightly darkened, dry and crispy on the outside, and soft on the inside, about 20 to 30 minutes.

Sprinkle the spices over the chickpeas and stir to coat evenly. Serve while the chickpeas are still warm and crispy. They will gradually lose their crispiness as they cool, becoming chewy.

Cinnamon Apples
Serves 4

- 2 tablespoons fresh orange juice
- 1 tablespoon unsalted butter
- 1/2 cup packed brown sugar
- 4 apples (McIntosh, Gala, Braeburn, Honeycrisp, or Fuji), sliced
- 1 teaspoon cinnamon
- 1/4 teaspoon salt
- 1/4 teaspoon nutmeg (optional)

Place a sauté pan over medium heat. Add the orange juice and butter. Swirl the pan to melt the butter. Add the brown sugar. Stir to dissolve the sugar. Add the apples, cinnamon, salt, and nutmeg. Coat the apples well with the mixture. Sauté over medium low heat until tender, about 5–8 minutes.

Serve warm sprinkled with toasted nuts and/or granola.

Kale Chips
Yield: 2 cups

- 4 cups kale, cut into bite sized pieces
- 1–2 tablespoons canola or safflower oil
- 1/2 teaspoon salt
- Spices of choice: curry powder, ancho powder, garlic powder, onion powder, chili powder, cumin, coriander, garam masala, paprika, etc.

Preheat oven to 350°F.

Wash kale well in cold water. Dry the leaves by spinning in a salad spinner or rubbing between two towels. The goal is to remove as much water as possible before baking.

Place the kale in a bowl. Add the oil, salt, and spices of choice. Toss to coat the kale well. Spread onto a baking sheet. Bake until slightly crispy and golden brown, about 10–15 minutes.

Brown Butter Cardamom Cookies
Yield: 2 dozen cookies

- 1 cup unsalted butter
- 2 cups AP flour
- 1 1/2 teaspoons ground cardamom
- 1/2 teaspoon salt
- 3/4 cup sugar
- 1 egg yolk
- 1 tablespoon heavy cream
- 1 1/2 teaspoons vanilla extract
- 1 teaspoon orange zest
- 1 to 2 cups powdered sugar

Place the butter in a sauté pan set over medium heat. Melt and brown the butter until it turns an amber color, about 3–5 minutes. Pour into a bowl and refrigerate until room temperature, about 15 minutes.

Preheat oven to 350°F.

In a small bowl, stir together the flour, cardamom, and salt. Set aside.

In a mixing bowl, mix together the butter, sugar, egg yolk, cream, vanilla, and orange zest. Mix until well combined. Stir in the flour mixture and mix until a stiff dough forms. If the mixture feels a little crumbly, add a little more cream. It should hold together when formed into balls.

Roll the dough into 1-inch balls and place on a baking sheet lined with parchment paper. Bake for 10–12 minutes. The bottom of the cookie will brown and the top will form cracks. Remove from the oven and cool for 1–2 minutes. Roll cookies in powdered sugar. Cool cookies completely. Roll in powdered sugar one last time. Keep in an airtight container.

5-Spice Salad
Serves 4–6

- 1 package soba or udon noodles
- 1/3 cup soy sauce
- 1 tablespoon sesame oil
- 2 teaspoons chili garlic paste (like Sambal)
- 1 to 2 tablespoons 5-spice powder
- 2 tablespoons canola or safflower oil
- 4 cloves garlic, minced
- 1 tablespoon fresh ginger, minced
- 3 carrots, shredded or julienned
- 2 cups broccoli florets
- 2 cups shredded savoy or Napa cabbage
- 3/4 cup vegetable or chicken stock
- 1/2 cup chopped scallions

Cook the noodles according to package directions. Toss the noodles in 1 to 2 tablespoons oil to prevent from sticking together. Set aside.

In a small bowl, mix together the soy sauce, sesame oil, chili paste, and five-spice powder. Set aside.

Place a large sauté pan or wok over medium high heat. Add the oil, garlic, and ginger. Sauté for 1 minute. Add the soy sauce mixture, carrots, and broccoli. Cook for 5 minutes or until the vegetables soften. Add the scallions and cooked noodles. Toss well to coat with the sauce. Serve warm or at room temperature.

Unit 2 Questions

1. In Experiment 1, which soup had the best overall flavor? What made it the best? Which soup was the saltiest (in flavor, regardless of actual sodium content)? Did the fat content of the soup alter the salty flavor of the soup? Why or why not?
2. In Experiment 2, how did each of the sodium free seasonings compare to the control? Which sodium free seasoning had the best overall flavor?
3. For Experiment 3, what were the differences between volume and weight measurements for the flour, sugar, and brown sugar? Would these differences cause any issues in baking if a recipe called for flour to be weighed and you used a volume measurement instead?
4. Which sodium-free seasoning(s) did the best at offering a good sodium free alternative?
5. What was your favorite spice used today? Describe the characteristics of the spice.
6. How would you describe the flavor of the following herbs and spices: rosemary, allspice, fennel, cayenne, cinnamon, and cardamom?

7. What does it mean to eat with your eyes?

8. In the ranking test, which item was your favorite? Why?

Conversion Exercises

1. 2 tablespoons = _____ teaspoons

2. 1 pound butter = _____ tablespoons = _____ cups = _____ ounces

3. 6.6 pounds = _____ kg

4. 1 gallon = _____ pints

5. 3 quarts = _____ cups

6. 350°F = _____ C

7. 1 tablespoon = _____ ounce

8. 24 ounces = _____ pounds

NOTE

1. Institute of Medicine (IOM), *Strategies to Reduce Sodium Intake in the United States* (Washington, DC: The National Academies Press, 2010), 91–98.

BIBLIOGRAPHY

Institute of Medicine (IOM). *Strategies to Reduce Sodium Intake in the United States*. Washington, DC: The National Academies Press, 2010.

Fruits, Vegetables, and Legumes

OBJECTIVES

- Differentiate between fruits, vegetables, and legumes
- Discuss effect of acids and bases in cooking vegetables
- Discuss effect of enzymatic browning on vegetables and fruit
- Evaluate different lentil varieties
- Practice basic cooking skills to prepare dishes

FRUITS AND VEGETABLES[1]

Botanically, fruits are the ovaries of a flowering plant. The plant ovaries contain seeds that are spread for new growth. Vegetables, on the other hand are either an edible plant or an edible portion of a plant that is consumed such as the flowers, leaves, stems, and/or roots of the plant.

Plant Pigments

Enhancing the aesthetic value of fruits and vegetables, plant pigments play many roles from plant metabolism to attracting pollinators. The four main pigments include chlorophylls, carotenoids, anthocyanins, and anthoxanthins.

Chlorophylls (Fat Soluble)

The green pigment found in the plant cell's chloroplast converts sunlight into chemical energy through photosynthesis. Vegetable examples include any green vegetable such as broccoli, dark leafy greens, or spinach.

Carotenoids (Fat Soluble)

Ranging in color from red to orange to yellow, carotenoids are divided into two classes: carotenes and xanthophylls. Carotenoids live in the chloroplasts and the chromoplasts of the plant. Carotenes are the precursors to vitamin A and include beta-carotene and lycopene. The yellow-orange xanthophylls include lutein, zeatin, and astaxanthin (found in salmon). Fruit and vegetable examples include carrots, tomatoes, pumpkins, and sweet potatoes.

Anthocyanins (Water Soluble)

The red, blue, and purple pigments are part of the flavonoid group anthocyanins. These are underlying pigments of chloroplasts. Due to their water solubility, their color may leach out into cooking liquid. These pigments are known for their antioxidant properties. Fruit and vegetable examples include blueberries, raspberries, red cabbage, eggplant, and the skins of radishes.

Anthoxanthins (Water Soluble)

Another class of flavonoids includes the white-to-pale-yellow pigment of anthoxanthins found in the plant cell's sap. Fruit and vegetable examples include apples, cauliflower, onions, and potatoes.

Betalaine (Water Soluble)

This is a minor group of pigments in the flavonoid family. A vegetable example is beets.

Altering Cell Structure

Adding acids and bases to fruits and vegetables during the cooking process alters the cell structures of the plants, resulting in changes to the pigment and texture of the vegetables and fruit. Heat and different cooking methods also affect the texture and color of the vegetables and fruits. In some cases, heat destroys nutrients in the produce; in other cases, heat enhances nutrients. Lycopene in tomatoes, for example, is more readily available for absorption after the tomatoes have been cooked. Additionally, overcooking fruits and vegetables can change the pigment to dull olive-gray color, as in the case of chlorophylls, or to a brownish color in anthoxanthins.

SELECTING AND STORING PRODUCE

Produce is typically sold as either conventionally grown or organically grown. Conventional produce can be grown with the aid of chemical fertilizers and/or pesticides. Organic produce, marked with a seal from the United States Department of Agriculture (USDA), is grown without the use of synthetic chemical fertilizers or pesticides.[2] Additionally, organic growers do not use GMOs (genetically modified organisms) to grow fruits and vegetables.[3]

Fruits and vegetables can be purchased fresh, frozen, or canned. Fresh vegetables have undergone very little processing and therefore have a shorter shelf life. Frozen and canned fruit and vegetables are typically processed at the time of harvest. During the freezing or canning process, salt, sugar, or other preservatives may be added to improve quality and shelf stability.

Follow these guidelines for selecting and storing produce.

TABLE 3.1

Selecting Produce	Description
Freshness[4]	Avoid fruit and vegetables with signs of mold and rot
Appearance[5]	Avoid openly bruised or blemished fruit and vegetables unless you can use part of it
Touch	Fruits and vegetables that should be firm to the touch: ■ Apples ■ Carrots ■ Celery ■ Melons ■ Onions ■ Potatoes ■ Summer squash ■ Winter squash Produce that should have some "give" or be slightly soft: ■ Avocados ■ Citrus ■ Mangoes ■ Papaya ■ Pears ■ Stone fruits (nectarines, peaches, cherries, etc.) ■ Tomatoes Vegetables that should have dense, compact heads ■ Broccoli ■ Brussels sprouts ■ Cabbage ■ Cauliflower
Smell	Most fruit should have a sweet scent when ripe

The following table lists common conversions for both volume and weight that are used in cooking.

TABLE 3.2

Storing Produce	Description
Keep fruit and vegetables separate[6]	Fruit gives off ethylene gas as it continues to ripen, which can speed up the ripening of certain vegetables

(Continued)

Storing Produce	Description
To be stored at room temperature[7]	Avocados Bananas Garlic Lemons Limes Melon Onions* Potatoes* Tomatoes Stone fruits (except cherries) Winter squash
To be stored in the refrigerator or cooler[8]	Any cut or washed produce Asparagus Berries Broccoli Brussels sprouts Carrots Cauliflower Celery Dark leafy greens Eggplant Grapes Greens Herbs Lettuce Peas Peppers Summer squash

Potatoes and onions should be stored separately. Potatoes should be kept in a cool, dark location.

FOOD WASTE

Each year, millions of pounds of food are wasted in restaurants, supermarkets, and at home. Part of reducing food waste is to follow guidelines for proper storage of produce and using it before it starts to rot or spoil. However, there are many other ways to prevent food waste.

Plan Ahead
Create menus and shopping lists so you only purchase food needed for recipes.

Leftovers
Use or freeze leftovers. Some leftovers can be made into new, creative dishes.

Inventory
Take an inventory of food in the freezer, cooler, and pantry and use items that are nearly out of date.

Compost

Produce scraps can be composted to create garden soil. Either start your own compost pile or partner with a local farm or company that makes compost.

SEASONAL PRODUCE[9]

If consuming fresh produce, the most flavorful varieties will be on the ones found in season. Part of becoming a competent cook is choosing quality ingredients and knowing when produce is in season. Seasonality of produce varies from region to region but here is a list of when produce is generally in season.

Spring
Lettuces
Spinach
Kale
Swiss chard
Radishes

Early Summer (June)
Radishes
Bok Choy
Lettuces
Spinach
Kale
Swiss Chard
Strawberries

Summer (July / August)
Cucumbers
Cabbage
Summer Squash
Tomatoes
Beans
Peas
Sweet Corn
Melons
Eggplant
Peppers
Potatoes
Leeks
Peaches
Nectarines
Cherries
Blueberries
Raspberries
Broccoli
Cauliflower

Late Summer / Fall (August – October)
Winter squash
Potatoes
Onions
Leeks
Plums
Apples
Pears
Grapes

Winter (February)
Citrus

Year Round
Mushrooms
Herbs

Tips for Eating Seasonally

- Check out the local farmer's market
- Buy a CSA share at a local farm
- Plant a garden

Extend the Season by

- Freezing fresh vegetables and fruit
- Canning fresh vegetables
- Drying fruit and vegetables

LEGUMES

Legumes such as beans, lentils, and peas are unique vegetables. Since they are high in protein, legumes are often used as meat substitutes in vegetarian dishes. However, they lack one of the essential amino acids, methionine.[10] To make up for the lack of methionine, legumes are often paired with cereals and grains (like rice), which are low in the essential amino acid, lysine.[11] The combination of legumes and grains provide the body with a complete protein. Additionally, legumes are an excellent source of dietary fiber.[12]

Pulses versus Fresh Beans[13]

Pulses encompass the dried bean, dry pea, or lentil varieties of legumes. Fresh legumes include fresh peas, fresh beans (fava beans), and green beans. Other legumes are harvested for their oil like soybeans.

Beans can be purchased canned or dry. Dry beans tend to be less expensive compared to their canned counterparts. However, dry beans need to be rehydrated prior to cooking. There are two methods for rehydrating beans: soaked overnight or quick soak in hot water.

Soaking Overnight

Place beans in a container and cover by 3–4 inches with cool water. Place in the refrigerator for 8–10 hours. To cook, drain the beans and place in a saucepan. Cover by 2 inches with water. Bring to a boil. Reduce heat to low/simmer. Cover and cook until the beans are tender, 40–60 minutes depending on the bean.

Quick Soak

Place the beans in a saucepan and cover by 3 inches with water. Bring to a boil. Remove from heat. Cover and soak for 2 hours. The beans should be tender enough to use in a recipe.

As opposed to beans, lentils do not need to be soaked ahead of time. They cook quickly from their dry form and can be easily added to soups and stews.

India is the largest consumer of lentils and other legumes since they are a staple in Indian cuisine. Latin America also utilizes beans, which are often paired with rice at meals.

In the United States, Montana is the largest producer of lentils. Agriculturally speaking, lentils are beneficial to soils since they, along with other pulses, fix nitrogen and reduce the need for chemical fertilizers.

All beans and lentils are gluten free and can be ground into flour for gluten-free baking.

LENTIL EVALUATION

Evaluate different varieties of cooked lentils.

Green Lentils

- 1/4 cup green lentils
- 2 cups water
- Pinch of salt

Black Lentils

- 1/4 cup black lentils
- 2 cups water
- Pinch of salt

Split Red Lentils

- 1/4 cup split red lentils
- 2 cups water
- pinch of salt

French Green Lentils

- 1/4 cup French green lentils
- 1 1/2 cups water
- pinch of salt

For each lentil variety, the cooking method is the same.

Place the lentils, water, and salt in a saucepan. Bring to a boil over high heat. Reduce heat to low/simmer. Cover and simmer 25–30 minutes or until the lentils are tender. If water remains, drain lentils and discard the cooking liquid.

Lentil Variety	Color before cooking	Color after cooking	Texture	Flavor
Green				
Black				
Split red				
French green				

EXPERIMENTS

Experiment 1: pH Effect on Vegetables

Acids and bases change the texture and color of vegetables depending on the dominant pigment in the vegetable.

Three types of fresh vegetables will be cooked in an acid and base. Record results below.

Ingredients:

- Acid: cream of tartar
- Base: baking soda

■ Vegetables: 1 cup of each, divided into 2 equal portions
- broccoli stems and florets (pigment—chlorophyll)
- carrots cut into 1/2-inch chunks (pigment – carotenoids)
- red cabbage, shredded (pigment – anthocyanins)

Method:

1. Pour 1 cup of water into a pan and add 1/2 teaspoon baking soda. Bring to a boil. Place one portion of vegetables in the boiling water and reduce heat to simmer. Cover and cook for 10 minutes.
2. Pour one cup of water in a pan and add 2 teaspoons cream of tartar. Bring to a boil. Place one portion of the vegetables in the pan. Reduce heat to low. Cover and cook for 10 minutes.
3. Place vegetables in a bowl, along with cooking liquid. Set out for evaluation.

Broccoli

Cooking Method	Appearance of cooking liquid	Appearance of vegetable	Texture	Explanation of observation
Baking soda				
Cream of tartar				

Carrots

Cooking Method	Appearance of cooking liquid	Appearance of vegetable	Texture	Explanation of observation
Baking soda				
Cream of tartar				

Red Cabbage

Cooking Method	Appearance of cooking liquid	Appearance of vegetable	Texture	Explanation of observation
Baking soda				
Cream of tartar				

Experiment 2: Heat Effect on Vegetable Color and Texture

Determine the best method for cooking vegetables. Record the effects of heat on the vegetables below.

Vegetables: 1 cup each, divided into 3 equal portions

- broccoli florets (chlorophyll)
- carrots, sliced (carotenoids)

Variables: boiling, steaming, microwave

Method

1. Bring 1 cup water to a boil. Place one portion of the vegetables into the boiling water. Reduce heat to simmer. Cover and cook for 10 minutes.
2. Steam the second portion of the vegetable by placing it in a steam basket set over boiling water. Cover and steam vegetables for 10 minutes.
3. Place the third portion of the vegetable, along with 3 tablespoons water in a microwave proof bowl. Microwave on high for 1 minute.
4. Place vegetables along with cooking liquid in bowl for evaluation.

Broccoli

Cooking Method	Appearance of cooking liquid	Appearance of vegetable	Texture	Explanation of observation
Boiling				
Steaming				
Microwaving				

Carrots

Cooking Method	Appearance of cooking liquid	Appearance of vegetable	Texture	Explanation of observation
Boiling				
Steaming				
Microwaving				

Experiment 3: Enzymatic Browning

Enzymatic browning occurs when certain fruits and vegetables are exposed to oxygen and the flesh turns brown. This experiment tests several methods that reduce enzymatic browning in order to determine which is the best.

Control: exposed to air

Variables: sugar, lemon juice, Fruit-Fresh®, pineapple juice, plastic wrap

Method

1. Cut apple into 12 slices and place on a plate. Be sure to label each variation.
2. Leave 2 apple slices exposed to air.
3. Toss 2 apple slices with 1 tablespoon pineapple juice.
4. Toss 2 apple slices with 1 tablespoon lemon juice.
5. Sprinkle 2 apple slices with 1/2 teaspoon granulated sugar.
6. Sprinkle 2 apple slices with 1 teaspoon Fruit-Fresh®.
7. Cover 2 apple slices with plastic wrap.
8. Allow apple slices to sit for at least 10 minutes before recording results.

Variation	Appearance of the apple slices
Control – Exposed to air	
Pineapple juice	
Lemon juice	
Sugar	
Fruit Fresh	
Plastic wrap	

RECIPES

Steamed and Sautéed Vegetables

Serves 4

- 2 cups broccoli florets, cauliflower, sugar snap peas, or green beans
- 2–3 tablespoons canola or safflower oil
- Salt and pepper, to taste

Steam the vegetables in either the microwave or in a steamer on the stove. Steam until fork tender. Vegetables should be bright green.

Place the oil in a sauté pan set over medium heat. Add the vegetables. Toss to coat well. Reduce heat to low; sauté for 2–3 minutes. Season to taste with salt and pepper.

Optional additions:

- 1–2 cloves garlic, minced (add when the vegetables are sautéing)
- 1/2 teaspoon crushed red pepper flakes
- any herbs or spices

Sautéed Summer Squash
Serves 4

- 2 cups zucchini or yellow summer squash, sliced
- 1 tablespoon canola or safflower oil
- salt and pepper to taste

Place the oil in a sauté pan set over medium heat. Add the vegetables. Toss to coat well. Reduce heat to low; sauté for 2–3 minutes. Season to taste with salt and pepper.

This recipe can be modified for any vegetable that does not need to be steamed prior to sautéing. Other vegetables include peppers, asparagus, or shelled peas.

Optional additions:

- 1–2 cloves garlic, minced (add when the vegetables are sautéing)
- 1/2 teaspoon crushed red pepper flakes
- any herbs or spices
- 1/2 cup diced red bell peppers

Brussels Sprouts with Bacon and Balsamic Glaze
Serves 4

- 4 ounces thick-cut bacon, cut into 1/2-inch pieces
- 1 pound brussels sprouts, ends removed and cut in half lengthwise
- salt and pepper, to taste
- 2 tablespoons balsamic vinegar
- 2 cloves garlic, minced
- 1 tablespoon honey or maple syrup
- pinch red pepper flakes

Preheat oven to 425°F.

Heat a cast iron or ovenproof sauté pan over medium heat. Add the bacon and render down until crispy. Remove bacon from the pan and reserve. Add the brussels sprouts to the pan and toss to coat well in the hot bacon fat. Season lightly with salt and pepper.

Bake the brussels sprouts in the oven for 15 minutes. Meanwhile, in a small bowl, whisk together the balsamic vinegar, garlic, honey, and red pepper flakes. Season lightly with salt and pepper.

When the brussels sprouts have baked for 15 minutes, remove from the oven and pour the balsamic glaze over the sprouts and sprinkle with the reserved bacon. Bake for another 10–15 minutes or until the brussels sprouts are tender and golden brown. Serve warm.

Roasted Root Vegetables
Serves 4

- 3 pounds assorted root vegetables: carrots, parsnips, celeriac, potatoes, turnips, etc.; peeled (optional) and cut into 1-to-2-inch chunks
- 1/4 cup olive oil
- salt and black pepper
- chopped fresh rosemary or thyme*

Preheat oven to 425°F. Place vegetables on a baking pan and toss with the oil and season with salt and pepper.

Put the vegetables in the oven and roast without stirring for 20 minutes, then check. If they look dry and stick to the pan, drizzle with more oil. Continue roasting, stirring or turning the vegetables once, for another 20 minutes or so. Stir in the herbs, then return the pan to the oven for another 20–40 minutes, or until crisp. Remove from the oven. Serve hot.

*Additional options:

- 1/2 cup grated parmesan cheese (add with or in place of the herbs)
- any spices

Root Vegetable Mash
Serves 6

- 3 pounds mixed root vegetables: carrots, parsnips, celeriac, potatoes, turnips, etc.; peeled (optional) and cut into 1-to-2-inch chunks
- 3 garlic cloves, minced
- 2 tablespoons olive oil
- 1/2 cup sour cream (or crème fraiche)
- 1/2 cup whole milk greek yogurt
- 1 tablespoon finely chopped fresh sage, rosemary, thyme, or chives
- salt and pepper to taste

Place the vegetables in a large pot and cover with cold water and add 2 teaspoons salt. Bring to a boil over high heat, then reduce heat to medium and cook until vegetables are tender and easily pierced with a fork. Drain and return to the pot. Let cool 5 minutes. Add the garlic, olive oil, sour cream, and yogurt. Mash with a potato masher or in a food mill to desired consistency. Mix in fresh herbs. Add salt and pepper to taste.

Honey Sage Carrots

Serves 4

- 1 teaspoon unsalted butter
- 1 teaspoon olive oil
- 2 cups thinly sliced carrots
- 2 tablespoons honey
- 1 tablespoon fresh sage
- salt and pepper, to taste

Heat the butter and olive oil in sauté pan set over medium heat. Add the carrots; sauté until soft, about 5 minutes. Add the honey and sage. Season to taste with salt and pepper. Sauté for another 3 minutes, stirring frequently. Remove from heat and serve.

Ginger Glazed Broccolini

Serves 2

- 1 bunch broccolini, ends trimmed
- 1/4 cup balsamic vinegar
- 1/2 cup pineapple juice
- 2 tablespoons fresh ginger, minced

Steam the broccolini until fork tender. Set aside while you make the glaze.

In a saucepan, combine the vinegar, pineapple juice, and ginger. Bring to a boil. Reduce by about 1/2 or until it looks like maple syrup. Add the broccolini and stir to coat well with the sauce.

Kale and Cannellini Beans

Serves 4

- 2 tablespoons olive oil
- 1/4 cup onion, diced small
- 2 cloves garlic chopped
- pinch red pepper flakes
- 1 bunch kale, stems removed, leaves roughly chopped
- 1 15-ounce can cannellini beans, drained and rinsed
- salt and pepper, to taste

Heat the oil in a skillet set over medium high heat. Add the garlic and red pepper flakes. Cook for 1 minute. Add the kale and beans. Sauté for 2–3 minutes or until the kale wilts. Season to taste with salt and pepper. Serve.

Even though this can be served as a side dish, it can also be the base for soup or stew. Add Italian or andouille sausage for a heartier meal.

Orange and Beet Salad
Serves 6

- 4 beets, red and/or orange, washed well, peeled, and cut into quarters
- 2–4 tablespoons extra virgin olive oil
- 1 small fennel bulb, sliced thinly
- 1/2 red onion, sliced thinly
- 4 oranges, navel and/or blood oranges, peel and pith removed and cut into segments (or supremed)
- 1 tablespoon fresh lemon juice
- 1 tablespoons fresh lime juice
- 1/4 cup loosely packed chopped fresh cilantro and/or parsley leaves
- salt and pepper, to taste

Preheat oven to 400°F. Place the beets on a sheet pan lined with foil or parchment. Toss the beets with 1–2 tablespoons olive oil and season lightly with salt and pepper. Bake in until fork tender, about 30–40 minutes. Remove from oven and cool.

Place the beets, fennel, onion, and orange segments in a large bowl and toss with the lemon and lime juice. Season lightly with salt and pepper and drizzle with olive oil. Toss in the cilantro. Refrigerate for 30 minutes before serving.

Spicy Kale Salad
Serves 6

- 1/4 cup fresh lime juice
- 1 1/2 tablespoons light brown sugar
- 1 clove garlic, minced
- 1 small jalapeno or serrano pepper, seeded and minced
- 1/2 cup canola or safflower oil
- salt and pepper, to taste
- 1 bunch kale (curly or Tuscan), washed well, stem removed and chopped into bite-sized pieces
- 1 cup julienned vegetables such as carrots, beets, and radishes
- 1 cup thinly sliced cucumber
- 1/2 cup fresh herbs of choice such as cilantro, mint, and/or basil

Whisk together the lime juice, brown sugar, garlic, and serrano pepper. While whisking, add the oil. Season lightly with salt and pepper. Set aside.

In a large bowl, toss together the kale, vegetables, cucumber, and herbs. Drizzle with the dressing. Let sit for 30 minutes or up to 2 hours in the refrigerator before serving.

Applesauce

Yield: 1–2 cups

- 1 pound apples (Braeburn, Gala, Fuji, and/or McIntosh), peeled and diced
- 1 1/2 cup water
- 1–2 tablespoons honey
- 1 tablespoon sugar (optional)
- 1 teaspoon fresh lemon juice
- ground cinnamon (optional)

In a large pot, bring apples, water, honey, sugar, and lemon juice to a boil over medium high heat. Reduce heat and simmer until apples are very soft and falling apart, about 25 to 30 minutes.

Mash with a potato masher or pulse in a food processor until semi-smooth. Stir in cinnamon if using.

Grilled Peaches

Serves 4

- 1/2 cup unsalted butter, at room temperature
- 1/2 teaspoon ground cinnamon
- 2 tablespoons sugar
- 1/4 teaspoon salt
- 4 ripe peaches (or nectarines), halved and pitted
- 1 tablespoon canola oil

Heat grill to medium high.

In a small bowl, stir together the butter, cinnamon, sugar, and salt. Set aside.

Brush the peaches with canola oil. Place on the hot grill. Grill until golden brown and just cooked through, about 3–4 minutes. If the peaches start to burn, decrease the heat on the grill. Place on a platter and top each one with the butter mixture.

Serve with sweetened whipped cream or vanilla ice cream.

Leek, Potato, and Lentil Soup

Yield: 1 quart

- 1 tablespoon canola or olive oil
- 3 medium sized leeks, washed well and sliced thin (white and light green part only)
- 2 medium sized russet potatoes, peeled and diced
- 2/3 cup split red lentils
- 1 quart low-sodium chicken or vegetable stock
- 1/4 cup half and half (optional)
- pinch of red pepper flakes, aleppo pepper, or cayenne pepper
- salt and pepper, to taste

Heat the oil in a large pot set over medium low heat. Add the leeks and lightly sauté until soft, about 5–8 minutes. Add the potatoes, lentils, and stock. Season lightly with salt and pepper. Increase heat to medium high and bring to a boil. Reduce heat to low and simmer until the potatoes and lentils are soft, about 20 minutes. Using an immersion blend or food processor, puree the soup until smooth. Return soup to the pan and add the half and half if desired and the red pepper flakes. Adjust seasonings accordingly.

Pineapple Salsa
Yield: 4 cups

- 1 whole pineapple, peeled, cored, and diced small
- 1 cup red bell peppers, diced small
- 1 cup green bell peppers, diced small
- 1 cup red onion, diced small
- 1/2 cup fresh cilantro leaves, chopped fine
- 2 cloves garlic, minced
- 2 jalapeno or serrano peppers, minced
- juice of 3 limes
- salt, to taste

In a large bowl, mix together all ingredients. Adjust seasonings to taste. Refrigerate for at least 1 hour before serving. Serve with fish tacos, grilled fish or poultry, or roasted pork loin. Can also be served with tortilla chips.

Date Nut Balls
Makes 2 dozen

- 2 cups walnuts or almonds
- 1 cup shredded coconut (preferably unsweetened)
- 2 cups dried, pitted dates, sliced in half
- 2–3 tablespoons olive oil
- 1 teaspoon salt
- 1 teaspoon vanilla extract

In a food processor, pulse the nuts and coconut until coarsely ground. Add the dates, oil, salt, and vanilla. Pulse until the mixture is finely chopped. It will be a sticky mass.

Roll mixture into 1-inch balls. Place on a baking sheet. Refrigerate until firm, about one hour. Store in an airtight container under refrigeration for up to one week. These can be frozen for up to three months.

Ratatouille
Serves 6

Sauce

- 1 (15-ounce) can diced tomatoes
- 8 ounces roasted red peppers, drained if canned
- 1 garlic clove, chopped
- 1 shallot, chopped
- salt and pepper, to taste
- 1 tablespoon fresh oregano, chopped OR 1 teaspoon dried oregano
- 2 teaspoons sugar

Vegetables

- 1 zucchini, sliced thin
- 1 yellow squash, sliced thin
- 1 eggplant, sliced thin (preferably Japanese eggplant)
- 1 orange or yellow bell pepper, sliced into rings

Topping

- 3 garlic cloves, minced
- 3 tablespoons olive oil
- 1/2 teaspoon dried thyme or 2 teaspoons fresh thyme
- salt and pepper, to taste

Preheat oven to 375°F.

In a saucepan, combine the diced tomatoes, roasted bell pepper, garlic, and shallots. Season with salt and pepper. Cook over medium heat for 10–15 minutes. Transfer mixture to a blender and puree until smooth. Add the oregano and sugar. Taste and adjust seasonings accordingly.

Pour sauce into the bottom of a casserole dish. Layer the vegetables on the sauce in this order: eggplant on bottom, layer of bell peppers, and zucchini and summer squash alternated on the top. In a small bowl, combine the topping ingredients. Sprinkle topping over the top of the vegetables.

Cover with foil and bake for 30 minutes.

Celeriac Apple Salad
Serves 4–6

- 1 medium size celeriac, shredded and tossed with 1 tablespoon lemon juice to prevent browning
- 1 medium sized apple, shredded (recommend gala, braeburn, fuji, or honeycrisp varieties)
- 1/2 cup chopped flat-leaf parsley
- 3 tablespoons lemon juice
- 3 tablespoons orange juice
- 2 teaspoons dijon mustard
- 1 tablespoon minced shallot
- 1 clove garlic, minced
- 1/2 cup olive oil
- salt and pepper, to taste

In a large bowl, toss together the celeriac, apple, and parsley. Set aside.

In a small bowl, whisk together the lemon juice, orange juice, mustard, shallot, and garlic. While whisking, drizzle in the olive oil. Season to taste with salt and pepper.

Pour vinaigrette over celeriac and apple mixture. Toss to combine well. Serve chilled. Salad will keep up to one day if kept under refrigeration.

Yellow Split Pea Soup
Yield: 2 quarts

- 2 teaspoons canola or safflower oil
- 1/2 cup diced white or yellow onion
- 1/2 cup diced carrot
- 1/4 cup diced celery
- 1 clove garlic, minced
- 2 quarts low-sodium vegetable or chicken stock
- 2 cups yellow split peas, picked over
- 1 medium size russet or Yukon gold potato, peeled and diced
- 1/4 teaspoon turmeric
- pinch cayenne pepper
- salt and pepper, to taste

Heat oil in a soup pot set over medium heat. Add the onions, carrot, celery, and garlic. Sauté vegetables until soft, about 5–6 minutes. Season lightly with salt and pepper. Add the stock, peas, potato, and turmeric. Simmer until the split peas are tender, about 60 minutes. Using an immersion blend, puree the soup. Add cayenne pepper to taste and adjust seasonings accordingly. Serve with seasoned croutons.

Butternut Squash Soup

Yield: 1 quart

- 1 (3-pound) butternut squash, cut in half and seeds scooped out
- 2 tablespoons canola or safflower oil
- 2 medium sized leeks, diced (white and light green parts only)
- 1 cup diced carrots
- 2 tablespoons freshly grated ginger
- 2 clove garlic, minced
- 3–4 cups chicken or vegetable stock
- 1/2 teaspoon dried sage (or 1 tablespoon chopped fresh sage)
- salt and pepper, to taste

Preheat oven to 375ºF. Place the butternut squash on a sheet pan. Rub the flesh of the squash with 1 tablespoon oil. Turn squash flesh side down on the pan. Bake until fork tender, about 45–50 minutes. Set aside to cool about 10 minutes. Peel the skin off the flesh.

In a soup pot set over medium-low heat, add the remaining 1 tablespoon oil, leeks, carrots, ginger, and garlic. Sauté until carrots are tender, about 10 minutes. Season lightly salt and pepper.

Add the cooked squash, 3 cups stock, and sage. Simmer 10 minutes. Puree soup using a stand blender or immersion blender. Add more stock thinning to desired consistency. Adjust seasonings accordingly with salt and pepper. Serve hot with crusty bread or seasoned croutons.

Lentil Burgers

Yield: 8–10 burgers

- 2 cups low-sodium vegetable or chicken stock
- 1 cup green lentils
- 1 tablespoon oil
- 1/2 cup red onion, diced small
- 1 carrot, peeled, diced small
- 2 cloves garlic, minced
- 2 large eggs
- 2 tablespoons chopped parsley
- 3/4 cup bread crumbs
- 1/4 cup grated Parmesan cheese
- 1 teaspoon salt
- 1/2 teaspoon black pepper
- Pinch of cayenne pepper
- 1/4 to 1/3 cup canola or safflower oil for frying

In a saucepan, combine the stock and lentils. Bring to a boil. Cover and reduce heat to low. Simmer until lentils are soft, about 20–30 minutes. Drain off excess liquid.

Place lentils, onions, carrots, and garlic in food processor. Pulse 5–10 times to puree mixture.

Scrape mixture into a bowl and add the eggs, parsley, breadcrumbs, parmesan cheese, salt, pepper, and cayenne. Form into patties.

In a large nonstick skillet, heat oil over medium high heat. Fry the lentil burger until golden brown on each side.

Top with herbed goat cheese or other cheese and serve with regular burger toppings.

Chickpea Salad
Yield: about 2 cups

Salad

- 1 (15-ounce) can chickpeas, drained and rinsed
- 1/2 cup small diced red bell pepper
- 1/2 cup small diced red onion
- 1 celery rib, diced small
- 1/4 cup chopped flat leaf parsley

Vinaigrette

- 2 tablespoons fresh lemon juice
- 1 tablespoon plain greek yogurt
- 2 teaspoons red wine vinegar
- 1 garlic clove, minced
- 1/2 teaspoon ground cumin
- 1/3 cup olive oil
- salt and pepper, to taste

In a medium bowl, toss together the salad ingredients. Set aside.

In a small bowl, whisk together the lemon juice, yogurt, vinegar, garlic, and cumin. Whisk in the olive oil. Season to taste with salt and pepper.

Pour vinaigrette over salad ingredients and stir to coat well. Refrigerate for 30 minutes before serving. Salad can be made up to 2 days ahead of time. Keep refrigerated.

Masur Dal
Serves 4

- 1/4 pound (4 ounces) split red lentils
- 1/4 cup ghee or clarified butter, divided (or use oil)
- 1/2 yellow onion, diced small
- 1 clove garlic, minced
- 1 serrano pepper, minced
- 2 teaspoons ground coriander
- 1/2 teaspoon turmeric
- 1/2 teaspoon ground cumin
- salt and pepper, to taste
- 2 tablespoons sour cream
- 1 teaspoon coriander seeds
- 2 shallots, sliced thin

Place the lentils in a saucepot. Cover by 2 inches with water. Bring to a boil over medium high heat. Cover and reduce heat to low. Cook until the lentils are soft, about 20–25 minutes. Drain well, reserving the liquid.

Heat 2 tablespoons of the ghee in a sauté pan set over medium heat. Add the onion, garlic, and pepper. Sauté for 3–4 minutes. Add the ground coriander, turmeric, and cumin. Season lightly with salt and pepper. Sauté for 1–2 minutes. Pour in the lentils and heat through. Add the sour cream. Adjust seasonings accordingly. Add reserved lentil cooking liquid if the mixture is too thick.

In a sauté pan, heat the remaining 2 tablespoons ghee over medium heat. Add the coriander seeds and shallots. Cook for about 1–2 minutes. Add to the stew right before serving.

Falafel
Yield: 1 dozen

- 1 (15-ounce) can chickpeas, drained and rinsed
- 1/2 red onion, chopped
- 1/4 cup chopped parsley
- 1/4 to 1/2 cup AP flour (or rice flour)
- 2 cloves garlic, chopped
- 2 tablespoons lemon juice
- 2 teaspoons ground cumin
- 1 teaspoon salt
- 1/2 teaspoon ground coriander
- 1/2 teaspoon baking soda
- 1/4 teaspoon cayenne pepper
- 1/4 teaspoon black pepper
- 1/2 cup canola or safflower oil

Combine the chickpeas, onion, parsley, flour, garlic, lemon juice, cumin, salt, coriander, baking soda, cayenne, and black pepper in a food processor. Pulse several times until the mixture forms a paste.

Scrape mixture into a bowl. Let stand for 10–15 minutes. If the mixture is too dry, add a little water. It should hold the shape of a ball or small patty.

Heat oil in a skillet set over medium high heat until hot. Test one patty in the oil. The oil is hot enough when it the patty immediately bubbles around the edges. Fry the first patty in the oil. If it breaks apart, add 1–2 tablespoons more flour to the remaining falafel mixture.

Form the remaining mixture into patties and pan fry until golden brown on each side. Serve hot in pita with yogurt or tahini sauce (see below) and fresh vegetables such as sliced tomatoes, cucumbers, and onion.

Yogurt sauce: Mix together 1 cup plain greek yogurt, 2 tablespoons olive oil, 1 tablespoon fresh lemon juice, 1 minced garlic clove, salt and pepper. Optional addition: 2 tablespoons crumbled feta cheese.

Tahini sauce: Mix together 1 cup tahini, 2 tablespoons plain greek yogurt, 1 tablespoon lemon juice, salt, pepper, sugar to taste, and hot water to thin as necessary.

Lima Bean (Butter Bean) Puree with Sautéed Vegetables
Serves 4–6

Beans

- 1 pound dried lima beans (butter beans)
- 1 teaspoon salt
- 1/2 cup olive oil
- 1/2 cup fresh parsley
- 1/2 cup grated parmesan cheese
- 3 cloves garlic, minced

Vegetables

- 1 tablespoon canola or safflower oil
- 1 white or yellow onion, diced
- 1 fennel bulb, julienned
- 1 cup celeriac, peeled and diced small
- 1–2 cups low-sodium vegetable stock
- 1 bunch kale (any variety) or swiss chard, chopped
- salt and pepper, to taste

Beans[i]

Place the beans in a large container. Cover by 2 inches with cool water. Refrigerate 8–12 hours. Drain beans and place in a large stockpot. Cover by 2 inches with fresh water. Bring to a boil. Cover and reduce heat to simmer. Cook for 1 hour or until tender.

Drain off excess liquid from cooked beans. Place beans in a food processor along with the salt, olive oil, parsley, parmesan, and garlic. Pulse several times to until semi-smooth. Adjust seasonings to taste. Set aside.

Vegetables

Heat the oil in a sauté pan set over medium heat. Add the onion, fennel, and celeriac. Sauté for 5–6 minutes or until the onions and fennel begin to soften. Season lightly with salt and pepper. Pour in the stock. Cover with a lid and reduce heat to low. Simmer for 10–15 minutes or until the celeriac is tender. Season lightly with salt and pepper. Add the kale or chard. Toss to coat well. Cook for 1 minute or until the greens have wilted slightly.

Serve the vegetables over the pureed beans along with toasted bread.

Mexican-Style Pinto Beans

Serves 4

- 1/2 pound dried beans
- 6 ounces bacon (optional: see note), cut into small pieces
- 1 white onion, diced small
- 1 roasted poblano pepper, seeded and diced small
- 3 cloves garlic, minced
- 3 cups low sodium chicken or vegetable stock
- 1 bay leaf
- 1 teaspoon dried oregano
- 1 (14.5 ounce) can diced tomatoes
- salt and pepper, to taste
- 2–3 tablespoons chopped cilantro

Place the beans in a large container. Cover by 2 inches with cool water. Refrigerate 8–12 hours. Drain beans and set aside.

Place the bacon in a medium saucepot set over medium heat. Cook the bacon until crispy. Remove from the pan, leaving the bacon fat in the pan. Set cooked bacon aside. Add the onion and poblano. Sauté for 5 minutes. Add the garlic; sauté for 1 minute. Add the beans, stock, bay leaf, and oregano. Bring to a boil. Cover and reduce heat to medium low. Cook until the beans are tender, about 40 minutes. Add the tomatoes and season with salt and pepper. Cook for 10–15 minutes longer. Adjust seasonings to taste. Stir in chopped cilantro and cooked bacon.

---

i *Alternatively, the beans can be cooked from the dry state in a pressure cooker according to manufacturer's instructions

Note: to make this vegan, omit the bacon and sauté the vegetables in 2 tablespoons canola oil.

Mung Bean Bowl
Serves 4

Mung Bean Bowl

- 1 cup dry mung beans
- 1/2 cup dry quinoa
- 3 cups water
- 1 tablespoon canola, safflower, or avocado oil
- 1 bunch kale or Swiss chard, roughly chopped
- salt and pepper, to taste
- 1 red onion, julienned
- 2 carrots, shredded
- 1/2 cup pepitas (pumpkin seeds), lightly toasted
- 1/4 cup feta cheese

Cilantro Yogurt Vinaigrette

- 1 cup full-fat greek yogurt
- 1/2 cup fresh cilantro
- 3 tablespoons olive oil
- 2 tablespoons fresh lime juice
- 1 serrano chili, chopped (optional)
- 2 garlic cloves, chopped
- salt and pepper, to taste

Bowl

Place the mung beans and 2 cups of water in a sauce pot. Place over medium high heat and bring to a boil. Cover and reduce heat to low. Simmer until the beans are soft, about 40–45 minutes. Drain off any excess liquid. Season lightly with salt and pepper. Set aside.

Place the quinoa and 1 cup of water in a sauce pot. Place over medium high heat and bring to a boil. Cover and reduce heat to low. Simmer until the quinoa is soft, about 20–30 minutes. Drain off any excess liquid. Season lightly with salt and pepper. Set aside.

Heat the oil in a sauté pan over medium heat. Add the kale. Season lightly with salt and pepper. Sautée for 1–2 minutes or until wilted slightly.

In a large bowl, combine the cooked beans and quinoa. To serve, layer a mound of the bean quinoa mixture in the bottom of the bowl. Add the kale, onions, carrots, pepitas, and feta on top. Drizzle with the yogurt vinaigrette.

Vinaigrette

Place all vinaigrette ingredients in a blender. Blend until smooth. Adjust seasonings to taste.

Roasted Red Pepper Hummus

Yield: 1–2 cups

- 1 (15-ounce) chickpeas, drained and rinsed
- 1 cup roasted red bell peppers (drained if from a jar)
- 2 garlic cloves
- juice of 1 lemon
- 3 tablespoons tahini
- 4 tablespoons olive oil
- salt and pepper, to taste

Place the chickpeas, peppers, garlic, lemon juice, and tahini in a food processor. Pulse several times to chop up the mixture. While the food processor is running, drizzle in the oil through the feed tube. Scrape down the sides of the bowl as necessary. Mixture should be creamy and thick. Season to taste with salt and pepper. Refrigerate for one hour before serving.

Serve with fresh vegetables, pita bread, or tortilla chips.

Red Lentil Puree

Yield: 1–2 cups

- 1 cup split red lentils
- 1 clove garlic
- juice 1 lemon
- 2 tablespoons fresh parsley
- 3 tablespoons olive oil
- salt and pepper, to taste
- spices as desired: ground coriander, garam masala, ground cumin, turmeric, etc.

Place the lentils in a saucepot. Cover by 2 inches with water. Bring to a boil over medium high heat. Cover and reduce heat to low. Cook until the lentils are soft, about 20–25 minutes. Drain well.

Place 1/2 of the lentils in a food processor and add the garlic, lemon juice, and parsley. Pulse until smooth. Add the olive oil and pulse until smooth. Pour into a bowl and add the remaining lentils, salt, pepper, and spices. Adjust seasonings accordingly.

Serve with fresh vegetables, pita bread, or tortilla chips.

White Bean Dip

Yield: 1–2 cups

- 2–3 tablespoons olive oil
- 1 tablespoon finely chopped fresh rosemary
- 2 cloves garlic, chopped
- 1 (15-ounce) can cannellini beans, drained and rinsed
- 1/2 teaspoon salt
- 1/2 teaspoon pepper
- 1 tablespoon fresh lemon juice

Heat 1 tablespoon olive oil in a small skillet over medium heat. Add the rosemary and garlic and cook for 1–2 minutes. Remove from heat.

Combine the rosemary mixture and beans. Puree until semi-smooth. Add the salt, pepper, and lemon juice. Add more olive oil if the mixture is too thick. Refrigerate until ready to serve.

Serve with fresh vegetables or pita chips.

Unit 3 Questions

1. Discuss the differences between the various method used to prevent enzymatic browning of the apples. For each method discuss why it worked or did not work. Which method prevented the browning the best?
2. Based on the results in experiment 1 using broccoli, carrots, and red cabbage, how do both acids and bases affect the color and texture of the vegetables? Explain what is happening at the cellular level.
3. Compare and contrast the different cooking methods of the broccoli and carrots. Did one method work the best in keeping the color of the vegetable bright? For each method, which cooking liquid contained the least amount of the chlorophyll or carotenoid from the vegetables? Why do you think this is?
4. When is the best time to add acid to dried beans when they are cooking?

NOTES

1. Vickie A. Vaclavik and Elizabeth W. Christian, *Essentials of Food Science*, 4th ed. (New York: Springer, 2014), 87–92.
2. United States Department of Agriculture (USDA), "Organic Standards," accessed May 7, 2019, https://www.ams.usda.gov/grades-standards/organic-standards.
3. United States Department of Agriculture (USDA), "Can GMOs be used in Organic Agricultural Products?" Accessed May 7, 2019, https://www.ams.usda.gov/publications/content/can-gmos-be-used-organic-products.
4. Food and Drug Administration (FDA), "Selecting and Serving Produce Safely," accessed May 7, 2019, https://www.fda.gov/food/buy-store-serve-safe-food/selecting-and-serving-produce-safely.
5. Food and Drug Administration, "Selecting and Serving Produce Safely."
6. UC San Diego Center for Community Health, "Ethylene in Fruits and Vegetables," accessed May 7, 2019, https://ucsdcommunityhealth.org/wp-content/uploads/2017/09/ethylene.pdf.

7. UC Davis, "Storing Fresh Fruits and Vegetables for Better Taste," accessed May 7, 2019, http://ucce.ucdavis.edu/files/datastore/234-1920.pdf.

8. UC Davis.

9. USDA SNAP-Ed Connection, *Seasonal Produce Guide*, accessed May 7, 2019, https://snaped.fns.usda.gov/seasonal-produce-guide.

10. Grains and Legumes Nutrition Council, "Legumes and Nutrition," accessed May 7, 2019, https://www.glnc.org.au/legumes/legumes-nutrition/.

11. Grains and Legumes Nutrition Council.

12. Grains and Legumes Nutrition Council.

13. "What are Pulses?" Pulses, accessed May 7, 2019, https://pulses.org/nap/what-are-pulses/.

BIBLIOGRAPHY

Food and Drug Administration (FDA). "Selecting and Serving Produce Safely," updated March 14, 2018, accessed May 7, 2019, https://www.fda.gov/food/buy-store-serve-safe-food/selecting-and-serving-produce-safely.

Grains and Legumes Nutrition Council, "Legumes and Nutrition." Accessed May 7, 2019. https://www.glnc.org.au/legumes/legumes-nutrition/.

Pulses. "What are Pulses?" Accessed May 7, 2019. https://pulses.org/nap/what-are-pulses/.

UC Davis. "Storing Fresh Fruits and Vegetables for Better Taste." Accessed May 7, 2019. http://ucce.ucdavis.edu/files/datastore/234-1920.pdf.

UC San Diego Center for Community Health, "Ethylene in Fruits and Vegetables." Accessed May 7, 2019. https://ucsdcommunityhealth.org/wp-content/uploads/2017/09/ethylene.pdf.

United States Department of Agriculture (USDA). "Can GMOs be used in Organic Agricultural Products?" Accessed May 7, 2019. https://www.ams.usda.gov/publications/content/can-gmos-be-used-organic-products.

United States Department of Agriculture (USDA). "Organic Standards." Accessed May 7, 2019. https://www.ams.usda.gov/grades-standards/organic-standards.

USDA SNAP-Ed Connection. "Seasonal Produce Guide." Accessed May 7, 2019. https://snaped.fns.usda.gov/seasonal-produce-guide.

Vaclavik, Vickie A., and Elizabeth W. Christian. *Essentials of Food Science*, 4th Edition. New York: Springer, 2014.

Dairy

- Evaluate different types of milk and cheese products
- Discuss coagulation effects of milk products
- Discuss differences in cooking with dairy and non-dairy products
- Use basic cooking skills to prepare dishes

DAIRY

An all-encompassing term, dairy includes many products produced from the milk of mammals, primarily cows, goats, and sheep. Dairy products can be consumed raw, pasteurized, or cultured.

Pasteurization[1]

Most dairy products sold commercially are pasteurized, a process in which the milk (or other food product) is heated to a certain temperature to eliminate pathogens. Dairy that is labeled as "pasteurized" has been heated to 161.6°F for 15 seconds. Some dairy has been ultra-pasteurized where it was heated to 280°F for 2 seconds. Pasteurized products have a shelf life of 3–4 week whereas ultra-pasteurized have a shelf life of many months.

Homogenization[2]

Many dairy products are labeled as "homogenized." In the process of homogenization, fat molecules are broken down so they stay integrated in the milk. This is opposed to non-homogenized dairy where the fat separates and sits in a cream layer on the top.

Buttermilk[3]

Traditionally, buttermilk was the liquid present after cream was churned into butter. During the churning process, the liquid fermented and turned sour. Today, buttermilk is made by adding bacterial culture and enzymes to low-fat milk.

Canned Milk[4]

Canned milk is sold as either evaporated or sweetened condensed. In evaporated milk, about 50% of the water is removed. Sweetened condensed milk is similar to evaporated milk but with sugar added. It is comprised of about 55% sugar.

CULTURED DAIRY

To culture milk, bacteria and/or enzymes are introduced to milk and given time to ferment, changing the nature of the milk. Common cultured milk products include yogurt, cheese, kefir, crème fraiche, sour cream, clotted cream, cheese, and buttermilk. In the process of culturing, the milk sugar, lactose, is converted into lactic acid.

Cheese[5]

Cheese is one of the most popular dairy products with over two thousand varieties available around the world. Cheese is simply made by coagulating milk from cows, sheep, or goats to separate the curds from the whey. Curds are made from casein, a protein that coagulates in the presence of acid. Whey is the remaining liquid after the casein has been coagulated. In cheese making, particular strands of bacteria and/or fungi are added to cheese, creating unique flavors and textures. As cheese ripens, it loses moisture and creates a crumbly, hard texture. Cheese is divided into categories: fresh, semi-soft, semi-hard, hard, soft-ripened (or bloomy rind), firm, hard, blue-veined, wash-rind, and brined cheese.

Fresh Cheese

Unripened cheese that has been coagulated with an acid. It is usually eaten soon after being made and does not contain a rind

Texture: soft, creamy

Examples: cottage cheese, ricotta, mozzarella

Semi-Soft Cheese

Curds are lightly pressed and rinsed or brushed with salt-water solution to encourage mold growth

Texture: soft, rubbery

Examples: Munster, Port-Salut

Semi-Hard Cheese

Curds are pressed and molded. They fermented for 3–9 months and have less moisture than fresh or semi-soft cheese. The rinds can be natural, wax, or made from cloth

Texture: firm, dense; some have air pockets (holes)

Examples: cheddar, gouda, emmental

Hard Cheese

Cheeses that have been aged for several months to ripen, resulting in a dry texture

Texture: dry, crumbly

Examples: parmesan, asiago

Blue-Veined Cheese

Pressed cheese curds that have been inoculated with blue-green fungi/mold

Texture: varies based on variety—soft to semi-firm

Examples: roquefort, gorgonzola, stilton, maytag blue

Bloomy Rind Cheese

Cheese that has been ripened with a layer of mold on the surface

Texture: interior is soft and creamy

Examples: brie and camembert

Washed-Rind Cheese

Soft, semi-hard, or hard cheeses that have been washed with a salt-water brine, beer, or wine to encourage bacterial growth. These cheeses are usually described as "stinky" but typically have a mild flavor

Texture: depends on the variety

Examples: taleggio, limburger

Brined Cheese

This is cheese that has been pickled or brined in a solution

Texture: soft, crumbly

Example: Feta

Making Basic Soft Cheese

To make cheese, acid and rennet are added to full-fat milk to separate the curds and whey. Rennet is made from enzymes that assist the acid in coagulating the milk. Many different types of acid are used including vinegar, lemon juice, and citric acid.

Once the curds and whey are separated, the curds are removed and pressed together to form cheese.

Processed Cheese

Processed cheese consists of some natural cheese ingredients blended with emulsifiers and preservatives to promote a longer shelf-life. American cheese is an example of processed cheese.

MILK VARIETIES: DAIRY AND NON-DAIRY

Dairy Milk

Dairy milk comes from the mammary glands of mammals. Commercial dairy milk is usually fortified with vitamins A and D.

Cow

Cow milk generally comes from certain breeds of cattle: Jerseys, Holsteins, Guernsey, and Brown Swiss. Cows were domesticated around 3000 BCE. Cow milk provides a wide variety of products including whole milk, 2%, 1%, non-fat, heavy cream, half-and-half, and butter.

Sheep

Sheep milk is mainly used for cheese making notably Roquefort. It is rich in fat and protein.

Goat

Goat milk is used for drinking and cheese making. Goats are popular in mountainous regions such as Italy, Greece, South America, and Central America. They graze on many types of plants and can handle rock or mountainous terrain better than cows.

Water Buffalo

Water buffalo was used as draft animal starting around 3000 BCE. In Italy, milk from the water buffalo is used for making fresh mozzarella; it produces richer, superior cheese to mozzarella made with cow's milk.

Non-Dairy Milk

Non-dairy milks are plant-based and a good alternative for those with milk allergies, lactose intolerance, or those who are following a vegan diet.

Coconut

This milk is derived from grated flesh of coconuts. It can be purchased in cans or cartons. Fat content varies among manufacturers.

Almond

Almond milk is made by soaking and grinding almonds and then straining the mixture to produce a milk-like liquid. It contains very little protein.

Soy

Soy milk is made from soybeans. Dry soybeans are soaked, ground, and strained to produce a milk-like liquid. Soy milk contains protein.

Rice

Rice milk is made from rice. The process to make rice milk involves boiling rice and blending it with water before straining it.

Hemp

Hemp milk is made from hemp seeds that have been soaked, ground, and strained.

Other nut milks

Other nuts, such as cashews, walnuts, hazelnuts, and pistachios can be used to make non-dairy milks in the same manner as almond milk.

Oat

Steel cut or whole oat groats are soaked in water, blended, and strained.

MILK EVALUATION

Taste and evaluate different varieties of dairy and non-dairy milk products.

Milk Product	Flavor	Aroma	Mouthfeel	Fat Content	Protein Content
Fat-free					
1% milk					
2% milk					
Whole milk					
Goat milk					
Almond milk					
Soy milk					
Hemp or oat milk					

CHEESE EVALUATION

Taste and evaluate different varieties dairy and non-dairy cheeses.

Cheese	Appearance	Flavor	Aroma	Texture	Fat Content

EXPERIMENTS

Experiment 1: Pudding Variations

Make and evaluate pudding made with different types of dairy and non-dairy milk.

Basic Recipe (Control)

- 1 cup whole milk
- 1/4 cup sugar
- 1 1/2 tablespoons* cornstarch
- pinch of salt
- 1/2 teaspoon vanilla extract

1 1/2 tablespoons = 1 tablespoon + 1 1/2 teaspoons

Whisk together the ingredients in a saucepan. Place over medium heat and bring to a boil. Cook for 1 minute. Remove from heat and pour into a bowl. Cover with plastic wrap and refrigerate until cold, about 1–2 hours.

Variations
In place of the whole milk use:

- Fat-free milk
- Almond milk
- Soy milk
- Full-fat coconut milk
- Lite coconut milk

Type of Milk	Flavor	Mouthfeel	Texture	Appearance
Whole milk (control)				
Fat-free				
Almond				
Soy				
Full-fat coconut milk				
Lite coconut milk				

Experiment 2: Coagulation of Milk Products

Test the coagulation of various types of dairy and non-dairy milk.

Basic Recipe (Control)

- 1 cup whole milk
- 1 tablespoon vinegar

Heat the milk in a saucepan until it reaches 130°F. Add the vinegar. Remove from the heat and let it stand at room temperature for 20 minutes. Strain the curds from the whey. Save both the whey and curd for evaluation.

Variations

In place of the whole milk, substitute:

- Rice milk
- Soy milk
- Full-fat coconut milk
- Lite coconut milk
- 1% milk
- Goat milk

Milk	Size of Curd	Volume of whey left over after coagulation
Whole milk (Control)		
Rice milk		
Soy milk		
Full-fat coconut milk		
Lite coconut milk		
1% milk		
Goat milk		

RECIPES

Fresh Mozzarella

Yield: 8 ounces mozzarella

- 1/2 cup distilled water
- 2 teaspoons citric acid
- 1/4 rennet tablet or 1/4 teaspoon single strength liquid rennet*
- 1 gallon whole milk (not ultra-pasteurized)
- 1 teaspoon cheese or kosher salt

If using double-strength rennet, decrease amount by half.

This recipe utilizes an Instant Pot to make fresh mozzarella.

Divide the water into 2 small bowls (1/4 cup water per bowl). To one cup add the citric acid. To the other cup, add the rennet. Stir to combine. Set aside.

Pour the milk into the Instant Pot. Press "yogurt" until it reads "boil." Warm the milk to 55°F. Pour in the citric acid while whisking briskly. Heat the milk until it reaches 88°F. Press cancel to turn off the Instant Pot.

Stir in the rennet, using an up and down motion. Place lid on the pot and allow to sit for 5–10 minutes or until a clear separation of the curds and whey forms. The whey should be clear and yellow. If it appears milky, allow it to sit for 5 minutes longer.

With a knife, cut the curds in a checkerboard pattern. Press "yogurt" until it says "boil." Heat the mixture to 105°F. Press cancel and put lid on the pot; allow to sit for 1 minute.

With a slotted spoon, scoop the curds into a strainer lined with cheesecloth. Press the curds to remove excess whey. Transfer the curds into a glass bowl. Microwave for 1 minute.

While wearing gloves (double layer if needed), gently fold the cheese over a few times, pouring off excess whey. Microwave curds for another 30–35 seconds. Pour off excess whey. Sprinkle with salt. Continue to fold and knead the curds until smooth, silky, and stretches like taffy.

Form into a ball (or several small balls). Enjoy the fresh mozzarella. To keep in the refrigerator, place in a brine (1 quart water plus 2–3 tablespoons salt + 2–3 tablespoons whey). Fresh mozzarella will keep for up to one week under refrigeration.

Buttermilk Cheese
Yield: about 1 cup

- 1 quart whole milk
- 1 1/2 cups low-fat buttermilk
- 2 teaspoons Kosher salt
- Chopped fresh herbs: chives, parsley, thyme, and/or basil
- Freshly ground black pepper

Line a colander or wire strainer with 3 layers of cheesecloth. Set colander over a large bowl.

Combine milk, buttermilk, and salt in a 2- or 3-quart saucepan. Place over medium-high heat. Cook until mixture has separated into curds and whey, about 8 minutes. Separation of the curds will happen around 180°F and the curds will clump together.

Ladle the contents of the saucepan into the prepared colander. Let the whey drain for 1–2 minutes. Lift the corners of the cheesecloth and gather then together. Gently twist the gathered cloth over the cheese and gently press out the excess whey.

The cheese can be unwrapped immediately and served warm or let stand until cooled to room temperature, about 10 minutes. At this point, mix in the herbs and black pepper. Serve.

To serve a firmer cheese, transfer the cheese in its cloth to a small flat-bottomed dish or pie plate. Refrigerate until cold. Unwrap the cheese and gently invert onto the plate. Discard the cloth. Tend the cheese with plastic wrap and keep refrigerated up to two days. Remove from refrigerator and let stand for 10 minutes at room temperature before serving.

Fresh Ricotta Cheese
Yield: about 2 cups

- 1 quart whole milk
- 2 cups heavy cream
- 1 1/2 teaspoons salt
- 2 tablespoons fresh lemon juice
- 1 tablespoon white vinegar

Set a large colander or wire mesh strainer over a deep bowl. Dampen 2 layers of cheesecloth with water and line the colander with the cheesecloth.

Pour the milk and cream into a saucepan. Stir in the salt. Bring to a full boil over medium heat, stirring occasionally. Turn off the heat and stir in the lemon juice and vinegar. Allow the mixture to stand for 1 minute until it separates into curds and whey.

Pour the mixture into the cheesecloth-lined sieve and allow it to drain into the bowl at room temperature for 20 to 25 minutes, occasionally discarding the liquid that collects in the bowl. The longer you let the mixture drain, the thicker the ricotta. Transfer the ricotta to a bowl, discarding the cheesecloth and any remaining whey. Use immediately or cover with plastic wrap and refrigerate. The ricotta will keep under refrigeration for up to five days.

Fresh Goat Cheese
Yield: about 1 cup

- 1 quart goat milk (preferably not ultra-pasteurized)
- 1/3 cup fresh lemon juice
- 2 tablespoons white vinegar
- 1/2 teaspoon salt
- fresh herbs of choice

Set a large colander or wire mesh strainer over a deep bowl. Dampen 2 layers of cheesecloth with water and line the colander with the cheesecloth.

In a 2-quart saucepan, heat the goat milk until it reaches 180°F.

Remove from heat and immediately add the lemon juice. Stir until combined. Add the vinegar and stir briefly. Let sit for 30 minutes.

The curds will be very small and look like tiny specks.

Gently ladle the mixture into the cheesecloth. Add salt and stir. Gather the ends of the cheesecloth and tie them with string. Hang this above a bowl or hang it off the faucet (be sure the sink is cleaned.

Allow the mixture to drain for 1 hour. Unwrap the cheese and place on a board. Sprinkle with fresh herbs. Refrigerate until cold.

Queso Fresco
Yield: 2–3 cups

- 1/2 gallon whole milk (not ultra-pasteurized)
- 1/3 cup fresh juice from about 2–3 lemons or 1/3 cup white vinegar
- 1 teaspoon Kosher or sea salt

Line colander with four layers of cheesecloth. Heat milk in a large pot over medium-low heat, stirring frequently, until it registers 165 to 180°F on an instant-read thermometer. Add the lemon juice or vinegar 1 tablespoon at a time, stirring gently after each addition. Stop adding the acid when the curds separate from the whey: you will see white clumps of curd suspended in a pale translucent whey. Let sit uncovered for 20 minutes.

Using slotted spoon or wire skimmer, transfer curds to prepared colander and allow to drain until desired texture is reached, about 20 minutes if using for pressed cheese (see step 3), or an hour for fresh curds. Gently stir in salt to taste.

For pressed cheese, gather curds into a ball in the middle of the cloth and press them into a hockey-puck shape. Tie the cloth closed around the cheese. Place the bound cheese back in the colander and place a heavy can or pan on top. Let sit until cheese has reached desired texture, about an hour and a half.

Non Dairy Yogurt

- 1 (14-ounce) can full fat coconut milk
- 1 1/2 cups unsweetened, additive free almond milk (or use homemade)
- 1 tablespoon honey
- 1 1/2 tablespoons tapioca starch/flour
- 1 (5 gram) packet powdered yogurt starter

Set up an ice bath. Set aside.

In a medium saucepan, combine the coconut milk, almond milk, and honey. Set over medium heat. Heat the milk mixture until it begins to steam and is at 150°F.

In a small bowl, stir together 1/4 cup of the hot milk and tapioca starch; whisk until smooth. Add to the rest of the milk.

Cook, stirring frequently to prevent burning, until the milk mixture thickens and is 180–185°F. Pour into a bowl and place in the ice bath. Cool milk mixture to 115°F. Remove from the ice bath.

Sprinkle the yogurt starter over the surface of the milk; whisk until thoroughly combined. Pour into a 1-quart jar and securely place a kitchen towel over the top.

Transfer jar to an oven and turn on the oven light. Place the jar close to the oven light. Let the yogurt sit for 12 hours.

Remove the towel and seal with a lid. Refrigerate until chilled, 4–5 hours.

Crème Fraîche
Yield: 1 cup

- 1 cup cream
- 2 tablespoons buttermilk

Mix cream and buttermilk together in a glass bowl/jar/container. Cover and let sit at room temperature for 8–24 hours or until thick. Stir well and refrigerate for up to ten days.

Soy Milk Rice Pudding
Serves 4

- 1 cup water
- 1/4 teaspoon salt
- 1/2 cup arborio rice
- 2 cups plain soy milk
- 2 tablespoons honey or maple syrup
- 1 teaspoon vanilla extract

In a medium saucepan, bring to a boil the water and salt. Add the rice. Reduce heat to low; cover and cook for 12 minutes. Increase heat to medium-low. Stir in 1/2 cup soy milk, stirring constantly until the milk is absorbed. Continue adding the soy milk, 1/2 cup at a time, stirring constantly until the milk is absorbed and the rice is creamy and tender. Stir in the honey and vanilla.

Kefir
Yield: 1 cup

- 1 cup whole milk
- 1 teaspoon active kefir grains
- 1 pint-size glass jar

Combine the milk and grains in the jar. Cover with cheesecloth and secure with a rubber band.

Allow to ferment for 12–48 hours at room temperature (70°F). Keep away from direct sunlight. Check after 12–15 hours. You are looking for milk that is thickened and tastes tangy. The milk ferments faster at warmer temperatures and slower at cooler temperatures.

When the kefir is ready, strain it to remove the kefir grains. Reserve the grains for the next batch of kefir. Keep grains in milk stored in the refrigerator if you do not want to make another batch of kefir.

Keep kefir refrigerated for up to one week. At this point, you can add sweeteners and flavorings such as maple syrup, brown rice syrup, sugar, and/or pureed fruit.

Yogurt (Instant Pot)
Yield: 8–9 cups

- 1 gallon whole milk
- 1/4 cup plain greek yogurt

Pour the milk into the instant pot. Close and lock the lid. Set the valve to "Sealing." Select "Yogurt" on the Instant Pot until the display reads "boil." Let the Instant pot complete the boiling stage. Once it is done boiling, remove the inner pot and cool the milk down to 110–115°F. This can take 45 minutes to an hour. Speed up the process by placing the milk in an ice bath.

Whisk in the 1/4 cup yogurt (the starter) in to the milk. Place the inner pot back into the instant pot. Close and lock the lid and set the valve to Sealing. Press the "yogurt" button and adjust the temperature to "normal." The standard time incubation time will be 8 hours.

When the yogurt is done, release the lid. Place a colander over a large bowl and line with cheesecloth or a clean flour sack towel. Pour the yogurt into the colander and all the whey to drain off the yogurt. The yogurt can be drained for about 1 hour or up to 8 hours for a greek-style thick yogurt. When the yogurt is strained to desired consistency, it's ready to use.

Caprese Salad
Serves 4

- 8 ounces fresh mozzarella, sliced
- 2–3 medium fresh tomatoes, sliced
- 2 ounces whole basil leaves
- 3 tablespoons olive oil
- juice of 1 lemon
- 1 clove garlic, minced
- salt and pepper, to taste

Decoratively alternate the mozzarella, tomatoes, and basil on a plate. In a small bowl, whisk together the oil, lemon juice, garlic, salt, and pepper. Pour mixture over the cheese and tomatoes. Serve immediately.

Ricotta Cannellini Bean Dip
Yield: about 2 cups

- 2–4 tablespoons olive oil
- 1 tablespoon fresh rosemary, chopped
- 1 clove garlic, minced
- 1 cup ricotta cheese
- 1 (15-ounce) can cannellini beans, drained and rinsed
- 1 tablespoon lemon juice
- Salt and pepper, to taste

Heat 1 tablespoon oil in a skillet. Add the rosemary and garlic. Lightly sauté for 1 minute. Set aside. Place the ricotta, beans, lemon juice, and rosemary/garlic mixture in a food processor. Pulse to combine well. With the motor running, add the remaining olive oil to desired creamy consistency. Season to taste with salt and pepper. Serve with crackers, toasted bread, or pita chips.

Carrot Tart with Ricotta and Herbs
Serves 6

- 1 1/2 cups ricotta cheese
- 2 tablespoons heavy cream
- salt and pepper, to taste
- 3 tablespoons olive oil
- 1 shallot, thinly sliced
- 3 medium carrots, thinly sliced into rounds
- 1 package frozen puff pastry, thawed
- 1 large egg + 1 tablespoon water, mixed together
- 1/4 cup chopped fresh herbs of choice: chives, parsley, basil, oregano, thyme, and/or sage

Preheat oven to 425°F. Line a sheet pan with parchment paper. Set aside.

In a small bowl, whisk together the ricotta and cream. Season with salt and pepper. Set aside.

In a skillet set over medium heat, heat 2 tablespoons oil. Add the shallot and sauté until it starts to soften and brown slightly, about 5 minutes. Add the carrots and sauté for 2–3 more minutes. Season lightly with salt and pepper. Set aside.

On a lightly floured surface, roll the puff pastry dough out to smooth out the creases. Transfer pastry to the sheet pan. With the tip of a sharp knife, score a 1-inch border around the puff pastry. Brush with the egg wash. Bake until golden brown and puffed, about 10–15 minutes.

Remove from the oven and spread ricotta mixture over the pastry, staying within the border. Scatter shallots and carrots over the top. Bake until the carrots are tender and the onions begin to caramelize, about 15 minutes.

Toss the herbs in remaining 1 tablespoon olive oil. Season with salt and pepper. Drizzle over the tart.

Goat Cheese Crostini with Fig-Olive Tapenade
Serves 6–8

- 15 (1/4-inch thick) baguette slices
- 3 tablespoons olive oil
- 1/2 cup pitted Kalamata olives
- 1/2 cup stemmed and halved dried figs
- 1/4 cup chopped walnuts
- 2 tablespoons fresh thyme (or basil or parsley)
- 1 tablespoon balsamic vinegar
- salt and pepper, to taste
- 3 ounces goat cheese
- fresh herbs (basil, thyme, or parsley) for garnish

Preheat oven to 425°F. Brush the bread slices with 1 tablespoon olive oil and place on a sheet pan. Bake until crisp and golden brown, about 8–10 minutes. Remove from oven and cool.

In a food processor, pulse the olives, figs, walnuts, and 2 teaspoons thyme until roughly chopped. Add the remaining oil, balsamic, salt, and pepper. Pulse to combine.

In a small bowl, mix together the goat cheese and remaining fresh thyme.

Spread goat cheese on the bread slices and top with the tapenade.

Fresh Butter
Yield: 8 ounces

- 1 pint heavy cream
- pinch of salt

Place the cream in the bowl of a stand mixer. With the flat beater, whip the cream until it starts to separate and slosh around, about 15–25 minutes. At this point, you will see yellow butter solids and fresh buttermilk. Stop whipping and drain off the buttermilk (reserve). Wrap the solid butter mass in plastic wrap. Add salt to it if desired. Refrigerate up to two weeks.

Lavender Honey Butter
Yield: 1 cup

- 1 cup softened butter
- 1 tablespoon fresh lavender or 1 1/2 teaspoons dried lavender, crushed
- 1 tablespoon honey
- pinch of salt

Mix ingredients together in a small bowl. Refrigerate until ready to use. Will keep for up to one week under refrigeration.

Buttermilk Biscuits
Yield: about 1 dozen

- 2 cups AP flour
- 1 tablespoon sugar
- 2 teaspoons baking powder
- 1/4 teaspoon baking soda
- 1 teaspoon salt
- 1/2 cup cold unsalted butter, cut into cubes
- 3/4 cup buttermilk

Preheat oven to 425°F.

Mix together the flour, sugar, baking powder, baking soda, and salt. Using a pastry blender, cut the butter into the flour mixture until the butter is in small pieces and distributed throughout the flour. Stir in the milk to make a sticky dough. Do not overmix.

Dust the counter with flour and knead the dough slightly to smooth it out. Roll it out to about 1/2-inch thick. Cut into shapes with a round biscuit cutter. Place on a sheet pan lined with parchment. Bake until golden brown, about 15 minutes.

Note: For this recipe, you can use the fresh butter and buttermilk made in the fresh butter recipe.

Yogurt Cheese
Yield: 1 1/2 cups

- 2 cups greek yogurt
- 1 tablespoon parsley, chopped
- 1 tablespoon fresh chives, chopped
- 1 clove garlic, minced
- salt and pepper, to taste

Fold a large piece of cheesecloth twice to form four layers in a roughly eighteen-inch square. Place in a sieve set over a large bowl, and spoon yogurt into center. Gathering the four corners, tie a piece of kitchen twine just above yogurt to form a tight bundle. Let yogurt (still in sieve over bowl) drain in refrigerator at least 8 hours and up to 24 hours.

Cut open cheesecloth. Transfer yogurt cheese to a bowl; set whey aside for another use. Stir chives, parsley, garlic, salt, and pepper into yogurt cheese. Serve with crudités and bread.

Lassi
Yield: about 2 cups

- 2 cups plain yogurt
- 1 cup chilled sparkling water or cold milk
- 2 1/2 cups mango chunks
- 1 tablespoon honey or agave
- 1/2 teaspoon ground cardamom

Mix yogurt and water in a blender. Blend until creamy and smooth. Add the mango, honey, and cardamom. Blend until smooth and creamy.

Kefir Ice Cream
Yield: 1 quart

- 3 large egg yolks
- 2 tablespoons sugar
- 2 cups heavy cream
- 2 1/2 cups milk kefir (any flavor)
- 1/2 cup liquid sweetener of choice (honey, maple syrup, or agave)
- 2 teaspoons vanilla extract

Make an ice bath in a large bowl. Set aside.

In a small bowl, whisk together the egg yolks and sugar. Set aside.

In a saucepan set over medium heat, bring the cream just to a boil. Ladle about 1/4 cup of the hot cream into the egg yolk mixture to temper it, whisking constantly. Add the tempered egg yolk mixture to the remaining hot cream. Cook over medium low heat until the mixture is slightly thickened, and the temperature reaches 170°F. This may take 3–5 minutes.

Pour the mixture into a stainless steel bowl. Place the bowl into the ice bath and stir until cool to the touch.

Add the kefir, sweetener, and vanilla to the cream mixture. Mix well.

Pour the mixture into the bowl of an ice cream maker. Churn according to manufacturer's instructions.

Serve when finished or freeze in a separate container until ready to serve.

Strawberry Frozen Yogurt
Yield: 1 quart

- 1 pound fresh or frozen strawberries (thawed, if frozen)
- 1 to 1 1/2 cups sugar (depends on how sweet the strawberries are)
- 2 cups plain or vanilla greek yogurt (or non-dairy yogurt)
- 2 teaspoons lemon juice

Toss together the strawberries and sugar. Let the mixture sit at room temperature for one hour. Place the strawberries, yogurt, and lemon juice in a blender. Puree until smooth. Freeze the mixture according to ice cream maker instructions.

Almond Milk (or Other Nut Milks)
Yield: 1 quart

- 1 cup almonds (or walnuts or cashews)
- 4 cups water

Place the almonds and water in a container. Refrigerate for 12 hours. Pour the almonds and water into a blender and grind until finely chopped.

Strain mixture through a mesh strainer lined with cheese cloth. Squeeze out the almond milk. Add vanilla or sweetener if desired.

The almond solids can be used in recipes. The almond milk will keep for one week in the refrigerator.

Coconut Ice Cream

Yield: 1 quart

- 1 (13- to 15-ounce) can full-fat coconut milk
- 1/2 cup sweetener, such as agave syrup, maple syrup, honey, turbinado sugar, or cane sugar
- 1/4 teaspoon salt
- 1 tablespoon cornstarch, or 2 teaspoons arrowroot starch
- 1 (13–15 ounce) can coconut cream
- 1 teaspoon vanilla extract
- optional mix-ins: nuts, chocolate chips, fruit purée, cacao nibs, etc.

Pour the coconut milk into a saucepan. Remove 2 tablespoons of the coconut milk and put in a small bowl. Set aside.

Add the sweetener of choice and salt to the pan with the remaining coconut milk. Bring to a simmer over medium high heat.

Whisk together the cornstarch and reserved 2 tablespoons coconut milk. Pour mixture into the pan and simmer over medium high until the mixture starts to thicken, about 6–8 minutes. Once the mixture starts to boil (it will "blop"), it has reached its full thickening power. Remove from heat and pour into to a stainless steel bowl. Place the bowl in an ice bath and stir until the mixture is cooled to room temperature. Stir in the coconut cream and vanilla extract.

Freeze the mixture according to ice cream maker instructions. Keep frozen until ready to serve.

Add optional mix ins while ice cream is churning.

If coconut cream is not available, increase coconut milk to 2 15-oz cans and cornstarch to 2 tablespoons.

Dairy Free Ice Cream

Yield: 1 pint

- 2 cups dairy-free milk of choice
- 1/2 cup nut or seed butter of choice
- 1/3 cup sweetener of choice
- 1/2 teaspoon salt
- 1 1/2 teaspoon vanilla extract
- 1/2 ripe banana (optional)
- optional mix-ins: cocoa powder (2–3 tablespoons), nuts, chocolate chips, fruit purée, cacao nibs, etc.

Whisk together all ingredients. Pour mixture into ice cream maker and proceed to churn it according to manufacturer's instructions. Either eat straight from the machine or freeze an hour for a firmer texture.

Coconut Squash Soup
Yield: 1 quart

- 1 acorn squash, cut in half and seeds removed
- 1/4 cup canola or safflower oil
- 1 leek, diced and cleaned well
- 1 serrano or Thai chili pepper, coarsely chopped
- 2 cloves garlic, chopped
- 2 tablespoons fresh ginger, minced
- 1 14-ounce can full-fat coconut milk
- salt and pepper to taste
- juice of 1 lime
- vegetable stock as needed for thinning
- chopped fresh cilantro for garnish

Preheat oven to 375°F.

Rub 2 tablespoon of the oil over the flesh of the squash. Place flesh side down on a sheet pan. Bake until fork tender, about 30 minutes. Remove from oven. Set aside to cool for 10 minutes.

Heat remaining 2 tablespoons oil in a saucepot. Add the leek, chili pepper, garlic, and ginger. Sauté for 3–4 minutes.

Scrape the skin off the squash and place the flesh in the pan. Add the coconut milk. Puree the mixture with an immersion blender until smooth. Season to taste with salt and pepper. Add lime juice. Adjust consistency with vegetable stock. Cook over medium low heat for 10 minutes to allow flavors to develop. Garnish with cilantro. Serve hot.

Unit 4 Questions

1. Describe the differences between the milk varieties tasted. Include in your description information about fat content, mouthfeel, texture, and flavor. How does fat content correlate to mouthfeel?
2. Describe the differences between the assortment of cheeses tasted. Be sure to concentrate on flavor and texture differences.
3. What is rennet? What is its purpose in cheese making?
4. Name 2 different microbes (bacteria or mold) used for cheese making. For each microbe, what type of cheese do they make?
5. Describe the differences in the coagulation of the different types of milk in Experiment 2. Why did some of them coagulate better than others?
6. Describe the differences in flavor, texture, and mouthfeel between the puddings made in experiment 1. Which pudding did you prefer? Why?
7. Why is raw milk preferred for cheese making? What are some food safety concerns with raw milk?
8. What is shelf-stable milk and how is it different than milk sold in the refrigerated section?

NOTES

1. International Dairy Foods Association (IDFA), "Pasteurization," accessed May 7, 2019, https://www.idfa.org/news-views/media-kits/milk/pasteurization.

2. Encyclopedia Britannica, "Homogenization," accessed May 7, 2019, https://www.britannica.com/science/homogenization.

3. Harold McGee, *On Food and Cooking: The Science and Lore of the Kitchen* (New York: Scribner, 2004), 50.

4. McGee, *On Food and Cooking*.

5. The Cheese Store, "The Major Types and Kinds of Cheese," accessed May 7, 2019 https://cheese-store.com/the-major-types-and-kinds-of-cheese/.

BIBLIOGRAPHY

The Cheese Store. "The Major Types and Kinds of Cheese." accessed May 14, 2019. https://cheese-store.com/the-major-types-and-kinds-of-cheese/.

Encyclopedia Britannica. "Homogenization." Accessed May 7, 2019. https://www.britannica.com/science/homogenization.

International Dairy Foods Association (IDFA). "Pasteurization." Accessed May 7, 2019. https://www.idfa.org/news-views/media-kits/milk/pasteurization.

McGee, Harold. *On Food and Cooking: The Science and Lore of the Kitchen.* New York: Scribner, 2004.

Protein

Meat, Poultry, Seafood, and Plant Based

OBJECTIVES

- ■ Identify different cuts of meat
- ■ Explain how to select meat, poultry, and seafood
- ■ Explain different grades of beef
- ■ Define terms found on meat and poultry labels
- ■ Demonstrate how to cut up a chicken
- ■ Demonstrate and evaluate different cooking techniques for meat, poultry, seafood
- ■ Discuss meat substitutes in vegetarian and vegan cooking
- ■ Use basic cooking skills to prepare dishes

MEAT

The term "meat" describes the muscle from mammalian animals such as cattle, goat, sheep, hogs, and bison, along with wild game like elk and deer.

In the United States, the two main sources of meat are beef and pork.[1] Generally, the most tender cuts of meat originate from muscles that the animal uses the least. Muscle that is worked extensively by the animal, such as the hind legs, creates more connective tissues resulting in tougher pieces of meat.[2] Because of this connective tissue, these pieces require longer cooking times.

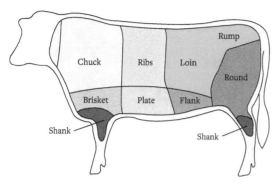

FIGURE 5.1 Cuts of Beef

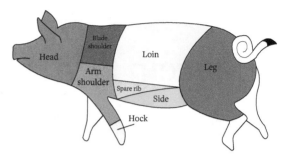

FIGURE 5.2 Cuts of Pork

Selecting Meat

When choosing meat to purchase, follow a set of guidelines to ensure the best quality.

TABLE 5.1

Selecting Meat	Description
Color	Color of the meat will vary according to the type of animal. Look for rich, vibrant, uniform color.
Marbling	Marbling refers to the amount of fat dispersed in the muscle. Look for marbling when selecting beef. It is associated with a higher quality and better flavor.
Odor/Smell	Meat should have a pleasant odor. Meat that is starting to turn bad will have an off-odor.
Firmness	Choose meat that is firm to the touch but not tough or soft. When poked, the meat should retain its shape.

The United States Department of Agriculture (USDA) grades beef based on the marbling of beef.

TABLE 5.2

USDA Beef Grades[3]	Description
Prime	Best quality with high amounts of marbling. Found in restaurants
Choice	High quality, good amounts of marbling; found in supermarkets
Select	Leaner with less marbling; found in supermarkets
Utility, cutter, canner	Low quality used for ground meat and hot dogs

Increasingly, consumers are curious about selecting more sustainably raised meat and pork. Conventionally raised beef starts out on pasture until 7–9 months old and is then moved to a feedlot where it is fed a diet of corn and soy for 3–4 months before being slaughtered. This is opposed to grass-fed beef, which stays at pasture longer and is slaughtered between 18–24 months. Typically, conventionally raised cattle and hogs are given antibiotics to prevent disease. Depending on the farming operation, some hogs may spend their time in CAFOs, concentrated animal feeding operations and are ready for market at 6 months.

Proper Cooking Temperatures

Test the internal temperature of the meat by inserting an instant-read or digital probe thermometer into the thickest part of the muscle.

TABLE 5.3

Steak	Ground Beef	Pork
Rare: 125°F Medium rare: 135°F Medium: 145°F Medium well: 155°F Well: 165°F	Hamburger: 155°F	Chops or roasts: 145°F Sausage: 165°F Ribs: 160°F

POULTRY

Chicken is not the only source of poultry. Poultry, however, covers a range of animals – chickens, duck, pheasant, turkey, and Cornish game hens.

Chicken and turkey are broken down into white meat and dark meat. The white meat includes wings and breasts of the birds while dark meat is from the legs and thighs.

TABLE 5.4

Selecting Poultry	Description
Color	Color of the chicken or turkey should be pale pink
Odor/Smell	Poultry should have a pleasant odor. Poultry that is starting to turn bad will have a strong, unpleasant odor.
Firmness	Choose poultry with firm, plump flesh

Cooking Temperatures

TABLE 5.5

Chicken and Turkey
White meat (breast, wing): 165°F Dark meat (thigh, leg): 175°F

Breaking Down Poultry

Poultry can be broken down into eight pieces: two breasts, two legs, two thighs, and two wings. Using a sharp boning knife, cut in between each joint. The breast can be cut away from the bone of have the rib cage left attached to the meat.

Terminology on Food Labels (Meat and Poultry)

When selecting meat and poultry, it is also important to understand terms that may be on the label.

Organic[4]

The USDA specifies organic guidelines. Organic meat and poultry can only consume organic feed and cannot be given hormones or antibiotics. The animals must also have access to the outdoors.

Pasture-Raised[5]

The USDA does not certify this term, but it refers to meat and poultry that has been raised outdoors on pasture. Some pastured meat may be fed grain to supplement the diet especially during the winter months.

Grass Fed[6]

Up until 2016, the USDA set standards for grass-fed beef stating the animals must only consume grasses after they are weaned from their mothers and may not be fed grain.

Grain-Finished

Finishing occurs right before the animal is butchered to increase the fat and marbling in the meat. All conventionally-raised cattle is finished on grain while some grass fed cattle may spend most of their lives on pasture and then have a diet of grain for the last couple of months.

Natural[7]

The USDA specifies that natural products may not have any artificial ingredients, colors, or preservatives and should be minimally processed.

No Hormones[8]

Hormones are prohibited for use in raising poultry according to the USDA. However, cattle can be given hormones. If the label says, "no hormones," this means that hormones were not administered to the livestock.

Kosher[9]

Kosher meat refers to the type of animal and how it is slaughtered. Beef and poultry producers must follow specific Jewish dietary laws in processing the animals for consumption.

Free Range[10]

Poultry producers must demonstrate that the birds have access to the outdoors, even if the animals choose to stay inside.

Cage Free[11]

Poultry is not kept in cages.

The USDA requires that muscle cuts and ground lamb, chicken, and goat indicate the source of where the meat was raised.

SEAFOOD

The world of seafood covers fish and shellfish. Fish are vertebrates whereas shellfish are invertebrates. There are nearly 30,000 species of fish which can be divided into subcategories from flatfish to fatty fish. Some of the most popular types of fish include tuna, salmon, mackerel, herring, cod, catfish, sold, halibut, and flounder. Salmon and mackerel are considered fatty fish and are good sources of omega-3 fatty acids. Shellfish include subcategories of crustaceans and mollusks. Shrimp, crabs, and lobsters are part of the crustacean family while clams, mussels, oysters, and scallops are part of the mollusk family.

Cooking Seafood

Seafood cooks very quickly and contains less connective tissue compared to meat. Cook fish at high temperatures to avoid mushy textures. Fish and shellfish should be cooked to an internal temperature of 145°F.

Selecting Seafood

TABLE 5.6

Selecting Seafood	Description
Odor/Smell	Fresh seafood should have a fresh ocean or seawater smell. Do not purchase seafood with a strong, "fishy" odor.
Flesh	Flesh of the fish should be firm and moist
Scales (if present)	Close to the skin and not flaking off
Mollusks	If purchased fresh, make sure they are alive. Clams and mussels will be closed. If they are open, tap the shell to see if they close.
Lobsters and crabs (if alive)	If purchasing live lobsters, look for ones that are active and curl their tails when picked up. For crabs, choose ones that have some movement.

Terminology on Food Labels (Seafood)

Around fifty percent of the seafood we consume is raised on farms or in aquaculture systems. It is a controlled system where fish are raised in pens that are often submerged in ponds, lakes, or salt water.

Seafood is caught in its natural environment by fishermen.

Line-Caught[15]

Fish is caught either off a long line that sits off the boat, or it is caught on individual lines.

Country of Origin Labeling (COOL)

Identifies where the seafood was raised or caught, similar to meat and poultry labeling.

Sustainable Seafood

The Monterey Bay Aquarium developed "Seafood Watch,"[16] providing guidelines for choosing sustainable seafood in stores and at restaurants. Each year, they update the list and consumers can find lists specific to the region in which they reside. They offer three categories for choosing seafood – best choices, good alternatives, and avoid. The best choices list is comprised of seafood that is well managed and caught or farmed in ways that do not cause harm to habitats or wildlife. For a comprehensive list of sustainably raised seafood, visit www.seafoodwatch.org or download their free app on your phone.

PLANT-BASED PROTEINS

A wide range of the plant kingdom serve as good sources of protein. All legumes, including beans and lentils, as well as grains and nuts, work together to create a complete source of protein. Legumes are discussed in detail in unit 3 and unit 8 covers grains and nuts.

To mimic the umami flavor of meat, several options are available, including the use of soy sauce and mushrooms.

Common sources of plant-based proteins:

- soybean products: tofu, tempeh
- seitan: meat-like product made from wheat
- TVP: textured vegetable protein
- jackfruit: a tropical fruit native to South India
- legumes: beans, lentils
- grains: most grains contain a source of protein
- tree nuts: almonds, pecans, walnuts, cashews, etc.

EXPERIMENTS

Experiment 1: Brining Chicken

Does brining chicken give it more flavor and juiciness?

Basic Recipe (control)—Sautéed Chicken Breast

- 2 tablespoons canola oil
- 1 teaspoon salt
- 1/4 teaspoon black pepper
- 2 boneless skinless chicken breasts, pounded slightly to even thickness

Heat the oil in a skillet or sauté pan set over medium heat. In a small bowl, mix the salt and pepper. Season both sides of the chicken breast with salt and pepper.

Place the chicken in the hot pan, skin-side down. Cook one side for 3–5 minutes. If it is browning too quickly, lower the heat to medium low. Flip when the side is nicely browned.

Flip the breast over and lower the heat to low. Continue to cook for another 5–8 minutes, or until internal temperature reaches 165°F. Allow chicken to rest for 5 minutes before slicing and serving.

Variations:
Brine the chicken breasts:

- 15 minutes
- 30 minutes
- 45 minutes

Brining solution

- 2 cups water
- 2 teaspoons kosher salt
- 1/2 teaspoon black peppercorns

Make the brining solution by bringing 1/2 cup of the water to a boil. Add the salt and peppercorns. Stir to dissolve the salt. Add the remaining 1 1/2 cups of water to bring the water temperature down to room temperature.

Add the chicken breasts to the brine and brine according the specified time above.

Sauté the chicken breasts in the same manner as the basic recipe. Do not season the brined chicken breasts before sautéing.

Chicken	Flavor	Juiciness	Texture	Additional Notes
Control—Basic Recipe				
15 minute brine				
30 minute brine				
45 minute brine				

Experiment 2: Dry-Rub Chicken Breasts

Does dry-rubbing meat or poultry make a difference in terms of flavor and juiciness?

Basic Recipe (control) – Sautéed Chicken Breast

- 2 tablespoons canola oil
- 1 1/2 teaspoons salt
- 1/4 teaspoon black pepper
- 2 boneless skinless chicken breasts, pounded slightly to even thickness

Heat the oil in a skillet or sauté pan set over medium heat. In a small bowl, mix the salt and pepper. Season both sides of the chicken breast with salt and pepper.

Place the chicken in the hot pan, skin-side down. Cook one side for 3–5 minutes. If it is browning too quickly, lower the heat to medium low. Flip when the side is nicely browned.

Flip the breast over and lower the heat to low. Continue to cook for another 5–8 minutes, or until internal temperature reaches 165°F. Allow chicken to rest for 5 minutes before slicing and serving.

Variations

Leave the chicken dry-rubbed for:

- 5 minutes at room temperature
- 15 minutes at room temperature
- 30 minutes at room temperature
- 1 hour under refrigeration

Mix the salt and pepper together and season the chicken breast before heating the oil in the pan. Once the chicken has been sitting for the specified amount of time, proceed with the recipe for sautéing the chicken breasts.

Chicken	Flavor	Juiciness	Texture	Additional Notes
Control—Basic Recipe				
5 minute dry rub				
15 minute dry rub				
30 minute dry rub				
1 hour dry rub				

EVALUATION OF GROUND MEAT

Evaluate different types of ground meat and meat alternatives.

Basic (Control)

- 1/3 pound ground beef (80/20)
- 1/2 teaspoon salt
- 1/2 teaspoon pepper
- 2 tablespoons canola oil

Combine the beef, salt, and pepper in a bowl. Form beef mixture into 2 patties. Heat the oil in a skillet set over medium heat. Sauté the beef patties in the hot oil for 3–4 minutes per side or until the internal temperatures reach 155°F. Rest for 5 minutes before serving.

Variations

In place of the ground beef, substitute:

- ground turkey (cook to internal temperature of 165°F)
- grass-fed ground beef (cook to internal temperature of 155°F)
- ground pork (cook to internal temperature of 155°F)
- ground lamb (cook to internal temperature of 155°F)
- frozen vegetable burger (cook according to package instructions)
- tofu or similar vegan sausage (cook according to package instructions)

Patty or sausage	Flavor	Texture	Fat Content
Basic recipe (control)			
Ground turkey			
Grass-fed beef			
Ground pork			
Ground lamb			
Vegetable burger			
Vegan sausage			
Beyond or Impossible burger			

RECIPES

Meatloaf

Serves 4–6

- 1/2 cup bread crumbs
- 1/4 cup milk
- 3/4 pound ground beef
- 1/4 pound ground pork
- 1/2 onion, minced
- 2 cloves garlic, minced
- 2 large eggs
- 1 tablespoon Worcestershire sauce
- 1/2 cup ketchup
- 2 tablespoons Dijon mustard
- 1 teaspoon salt
- 1 teaspoon pepper

Preheat oven to 375°F. Line a sheet pan with parchment paper.

In a large bowl, mix the breadcrumbs and milk. Let sit for 5 minutes to soften the bread-crumbs. Add the ground beef, pork, onion, garlic, eggs, Worcestershire, 1/4 cup of ketchup, Dijon, salt, and pepper. With your hands, mix the ingredients together. Scoop the mixture onto the sheet pan and form into a loaf shape. Spread the remaining ketchup over the top of the loaf. Bake for 45–60 minutes or until the internal temperature reaches 155°F. Allow to rest for 10 minutes before serving.

Swedish Meatballs

Serves 4–6

- 1/2 cup breadcrumbs
- 1/4 cup milk
- 12 ounces ground beef
- 12 ounces ground pork
- 1/2 cup onion, minced
- 1 large egg
- 1–2 teaspoons salt
- 1/2 teaspoon black pepper
- 1/4 teaspoon ground allspice
- 1/4 teaspoon nutmeg
- 3 tablespoons unsalted butter
- 1/4 cup all-purpose flour
- 3 cups low sodium beef stock
- 1/4 cup heavy cream

Preheat oven to 200°F.

Place the breadcrumbs in the milk. Set aside.

In a bowl, combine the bread crumb/milk mixture, beef, pork, onion, egg, 1 teaspoon salt, pepper, allspice, and nutmeg. Use your hands to combine the mixture. Roll into 1-ounce meatballs (about the size of a walnut).

Heat 2 tablespoons butter in a sauté pan set over medium-low heat. Add the meatballs and sauté until golden brown on all sides, about 7–10 minutes, or until the internal temperature reaches 155°F. Remove the meatballs and place in an oven proof dish. Keep warm in the oven.

Once all of the meatballs are finished cooking, decrease the heat to low and add the remaining tablespoon butter and the flour. Whisk the roux until lightly browned, about 1–2 minutes. Gradually add the beef stock and whisk until sauce begins to thicken. Add the cream and continue to cook until the gravy reaches the desired consistency. Adjust seasoning accordingly. Remove the meatballs from the oven and place in the gravy. Serve with buttered noodles.

Italian Meatballs
Serves 4–6

- 2 pounds ground beef
- 1 cup breadcrumbs
- 1/2 cup grated parmesan
- 2 large eggs
- 2 cloves garlic, minced
- 1 heaping tablespoon chopped fresh basil (or 1 teaspoon dried)
- 1 heaping tablespoon chopped fresh parsley
- 1 teaspoon salt
- 1/2 teaspoon black pepper
- 1/4 teaspoon ground cayenne pepper
- 3 tablespoons olive oil

Place the beef, breadcrumbs, parmesan, eggs, garlic, basil, parsley, salt, pepper, and cayenne pepper in large bowl. Mix with your hands to form a homogenized mass. Roll into meat balls about the size of a walnut.

Heat the oil in a large skillet set over medium heat. Working in batches, add the meatballs. Brown the bottom of the meatball before turning. Continue cooking until browned all over and the internal temperature reaches 155°F. Remove meatballs to a plate as each batch is finished. Let meatballs cool slightly. Serve with a red tomato sauce and pasta.

Grilled Marinated Steak
Serves 2

- 2 steaks (any cut)
- 1/4 cup olive oil
- 2 cloves garlic, minced
- 1 tablespoon fresh rosemary, finely chopped
- 1/2 teaspoon salt
- 1/2 teaspoon pepper

Place the steaks in a shallow dish. Set aside.

In a small bowl, whisk together the oil, garlic, rosemary, salt, and pepper. Pour marinade over the steaks and cover with plastic wrap. Allow to set for 30 minutes at room temperature for up to 2 hours in the refrigerator.

Preheat the grill until hot. Place steaks on the grill. Depending on thickness of the steak, grill for 2–6 minutes per side to achieve medium rare temperature. Allow steaks to rest for 10 minutes before serving.

Roast Beef
Serves 6

- 3 pound top round or sirloin beef roast
- 3–4 tablespoons oil
- Salt and pepper
- 4–5 ribs celery, cut into chunks
- 1 white onion, cut into chunks
- 3 carrots, cut into chunks
- 1 whole head of garlic, cut in half
- 2 bay leaves
- 3 sprigs rosemary
- 3–4 tablespoons flour
- 1 cup red wine
- 1 quart beef stock

Preheat oven to 350°F.

Rub the roast with the oil. Season all sides of the roast with salt and pepper. If using roast sirloin with a fat cap, score the fat with a knife.

Heat 1–2 tablespoons oil in a roasting pan over medium-high heat. Sear the beef until nice and brown on all sides. Remove beef roast from the pan. Turn off the heat. Add the celery, onion, carrots, garlic, bay leaves, and rosemary to the bottom of the pan. Place the roast on top of the vegetables.

Roast in the oven for 1 hour and 15 minutes (10 minutes less if you want medium rare). Remove from oven and remove roast from the pan. Rest for 30 minutes.

Make the gravy by placing the roasting pan over medium heat. Add the flour to the pan to make a roux. Cook for 3–4 minutes. Mash the vegetables with a potato masher. Add the red wine. Cook for 2 minutes. Add the stock and stir to incorporate. Reduce heat to low and simmer the gravy for 25 minutes.

Strain the gravy through a fine sieve. Slice the beef into thin slices. Serve with horseradish sauce and gravy alongside roasted root vegetables.

Beef Stew
Serves 4–5

- 1/4 cup all-purpose flour
- 1 pound beef stewing meat, trimmed and cut into 1-inch cubes
- 2–3 tablespoons canola oil
- 1 cup red wine
- 3 1/2 cups low sodium beef stock
- 2 bay leaves
- 2 sprigs fresh thyme
- 1 medium onion, chopped
- 5 medium carrots, cut into 1/2-inch rounds
- 2 large baking potatoes, cut into 1-inch cubes
- salt and pepper, to taste

In a shallow dish or bowl, season the flour with salt and pepper. Toss the beef in the flour, coating well and shaking off any excess.

Heat 2 tablespoons of the oil in a large pot or Dutch oven. Working in batches, cook the beef until browned on all sides. Remove and place in a dish. Add more oil as needed between batches and repeat until all the beef is browned.

Remove the beef from the pot and add the wine. Cook over medium-high heat, scraping the pan with a wooden spoon to loosen any browned bits. Add the beef, beef stock, bay leaves, and thyme. Bring to a boil, then reduce to a slow simmer.

Cover and cook, skimming broth periodically to remove any foam or impurities, until the beef is tender, about 1 1/2 hours. Add the onions and carrots and simmer, covered, for 10 minutes. Add the potatoes and simmer until vegetables are tender, about 30 minutes more. Add broth or water if the stew is dry. Season to taste with salt and pepper.

Pork Chops
Serves 4

Brine

- 3 cups water
- 3 tablespoons salt
- 1 teaspoon black peppercorns
- 2 garlic cloves, smashed

Pork Chops

- 4 bone-in pork chops
- 2 tablespoons olive oil
- 1–2 teaspoons salt
- 1–2 teaspoons pepper

Make the brine by bringing 1 cup of water to a boil with the salt. Add the peppercorns, garlic, and remaining 2 cups water. Let the brine cool to room temperature.

Place the pork chops in a shallow dish. Pour brine over the pork. Allow to sit for 30 minutes at room temperature or up to 4 hours in the refrigerator.

Preheat the oven to 400°F.

Remove the chops from the brine and pat dry with paper towels. Rub the pork with olive oil and season well with salt and pepper.

Heat an oven-proof sauté pan (preferably cast iron) over medium-high heat. Sear the pork chops for 1–2 minutes per side. Place pan and pork chops in the oven and bake for 6–10 minutes, depending on the thickness of the chops, or until the internal temperature of the pork reaches 145°F. Remove from oven and place on a platter. Rest for at least 10 minutes before serving.

Roast Pork Loin
Serves 5–6

- 1 (3–4 pound) pork loin
- 2 tablespoons canola or safflower oil
- 2 teaspoons salt
- 2 teaspoons pepper
- 4 cloves garlic, minced
- 2 tablespoons dijon mustard
- 2 tablespoons cider vinegar
- 1 tablespoon fresh sage, finely chopped
- 1 tablespoon fresh rosemary, finely chopped
- 1 onion, chopped
- 1 gala or fuji apple, cut into wedges
- 2 tablespoons flour
- 1 cup white wine
- 2 cups low-sodium chicken stock

Preheat oven to 375°F.

Trim and tie the pork loin. Rub the pork with olive oil and season well with salt and pepper.

Heat an ovenproof sauté pan (like a cast iron pan) or a roasting pan over medium-high heat. Sear the pork on all sides until nice and brown. Remove from the pan. Turn off the heat.

In a small bowl, whisk together the garlic, mustard, cider vinegar, sage, and rosemary. Set aside.

Fill the bottom of the pan with the onions and apples. Place the pork loin on the vegetables and rub the garlic mustard mixture over the top and sides of the pork loin.

Bake for 60 minutes or until the internal temperature reaches 145°F.

Rest for 10–15 minutes before slicing and serving.

Make a quick sauce from the pan drippings. Remove the onions and apples. Add flour to the pan to make a roux. Cook over medium heat for 2–3 minutes. Pour in white wine; reduce by half. Add 2–3 cups chicken stock. Bring to a boil and reduce heat to low. Simmer for 10–15 minutes or until slightly thickened. Adjust seasonings to taste.

Pork Tenderloin with Raspberry-Chipotle Sauce
Serves 3–4

Pork

- 2 tablespoons canola or safflower oil
- 1 clove garlic, minced
- 1 tablespoon fresh sage, finely chopped
- 1 tablespoon fresh thyme, finely chopped
- 1 teaspoon salt
- 1/2 teaspoon black pepper
- 1 pork tenderloin, trimmed of silver skin

Sauce

- 1 tablespoon canola or safflower oil
- 1/4 cup red onion, diced small
- 1 clove garlic, minced
- 1 chipotle pepper in Adobo sauce, minced
- 1 (10-ounce) bag frozen raspberries
- 1/2 cup raspberry vinegar (or balsamic vinegar)
- 1/2 cup sugar
- Salt and pepper, to taste

Prepare the pork by preheating the oven to 375°F. Combine the oil, garlic, sage, thyme, salt, and pepper in a small bowl. Rub mixture over the pork tenderloin. Let sit at room temperature for 15 minutes.

Start the sauce by heating the oil in saucepan set over medium heat. Add the onion, garlic, and chipotle pepper. Sauté until the onions are soft, about 5 minutes. Add the raspberries and cook until the berries start to get mushy. Add vinegar and sugar. Reduce heat to medium low and simmer until the sauce reduces by about half, about 20 minutes.

While the sauce is simmering, heat an oven-proof sauté pan (like cast iron pan) over medium-high heat. Sear the pork on all sides until nice and brown. Place the pan and pork in the hot oven and bake for 10–15 minutes or until the internal temperature reaches 145°F. Remove from the oven and rest for 10 minutes before slicing and serving.

Finish the sauce by straining it through a fine mesh strainer set over a bowl. Press the solids and scrape off any pulp on the bottom of the strainer. Pour the sauce back into a saucepan. Season with salt and pepper. Turn the heat to medium-high and cook the sauce until reduced slightly. The sauce can be reduced to a glaze consistency if desired.

Serve the sauce over the pork tenderloin.

Coq au Vin
Serves 6–8

- 1 (3- to 4-pound) chicken, cut into 8 pieces
- kosher salt and freshly ground black pepper
- 2 tablespoons olive oil
- 4 ounces bacon or pancetta, diced
- 1/2 pound carrots, cut into 1-inch pieces
- 1 yellow onion, sliced
- 2 garlic cloves, minced
- 1/4 cup cognac or brandy
- 1/2 bottle (375 ml) dry red wine
- 1 cup low-sodium chicken stock
- 10 fresh thyme sprigs
- 2 tablespoons unsalted butter, at room temperature
- 2 tablespoons all-purpose flour
- 8 ounces frozen pearl onions
- 8 ounces cremini mushrooms, stems removed and quartered

Preheat the oven to 250°F.

Pat the chicken with paper towels to remove any excess moisture. Season both sides of the chicken with salt and pepper. Set aside.

Heat the olive oil in a large Dutch oven set over medium heat. Add the bacon and cook 8–10 minutes, or until most of the fat is rendered off and bacon is starting to become crispy. Remove the bacon with a slotted spoon. Set aside.

After removing the bacon, brown the chicken pieces in batches in a single layer for about 5 minutes, turning to brown evenly. Remove the chicken to the plate with the bacon and continue to brown until all the chicken is done. Set aside.

Add the onions and carrots to the pan. Season with salt and pepper. Cook over medium heat for 10–12 minutes, stirring occasionally, until the onions are lightly browned. Add the garlic and cook for 1 more minute. Add the cognac. Cook for about 1 minute. Add the bacon, chicken, and any juices that collected on the plate into the pot. Add the wine, chicken stock, and thyme and bring to a simmer. Cover the pot with a tight fitting lid and place in the oven for 30–40 minutes, until the chicken reaches an internal temperature of 165°F. Remove from the oven and place on top of the stove. Alternately, you can cook this completely on the stove if placed over low heat.

In a small bowl, mix together 1 tablespoon of butter and the flour together to make a paste. Stir this into the stew. Heat the remaining tablespoon butter in a sauté pan set over medium heat. Add the pearled onions and mushrooms. Season lightly with salt and pepper. Cook for about 10 minutes.

Remove stew from oven and add the mushrooms and onions. Cook stew over low heat for 10 minutes. Adjust seasonings to taste. Serve hot with mashed potatoes and crusty bread.

Sautéed Chicken with Lemon Garlic Sauce
Serves 4

- 4 chicken breast cutlets
- salt and pepper
- 1/2 cup flour
- 6 tablespoons unsalted butter
- 1 tablespoon olive oil
- 2 tablespoons minced shallots
- 2 cloves garlic, minced
- 1/4 cup white wine
- 3 tablespoons fresh lemon juice

Season the chicken with salt and pepper. Place the flour in a shallow dish and season with salt and pepper. Dredge the chicken in the flour and shake off the excess. Set aside.

Melt 1 tablespoon butter in a skillet set over medium heat. Add the olive oil. Sauté the chicken in the butter/oil mixture, about 4–5 minutes per side or until the internal temperature reaches 165°F. Remove from the pan.

Add 1 tablespoon butter, shallots and garlic to the pan. Sauté for 1–2 minutes. Deglaze the pan with the wine and lemon juice. Reduce by half. Turn off the heat and whisk in the remaining 4 tablespoons of butter. Season the sauce accordingly. Serve sauce over the chicken.

Roast Chicken
Serves 4

- 1 (3–5 pound) whole roasting chicken, giblets removed
- 2-4 tablespoons olive oil
- 2 teaspoons salt
- 2 teaspoons pepper
- 1 lemon, cut into wedges
- 3 sprigs fresh thyme and/or rosemary

Preheat oven to 350ºF (or 400ºF).

Place the chicken breast-side-up in an ovenproof pan. Rub the chicken with the olive oil and season well with salt and pepper. Fill the cavity with the lemons and herbs. If desired, tie the legs together and tuck the wings under the bird.

Bake for 1 1/2 to 2 hours at 350ºF (or 45–75 minutes at 400ºF) or until the internal temperature reaches 165ºF.

Allow the chicken rest for at least 15 minutes before serving.

Chicken Fricassee
Serves 4

- 1 (3–4pound) chicken, cut into 8 pieces
- Salt and pepper, to taste
- 2 tablespoons unsalted butter
- 1/2 cup coarsely chopped onion
- 1 clove garlic, finely chopped
- 2 tablespoons flour
- 3/4 cup dry white wine
- 1/4 cup low-sodium chicken stock
- 1 bay leaf
- 2 sprigs fresh thyme or 1/2 teaspoon dried
- 1/2 cup heavy cream

Season the chicken with salt and pepper.

Heat the butter in a sauté pan set over medium heat. Add the chicken pieces skin-side down. Cook until nicely browned, about 4–5 minutes. Remove from the pan.

Add the onion and cook for 4–5 minutes. Add the garlic and season with salt and pepper.

Cook for 1 minute. Add the flour and stir to make a roux. Add the wine, chicken stock, bay leaf, and thyme. Bring to a boil. Reduce heat to low. Add the chicken back to the pan. Cover and cook over low heat for about 20 minutes or until the internal temperature of the chicken reaches 165ºF.

Add the cream. Adjust seasonings to taste. Serve with rice or potatoes.

Grilled Chicken
Serves 2

- 2 boneless, skinless chicken breasts
- 1 teaspoon canola or safflower oil
- salt and pepper

Lightly coat the chicken with the oil and season well with salt and pepper. Let sit at room temperature for 20–30 minutes.

Heat the grill to hot. Place the chicken on the grill, skin side down. Depending on the thickness, grill for 5–6 minutes per side or until the internal temperature reaches 165°F. Remove and allow to rest for 5–10 minutes before serving.

Sausage and Mussels
Serves 4–5

- 1 tablespoon olive oil
- 9 ounces andouille sausage or Spanish chorizo
- 2 cloves garlic, chopped
- 1 pound fresh or frozen mussels
- 1/2 cup dry white wine
- 1/4 cup chopped fresh parsley
- salt and pepper, to taste

Heat the oil in a large sauté pan set over medium heat. Add the sausage and garlic. Sauté for 3–5 minutes. Add the mussels and wine. Cover and cook until the mussels are cooked through (they will open if you are using fresh mussels), about 3–5 minutes. Add the parsley and season with salt and pepper. Serve with crusty bread.

Salmon with Asian BBQ Sauce
Serves 4

- 1 pound salmon filets, skin removed
- 2/3 cup hoisin sauce
- 2 tablespoons soy sauce
- 1 tablespoon minced fresh ginger
- 2 cloves garlic, minced
- 1 tablespoon sambal or Sriracha
- 1 teaspoon sesame oil

Preheat oven to 375°F. Line a sheet pan with foil. Grease the foil with oil.

Place the salmon on the pan, flesh side up. In a small bowl, stir together the hoisin, soy sauce, ginger, garlic, sambal, and sesame oil. Spread mixture over the salmon.

Bake until the salmon is done, about 10–15 minutes depending on the thickness of the filets. When done, salmon turns opaque in color and beings to flake. Serve with rice and steamed vegetables.

Trout
Serves 4

- 1 teaspoon ground coriander
- 1 teaspoon ground cumin
- 1 teaspoon paprika (mild, spicy, or smoked)
- 1 teaspoon garlic powder
- 1 teaspoon salt
- 1/2 teaspoon pepper
- 1 pound trout, cut into 4-ounce filets (can leave skin on for more flavor)
- 2–3 tablespoons canola or safflower oil

Mix together the coriander, cumin, paprika, garlic powder, salt, and pepper. Rub spice mixture over the trout.

Heat oil in a cast iron skillet set over medium high heat. Sear the trout in the hot oil until cooked through and browned, about 3–4 minutes per side.

Remove from pan and serve immediately. Serve with cooked vegetables and rice.

Calamari
Serves 4

- 1 pound squid – tubes and tentacles (cleaned); cut tubes into 1/4-inch rings and leave tentacles in tact
- 2 cups buttermilk
- 1/2 teaspoon Tabasco sauce
- 2 cups AP flour
- 1 teaspoon ground cayenne pepper
- 1 teaspoon salt
- 2–3 cups canola or safflower oil for frying
- Aioli for dipping

In a bowl, combine the squid, buttermilk, and tabasco. Soak the squid for 3–4 hours under refrigeration.

Place the flour in a bowl and season with the cayenne pepper and salt. Set this near the stove. Line a plate or baking sheet with paper towels. Set this near the stove.

In a 2-quart saucepan set over medium heat, heat the oil until it reaches 360°F. Drain the calamari from the buttermilk mixture and toss it in the flour mixture. Coat the calamari well. Fry the calamari in batches until it turns light golden brown.

Remove from the oil and drain on the paper towels. Season lightly with salt. Serve with aioli.

Whole Roasted Fish

Serves 4–6

- 2 whole fish that have been cleaned – scaled, gutted, and gills removed
- 1–2 tablespoons olive oil
- salt and pepper
- 8 lemon slices
- 2 bundles of herbs: thyme, oregano, dill, parsley, and/or chives
- 2 cloves garlic, minced

Preheat oven to 400°F.

Place the fish on a baking sheet. Cut 3 diagonal slices on each side of the fish. Rub the fish with the olive oil and season with salt and pepper (inside and out). Place 3–4 lemon slices in the cavity of the fish, along with the herbs and garlic.

Bake until the flesh is opaque and separates easily from the backbone, about 30 minutes for a 2–3 pound fish, 35–45 minutes for a 4-pound fish, or 45–60 minutes for a 6-pound fish.

Serve hot with rice.

Shrimp Scampi

Individual portion

- 1 tablespoon butter
- 1 tablespoon oil
- 2 cloves garlic, minced
- 2 ounces white wine
- salt and pepper
- pinch red pepper flakes
- 6–8 ounces shrimp, shelled
- 2 tablespoons parsley
- fresh lemon juice

Heat butter and oil in a sauté pan. Add garlic. Sauté 1 minute. Add wine, salt, pepper, and red pepper flakes. Reduce by half, about 1–2 minutes. Add shrimp. Sauté until they just turn pink, about 2–4 minutes, depending on the size. Add parsley and a squeeze of fresh lemon juice. Serve hot.

TVP Tacos
Serves 6

- 1 cup water
- 1 cup dry textured vegetable protein (TVP)
- 2 teaspoons soy sauce
- 1 tablespoon canola oil
- 1/2 teaspoon salt
- 1/2 teaspoon garlic powder
- 1/2 teaspoon onion powder
- 1/2 teaspoon chili powder
- taco accompaniments: salsa, guacamole, cheese, scallions, lettuce, tortillas

Bring 3/4 cup of water to a boil. Add the TVP to the water. Let it sit for 5–10 minutes or until all the water is absorbed.

In a sauté pan set over medium heat, combine the oil, rehydrated TVP, soy sauce, salt, seasonings, and remaining 1/4 cup of water. Stir occasionally until the water is absorbed and the taco "meat" is heated through. Adjust seasonings to taste. Serve with taco toppings.

Crispy Tofu
Serves 4

- 1 (14- to 16-ounce) block extra-firm tofu
- 1 teaspoon kosher salt
- 3 tablespoons cornstarch
- 2 tablespoons canola or safflower oil

Place the block of tofu on a plate lined with paper towels. Set a plate on top of it and add something heavy, like a can of beans or tomatoes. Press for 15–30 minutes.

Remove the weight and plate. Pat the tofu dry with more paper towels. Cut the tofu into cubes, thick rectangles, or sticks.

Place the tofu in a shallow dish and sprinkle with salt.

Sprinkle 1 tablespoon of the cornstarch over the tofu. Toss to coat evenly. Continue sprinkling and tossing until all the cornstarch is used.

After adding all the cornstarch, the tofu should be evenly coated with a sticky, gummy layer of cornstarch.

Set a large sauté pan (stainless steel or nonstick) or cast iron skillet over medium-high heat and add the oil. Heat until the oil starts to shimmer.

Add all of the tofu in a single layer. The tofu should sizzle upon contact — if not, wait a few minutes to let the pan heat before continuing.

At first, the tofu will stick to the pan (unless you are using a nonstick skillet). Wait until the tofu releases from the pan before browning the other side. Fry until both sides are browned and crispy.

Transfer the browned tofu to a cooling rack until all the tofu is done. Serve immediately with a dipping sauce.

Quick Dipping Sauce

- 3 tablespoons soy sauce
- 1 teaspoon sesame oil
- 1 teaspoon honey
- 1 teaspoon sambal

Mix and serve with the tofu.

Jackfruit Meatballs
Yield: 50–60 meatballs

- 20 ounces canned jackfruit, drained
- 2 cups water
- 1/2 to 1 cup chickpea or quinoa flour
- 2 teaspoons garam masala
- 1 teaspoon paprika
- 1 teaspoon ground cumin
- 1 teaspoon kosher salt
- 1 teaspoon garlic powder
- 1 teaspoon onion powder
- 1 teaspoon black pepper
- 1–2 tablespoons canola or safflower oil

Place the jackfruit and water in a saucepan. Bring to a boil and cook for 10–15 minutes. Drain off excess liquid. Cool. Place the jackfruit in a large bowl and shred with your hands or with 2 forks.

Add 1/2 cup flour, along with all the seasonings. Mix well. Add additional flour if the mixture is too sticky. Form into balls. Set aside.

To pan fry: Heat oil in a sauté pan set over medium high heat. Fry the balls in batches for 2–3 minutes per side.

To bake: preheat oven to 375°F. Place the balls on a sheet pan. Drizzle with oil. Bake for 15 minutes or until lightly golden brown.

Serve with tzatziki sauce if desired.

Unit 5 Questions

1. Describe the differences in flavor and texture among the ground meat patties and vegan/vegetarian options. Which one had the highest fat content and was it the most flavorful? Did you like the non-meat options? Why or why not?

2. In Experiment 1, describe the differences in flavor of the brined chicken breasts. How does brining time affect the moisture content of the chicken?

3. In Experiment 2, describe the differences in flavor of the dry rubbed chicken breasts. How does adding dry rub to the chicken affect the moisture content of the chicken?

4. Describe the texture and flavor of the TVP taco meat. Did you like it as a meat substitute? Why or why not?

5. What is silver skin?

6. How do you identify different cuts of meat if it is unlabeled?

7. Why do you let meat to sit out at room temperature for 30 minutes prior to cooking?

8. Why does meat need to rest after cooking and before serving?

9. Are there any nutritional differences between grass fed beef and conventionally raised beef? If so, what are they?

10. In a meatless recipe, what ingredients could you add to mimic the flavor of meat or enhance the umami flavor?

NOTES

1. Paul Westcott and James Hansen, "USDA Agricultural Projections to 2025," updated February 18, 2016, accessed May 14, 2019, https://www.ers.usda.gov/publications/pub-details/?pubid=37818.

2. Harold McGee, *On Food and Cooking: The Science and Lore of the Kitchen* (New York: Scribner, 2004), 129–130.

3. United States Department of Agriculture Food Safety and Inspection Service, "Inspection and Grading Meat and Poultry: What are the differences?" Accessed May 14, 2019, https://tinyurl.com/y4gstzrf.

4. USDA, "Organic Labeling," accessed May 14, 2019, https://www.ams.usda.gov/rules-regulations/organic/labeling.

5. Rachel Krantz, "'Wild-caught,' 'organic,' 'grass–fed': what do all these animal welfare labels actually mean?" Vox, accessed May 14, 2019, https://www.vox.com/future-perfect/2019/1/30/18197688/organic-cage-free-wild-caught-certified-humane.

6. Julia Calderone, "You may want to think twice before buying expensive grass-fed beef," accessed May 14, 2019, https://www.businessinsider.com/grass-fed-claims-beef-bogus-usda-packaging-2016-2.

7. USDA, "Meat and Poultry Labeling Terms," accessed May 14, 2019, https://www.fsis.usda.gov/wps/portal/fsis/topics/food-safety-education/get-answers/food-safety-fact-sheets/food-labeling/meat-and-poultry-labeling-terms/meat-and-poultry-labeling-terms.

8. USDA, "Meat and Poultry Labeling Terms."

9. USDA, "Meat and Poultry Labeling Terms."

10. USDA, "Meat and Poultry Labeling Terms."

11. Rachel Krantz, "'Wild-caught,' 'organic,' 'grass–fed': what do all these animal welfare labels actually mean?"

12. USDA, "USDA Amends Country of Origin Labeling Requirements, Final Rule Repeals Beef and Pork Requirements," accessed May 14, 2019, https://www.ams.usda.gov/press-release/usda-amends-country-origin-labeling-requirements-final-rule-repeals-beef-and-pork.

13. Rachel Nania, "What you need to know about farm-raised vs. wild-caught," accessed May 14, 2019, https://wtop.com/food-restaurant/2015/06/what-you-need-to-know-about-farm-raised-vs-wild-caught-fish/.

14. Rachel Nania, "What you need to know about farm-raised vs. wild-caught."

15. Monterey Bay Aquarium, Fishing and Farming Methods, accessed May 14, 2019, https://www.seafoodwatch.org/ocean-issues/fishing-and-farming-methods.

16. Monterey Bay Aquarium, Seafood Watch, accessed May 14, 2019, https://www.seafoodwatch.org/.

BIBLIOGRAPHY

Calderone, Julia. "You may want to think twice before buying expensive grass-fed beef." March 25, 2016. Business Insider, accessed May 14 2019, https://www.businessinsider.com/grass-fed-claims-beef-bogus-usda-packaging-2016-2.

Krantz, Rachel. "'Wild-caught,' 'organic,' 'grass-fed': what do all these animal welfare labels actually mean?" Vox. Accessed May 14, 2019. https://www.vox.com/future-perfect/2019/1/30/18197688/organic-cage-free-wild-caught-certified-humane.

McGee, Harold. *On Food and Cooking: The Science and Lore of the Kitchen.* New York: Scribner, 2004.

Monterey Bay Aquarium, "Fishing and Farming Methods," Seafood Watch, accessed May 14, 2019, https://www.seafoodwatch.org/ocean-issues/fishing-and-farming-methods.

Monterey Bay Aquarium. Seafood Watch. Accessed May 14, 2019. https://www.seafoodwatch.org/.

Nania, Rachel. "What you need to know about farm-raised vs. wild-caught." WTOP. June 2, 2015. Accessed May 14, 2019. https://wtop.com/food-restaurant/2015/06/what-you-need-to-know-about-farm-raised-vs-wild-caught-fish/.

United States Department of Agriculture (USDA) Food Safety and Inspection Service. "Inspection and Grading Meat and Poultry: What are the differences?" Updated June 3, 2014. Accessed May 14, 2019. https://www.fsis.usda.gov/wps/portal/fsis/topics/food-safety-education/get-answers/food-safety-fact-sheets/production-and-inspection/inspection-and-grading-of-meat-and-poultry-what-are-the-differences_/inspection-and-grading-differences/!ut/p/a1/jZFRT4MwEMc_DY9di8yF-UZIzIYOXBYd42Xp4FpIoCVtkcxPb8EHnRm69qV39_tf2__hDKc4E_S94tRUUtB6iLPFkWzJwl2GJEqW7iNZx2_b5CkMib-7t8DhDyD2b-tRPrID8p49uuOBObcINx1lLTYkqwSROORhEhe5BaZwyKQukKQNzRozmBukSwNhCq2TR5YMVFi6s-VLcwhjj9Po8lrmhRCY4kQw1QM-Za2dVGnVFfDgkFyJSAiooxUCBy0MfJLj8gvMfZ5ReJa_c69nbzVR-R7JJn_Bq7M4AuYNtm6yGt5Ggd-CMTJ861dCoZHqFmnbLo0ptUPDnFI3_czLiWvYZbLxiHXJKXU-BqeXJG6b1_TjOViR6qXZ-zr4BEpuht4!/#11.

USDA. "Meat and Poultry Labeling Terms." Updated August 10, 2015. Accessed May 14, 2019. https://www.fsis.usda.gov/wps/portal/fsis/topics/food-safety-education/get-answers/food-safety-fact-sheets/food-labeling/meat-and-poultry-labeling-terms/meat-and-poultry-labeling-terms.

USDA. "Organic Labeling." Accessed May 14, 2019. https://www.ams.usda.gov/rules-regulations/organic/labeling.

USDA. "USDA Amends Country of Origin Labeling Requirements, Final Rule Repeals Beef and Pork Requirements." February 29, 2016. Accessed May 14, 2019. https://www.ams.usda.gov/press-release/usda-amends-country-origin-labeling-requirements-final-rule-repeals-beef-and-pork.

Westcott, Paul and James Hansen. "USDA Agricultural Projections to 2025." Updated February 18, 2016. Accessed May 14, 2019, https://www.ers.usda.gov/webdocs/publications/37809/56725_oce-2016-1-d.pdf?v=0.

IMAGE CREDITS

Eggs

- Discuss applications of eggs in cooking and baking
- Discuss how to substitute eggs in baking
- Evaluate the effect of cooking time on hard-cooked eggs
- Evaluate different techniques for scrambling eggs
- Determine the best consistency of whipped egg whites
- Use basic cooking skills to prepare recipes

EGGS

Eggs are one of the most versatile foods used in cooking and baking. Their uses range from acting as binders, thickening sauces, and providing leavening and moisture to baked goods and acting as emulsifiers.

The anatomy of an egg[1] includes the egg yolk, albumin (egg white), shell, air pocket, and chalaza. The chalaza are the two membranes that hold the yolk in place in the shell. The eggshell is comprised of primarily calcium carbonate. The two main components of the egg, the yolk and the albumin, provide the nutrition. The egg yolk carries 75% of the total calories as well as most of the iron, thiamin, and vitamin A. Yolks are also the source of flavor and fat in the egg. The yellow color of the yolk is due to the chicken's diet and is a result of xanthophylls, a yellow pigment. Egg whites are comprised of mostly protein and water.

Eggs can be separated into egg whites and yolks or used whole, depending on the application. Cooking eggs, separated or whole, denatures the proteins.[2] This occurs when the protein structure unfolds, causing the proteins to form masses and glob together as evidenced by the opaque color of eggs when they are cooked. Heat, acid,

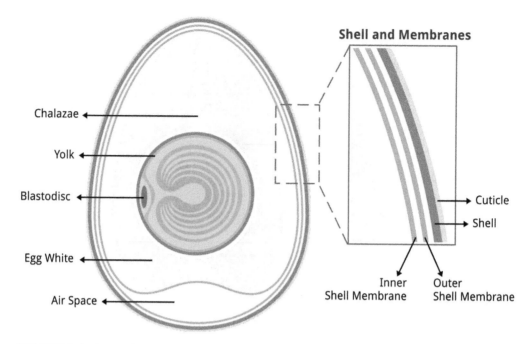

FIGURE 6.1 Anatomy of an egg.

and agitation are the primary ways proteins are denatured in cooking. Agitation refers to the rapid whipping or mixing of proteins. The best example of agitation is the whipping of egg whites to create a foam.

Egg Uses
Foams
Egg foams are formed from the denaturing of the proteins in the egg white. Using cream of tartar, an acid, stabilizes the egg whites[3] when whipped. Sugar can be added to sweeten the whites but should be added gradually after soft peaks form. Egg whites can be whipped to soft or stiff peaks. Over-whipping egg whites results in grainy texture that begins to separate and release water. Overwhipped whites are not suitable for baking.

Leavening
Whipped whole eggs or egg whites can be used as leavening in baking. When eggs are whipped, air is trapped. When heat is applied, the trapped air expands and rises, causing the product to puff.

Moisture
Eggs also provide moisture to many different types of recipes.

Flavor and Appearance
Because of their fat content, eggs can carry and distribute flavor in a recipe. In terms of appearance, eggs help facilitate the maillard reaction. The maillard reaction is a reaction of proteins and sugar and is responsible for the browning of foods.

Binders

Eggs are used as binders for meat and baked goods. They are added to meat mixtures such as meatloaf, pates, and meatballs to help the products hold their shape during baking.

Structure

In baking, eggs provide structure to the product.

Thickeners

Due to their high fat content, egg yolks are used as thickeners for sauces. Classic applications for egg yolks as thickeners include custards like crème brûlée or sauces such as crème anglaise. When using egg yolks for thickening hot sauces, the yolks need to be tempered to avoid curdling the eggs. Tempering refers to the gradual adding hot liquid to cold yolks to bring them to the same temperature of the liquid.

Emulsifiers

Egg yolks are often used as emulsifiers in making salad dressings. This is due to the proteins in the yolk that are either hydrophobic or hydrophilic. An important emulsifier, lecithin is a phospholipid with one end that is hydrophobic and the other that is hydrophilic. Emulsifiers keep oil from coalescing in water and help create a more homogenized mixture. Since fats and water do not mix, emulsifiers contain both hydrophobic and hydrophilic properties that attract the fat and water, holding them together. Two classic applications using eggs as emulsifiers are Hollandaise sauce and mayonnaise.

Examples of Egg Applications

Custards

Custards are usually baked in a hot water bath (bain marie) to ensure even cooking and prevent the eggs from scrambling and curdling. Crème brûlée, flan, and cheesecake are examples of custards.

Soufflé

Soufflés can be sweet or savory and have the reputation for being temperamental and finicky. Cooking temperature and time affects the rise and fall of soufflés. A higher cooking temperature results in a higher rise but a quicker fall after being removed from the oven. A thicker soufflé results less rising but consequently less falling after being removed from the oven. When making a soufflé, the egg whites need to be whipped to stiff peaks but not over whipped.

Hard- and Soft-Boiled Eggs

Eggs that are cooked in their shells are referred to as hard- or soft-boiled eggs depending on the length of time, they are cooked. When cooked in their shells, the eggs cook from the outside to the inside. A soft-boiled egg has a softer, less cooked yolk compared to a hard-boiled egg. Overcooking hard-boiled eggs results in a ferrous sulfur ring surrounding the yolk: a reaction of the iron in the egg yolk and the sulfur in the egg white.

Stages of Hard-Cooked Eggs

When cooking eggs, it's important to note that proteins start to denature at 145°F. At this point, the yolk begins to thicken and solidify.

Altitude adjustments: increase cooking time due to the decreased temp water at which water boils. For example, at 5000 feet above sea level, the boiling temp is 203°F, so you need to add 1–2 minutes to the cooking time for the eggs.

SELECTING EGGS

TABLE 6.1

Egg Quality[4]	Grade AA	Grade A	Grade B
Appearance of spread	Covers a small area	Covers a moderate area	Covers a wide area
Albumen Appearance	Albumin is thick; stands high Chalazae is prominent	Albumin is mostly thick, stands fairly high, chalazae prominent	Albumin is not very thick, chalazae not noticeable or absent; watery appearance
Yolk Appearance	Firm, round, and high	Firm and stands fairly high	Flattened and enlarged
Shell appearance	Usual shape, clean, unbroken	Usual shape, clean, unbroken	Abnormal shape, stains, pronounced ridges
Usage	Any use	Any use	Best for scrambling, baking

TABLE 6.2

Egg Sizes (average weight per egg)[5]					
Jumbo	Extra Large	Large	Medium	Small	Pee Wee
2.5 ounces	2.25 ounces	2 ounces	1.75 ounces	1.5 ounces	1.25 ounces

Substitutions[6]				
Jumbo	Extra Large	Large	Medium	Small
1	1	1	1	1
2	2	2	2	3
5	5	6	7	8
9	10	12	13	15
18	21	24	27	28
37	44	50	56	62

Equivalent Amounts

Egg Whites:

1 egg white = 2 tablespoons	8–10 large egg whites = 1 cup	6 extra large egg whites = 1 cup

Egg Yolks:

1 large egg yolk = 1 tablespoon	12–15 large egg yolks = 1 cup

Label Terminology

Some of the same labels discussed in Unit 5 are the same for eggs. However, there are a couple other labels specific to chicken eggs.

Omega 3[7]

Hens are given feed enriched with omega 3 fatty acids from algae, fish oil, or flax seed sources.

Vegetarian[8]

Hens are not fed any animal protein.

Egg Substitutes

Finding a great substitute for the many uses of eggs can be challenging. Gelatin and cornstarch are good for replacing yolks in custards since they provide thickening agents to the liquid.

In baking, ground flax seeds, ground chia seeds, and tofu can be used in place of whole eggs. Ground flax and chia provide additional fiber to the baked goods.

Finding a good substitute for egg whites is a challenge facing chefs since eggs have so many uses in the kitchen. One of the biggest challenges has been finding an appropriate substitute for whipped egg whites. Providing light, airy texture and lift to many dessert recipes, whipped egg whites are vital to baking and pastry.

Recently aquafaba was discovered to be an alternative to whipped egg whites. Aquafaba is made from whipped garbanzo bean (chickpea) liquid from canned garbanzo beans. The properties of both egg whites and aquafaba are similar. Each one has protein strands that become denatured after agitation (in this case, whipping), creating an opaque appearance and light, airy texture.

However, when it comes to flavor, neutral egg whites absorb any flavor presented to them. In contrast, aquafaba's flavor of chickpea/garbanzo bean sits in the background. If developing recipes, you may need to add stronger flavors to aquafaba to counteract the earthiness of the bean liquid.

TABLE 6.3

Egg Substitute	Amount to replace 1 large egg	Best Use
Ground flax seeds	1 tablespoon flax + 3 tablespoons water Soak for 15 minutes	Baking, binding, adding moisture
Ground chia seeds	1 tablespoon chia + 3 tablespoons water Soak for 15 minutes	Baking, binding, adding moisture
Commercial egg substitutes	Use according to package instructions	Baking
Mashed Banana	1/4 cup	Baking, binding, adding moisture
Unsweetened applesauce	1/4 cup	Baking, binding, adding moisture
Nut butters (peanut butter, almond butter, etc.)	3 tablespoons	Baking, binding, thickening
Mashed potatoes	1/4 cup	Baking, binding, thickening
Instant mashed potatoes	2 tablespoons rehydrated	Baking, binding, thickening
Silken tofu, blended	1/4 cup	Baking, binding, adding moisture
Water, vegetable oil, baking powder	2 tablespoons water + 1 tablespoon oil + 2 teaspoons baking powder	Baking – provides leavening and moisture
Baking soda and vinegar	1 teaspoon baking soda + 1 tablespoon vinegar	Provides aeration (leavening) similar to whipped egg whites
Aquafaba	3 tablespoons = 1 whole egg 2 tablespoons = 1 egg white	Can be used as a substitute for whole eggs in baking or as a substitute for whipped egg whites.

EVALUATION

Soft-Boiled Eggs

Objective: Assessing the different stages of protein denaturing in soft-boiled eggs.

Method

- 1 quart water
- 2 eggs

Bring the water to a boil in saucepan set over high heat. Add the eggs, cover the pan with a lid and remove from heat. Cook eggs according to the times below, adjusting for altitude. Higher altitudes require longer boiling time.

- 1–3 minute eggs
- 4–6 minute eggs
- 7–9 minute eggs

Soft-boiled egg	Appearance of Yolk	Appearance of White
1–3 minute		
4–6 minute		
7–9 minute		

EXPERIMENTS

Experiment 1: Hard-Boiled Eggs

Basic Recipe (Control)

- 1 quart water
- 2 eggs
- Ice water

Place the water and eggs in a sauce pan. Place pan over high heat and bring to a rolling boil. Boil for 1 minute. Cover and remove pan from heat. Let sit for 14 minutes. Drain and rinse eggs under cool water for 1–2 minutes. Submerge into ice water for 5 minutes. Peel off the shell.

Variations

Increase boiling time to:

- 30 minutes (Cover and cook for specified time, then proceed directly to draining and rinsing.)
- 60 minutes (Cover and cook for specified time, then proceed directly to draining and rinsing.)

Hard-boiled Egg	Appearance of the Egg Yolk	Appearance of the Egg White	If present, how pronounced is the ferrous sulfide ring?
Basic Recipe (control)			
30 minutes			
60 minutes			

Experiment 2: Scrambling Eggs

Objective: Determine the fluffiest, best tasting scrambled egg.

Basic Recipe (Control)

- 3 large eggs
- 1/4 teaspoon salt
- 1/8 teaspoon black pepper
- 1 tablespoon unsalted butter

Whisk together the eggs, salt, and pepper. Melt the butter in a nonstick pan set over medium-high heat. Pour the eggs into the pan. Flip and turn the eggs to scramble them as they cook. Continue until the eggs are fully cooked through. Serve hot.

Variation 1: Added Milk

- 3 large eggs
- 1 tablespoon whole milk
- 1/4 teaspoon salt
- 1/8 teaspoon black pepper
- 1 tablespoon unsalted butter

Whisk together the eggs, milk, salt, and pepper. Let the mixture sit at room temperature for 15 minutes.

Melt the butter in a nonstick pan set over medium-high heat. Pour the eggs into the pan. Flip and turn the eggs to scramble them as the cook. Continue until the eggs are fully cooked through. Serve hot.

Variation 2: Chilled Butter

- 3 large eggs
- 1/2 teaspoon salt
- 1/8 teaspoon black pepper
- 1 tablespoon cold unsalted butter, cut into cubes
- 1 tablespoon heavy cream

Whisk together the eggs, salt, and pepper. Let the mixture sit at room temperature for 15 minutes.

Add the chilled butter to the eggs and pour the mixture into a nonstick pan. Place over medium-low heat. Cook the eggs, stirring constantly until the butter melts and the eggs begin to set. Cook until the eggs are cooked through and no liquid remains.

Remove from the heat and stir in the cream. Serve immediately.

Variation 3: Whipped Eggs

- 3 large eggs
- 2 tablespoons whole milk
- salt and pepper, to taste
- 1 tablespoon butter

In a medium bowl, vigorously whip the eggs and milk until slightly thick and pale in color. Season with salt and pepper.

Melt the butter in a nonstick sauté pan set over medium heat. Pour the egg mixture into the pan. Flip and turn the eggs to scramble them as the cook. Continue until the eggs are fully cooked through. Serve hot.

Scrambled Egg	Appearance (color, fluffiness, etc.)	Flavor	Texture
Basic Recipe (control)			
Milk added			
Chilled Butter			
Whipped eggs			

Experiment 3: Egg Substitutes

Objective: Determine the best substitute for eggs in baking.

Basic Apple Cinnamon Muffin Recipe (control)

Yield: 6 muffins

- 1 cup AP flour
- ¼ cup sugar
- 1 1/2 teaspoons baking powder
- 1/2 teaspoon ground cinnamon
- 1/4 teaspoon salt
- 1/2 cup whole milk
- 1 large egg
- 2 tablespoons canola or safflower oil
- 1/2 teaspoon vanilla extract
- 1/2 cup shredded apple

Preheat oven to 425°F. Line a muffin pan with muffin/cupcake papers or lightly grease and flour the pan. Set aside.

In a small medium bowl, whisk together the flour, sugar, baking powder, cinnamon, and salt. In a small bowl, whisk together the milk, eggs, oil, and vanilla. Pour the wet ingredients into the dry ingredients. Stir until just combined (do not overmix). Fold in the apples.

Fill the muffin tins 3/4 of the way up. Bake for 15–20 minutes or until a toothpick inserted in the center comes out clean. Cool completely on a rack.

Variations:

In place of 1 large egg, substitute:

- ground flax seeds (1 tablespoon ground flax mixed with 3 tablespoons water; let sit for 15 minutes)
- ground chia seeds (1 tablespoon mixed with 3 tablespoons water; let sit for 15 minutes)
- commercial powdered egg substitute (use according to package directions)
- silken tofu (1/4 cup tofu blended until smooth)
- mashed banana (1/4 cup banana mashed until semi smooth)
- aquafaba (3 tablespoons aquafaba)

Muffin	Appearance	Flavor	Texture
Basic Recipe (control)			
Flax			
Chia			
Commercial powdered egg substitute			
Silken tofu			
Mashed banana			
Aquafaba			

RECIPES

Poached Eggs

Yield: 4 eggs

- water, as needed
- 1 teaspoon salt
- 2 tablespoons vinegar
- 4 large eggs

Bring water to a simmer in a shallow pan. Add the salt and vinegar. The water should not be boiling but at a strong simmer; little bubbles will form around the edges of the pan.

Crack one egg into a cup and carefully add it to the water. Gently coax the egg white around the yolk. Repeat with the other eggs. Cook the eggs for 3–5 minutes. The center of the egg should be "jiggly" or runny and the egg white should be set around the yolk. Remove with a slotted spoon.

Omelet

Yield: 1 omelet

- 1 tablespoon canola or safflower oil
- 2 ounces diced pancetta or bacon (optional)
- 1 clove garlic, minced
- 1 cup dark leafy greens of choice
  - swiss chard, chiffonade
  - kale, chiffonade
  - spinach
- 4 large eggs
- 2 tablespoons whole milk or half and half
- salt and pepper, to taste
- 1–2 tablespoons cheese of choice, such as
  - goat cheese
  - shredded cheddar
  - shredded gruyere
  - shredded pepper jack

Heat the oil in a nonstick skillet set over medium heat. Add the pancetta and cook until crispy. Remove from pan. Add the greens and garlic. Sauté for 2–3 minutes or until wilted. In a small bowl, whisk the eggs and milk; season with salt and pepper. Pour egg mixture into the pan. Stir until they begin to set, about 10–15 seconds. Pull the egg from the sides of the pan toward the center, allowing the raw egg to run underneath. Continue doing so for 30–40 seconds or so. Sprinkle the top with the cooked pancetta and goat cheese. When the eggs are nearly cooked through, flip one side of the omelet toward the center with a spatula. Slide the omelet onto a plate so it remains folded.

Quiche

Yield: 1 9-inch quiche

- 1 homemade or store bought single pie pastry
- 1–2 cups filling ingredients (mix and match)
  - ham, diced small
  - bacon or pancetta, cooked and crumbled
  - mushrooms, sliced
  - dark greens (kale, chard, spinach), chopped
  - onions, diced
  - broccoli florets, chopped
  - bell peppers, diced
  - zucchini or yellow summer squash, diced
- 1 cup shredded cheese (gruyere, swiss, cheddar) or crumbled goat cheese
- 3 large eggs
- 1 cup milk
- 1/2 cup cream
- 1 1/2 teaspoons salt
- 1/2 teaspoon pepper

Preheat oven 350°F. Roll out the pie crust and fit it into a 9-inch pie plate. Trim excess overhang. Fold and crimp overhang decoratively around the pie. Prick the bottom of the pie with a fork.

Cover the pie crust with parchment paper and fill with pie weights or dried beans. Make sure the foil and weights are snug against the sides of the crust. Bake for 20 minutes. Remove the weights and parchment. Bake until just starting to brown, about 10–15 minutes.

Sprinkle 1/2 the cheese over the bottom of the pie crust. Layer in the filling ingredients. Whisk together the eggs, milk, cream, and salt in a medium bowl. Pour the custard into the piecrust over the filling. Sprinkle the top with the remaining cheese.

Bake the quiche until the edges are set, about 30–40 minutes.

Cool for at least 20 minutes before serving. Quiche can be made ahead of time and kept under refrigeration 1–2 days. Serve cold, room temperature, or warmed. Reheat in 350°F oven until hot.

Frittata

Serves 4

- 1 tablespoon canola or safflower oil
- 2–3 cups vegetables of choice (mix and match as desired):
  - yukon gold potatoes, diced
  - dark greens (kale, chard, or spinach), chopped
  - broccoli florets
  - zucchini or yellow summer squash, sliced or diced
  - bell pepper, sliced or diced
  - mushrooms, chopped
- 2 cloves garlic, minced
- pinch red pepper flakes (optional)
- 8 large eggs
- 1/4 cup half and half or milk
- salt and pepper, to taste
- 1/2 to 1 cup cheese of choice
  - cheddar, shredded
  - goat cheese
  - feta cheese
  - monterey jack, shredded
  - gruyere, grated
  - provolone, shredded
- Optional addition: cooked bacon, sausage, or ham

Preheat to 400°F.

Place a 10-inch cast iron (or other nonstick oven proof skillet) over medium heat. Add the oil and cook the veggies in the hot oil, starting with potatoes (if using). Allow the potatoes to cook until tender, about 5–8 minutes. Add the other veggies; cook until soft or slightly wilted for the greens. Add the garlic, red pepper flakes, and season lightly with salt and pepper. If using, add the cooked bacon, sausage, or ham.

In a small bowl, whisk together the eggs, half-and-half, 1 teaspoon salt, and 1/2 teaspoon pepper.

Pour the egg mixture over the vegetables and cheese. Bake until the eggs are set, 10–15 minutes.

Cool in the pan for 5 minutes, then slice into wedges and serve.

Spanish Omelet
Serves 4–6

- 1 cup olive oil
- 2 pounds yukon gold potatoes, sliced thin
- 1 yellow onion, julienned
- 8 large eggs
- 1/4 cup chopped parsley
- 2 teaspoons salt
- 1 teaspoon black pepper

Heat oil in a large nonstick skillet (10–12-inch diameter) over medium heat. Add the potatoes and onions. Stir to coat with the oil. When the oil begins to bubble, reduce to medium-low heat. Turn the potatoes and onions occasionally. Cook until tender, about 20 minutes.

Using a slotted spoon, remove the potatoes and onions from the oil. Strain the olive oil and reserve 3 tablespoons.

In a medium-sized bowl, whisk together the eggs, parsley, salt, and pepper. Add the potatoes and onions.

Pour the 3 tablespoons oil back into the pan and place over medium heat. Pour in the egg mixture. Occasionally shake the mixture to be sure it isn't sticking to the bottom of the pan. When the bottom of the omelet has set, turn the heat to low and cover with a lid. Cook for 10 minutes. Carefully slip the omelet over and to brown the other side. Cook for 3–5 minutes or until eggs are set.

Serve warm.

Vanilla Ice Cream
Yield: 1 quart

- 3 cups half and half or whole milk
- 1 cup heavy cream
- 8 large egg yolks
- 9 ounces sugar
- 2 teaspoons vanilla extract

In a 2- or 3-quart saucepan, bring the cream and half and half to a strong simmer. In a bowl, whisk together the egg yolks and sugar until slightly more pale yellow in color.

Temper the yolks with the hot liquid by whisking 1/2 cup liquid into the egg yolks. Add the tempered yolks to the remaining hot liquid. Reduce heat to medium low and stir with a rubber spatula or wooden spoon until the mixture starts to thicken slightly (it will coat the back of a spoon). The temperature of the mixture should reach 170–190°F, depending on where you live. Do not allow the mixture boil and bubble.

Remove from the heat and pour in the vanilla. Pour the mixture into a stainless steel bowl set in an ice bath. Stir and cool the mixture until cool to the touch (should be around 45°F). At this point, you can refrigerate the mixture for 2–4 hours to develop flavors before making ice cream or you can churn it immediately into ice cream according to the ice cream machine instructions.

Crème Brûlée
Yield: 8 (4-ounce) servings

- 1 quart heavy cream
- 4 ounces sugar
- 10 large egg yolks
- 1 tablespoon vanilla
- sugar for topping

Preheat oven to 325°F. Place ramekins in a shallow pan. Set aside.

Bring the cream to a boil (be careful not to boil over).

In a separate bowl, whisk together the egg yolks, sugar, and vanilla. Gradually pour the hot cream into the egg mixture.

Pour the mixture into the ramekins, filling to the top.

Place the pan in the oven and fill half up the sides with hot water, creating a hot water bath. Bake for 20–30 minutes or until the center of the custards is set (only jiggles slightly). Remove from oven and remove ramekins from the hot water bath. Cool for 10–15 minutes at room temperature. Cool completely in the cooler.

Before serving, sprinkle a thin layer of sugar over the top. Caramelize the top with a torch. Serve immediately.

Flan
Yield: 4 (4-ounce) servings

- 1 1/2 cups sugar
- 2 tablespoons water
- 1/2 lemon, juiced
- 2 cups heavy cream
- 1 cinnamon stick (or 1/2 teaspoon ground cinnamon)
- 1 teaspoon vanilla extract
- 3 large eggs
- 2 large egg yolks
- pinch salt
- hot water for water bath

Place a 2-quart round flan mold sitting a large roasting pan next to the stove. Combine 1 cup of the sugar and 2 tablespoons of water in a saucepan. Cover over medium-high heat until the sugar begins to melt. Swirl the pan over the heat until the syrup darkens to a medium amber color, about 7–10 minutes. Do not stir. Remove from the heat and stir in the lemon juice. Pour into the flan mold. Tilt the mold ensuring the caramel evenly coats the bottom. Set aside.

Preheat the oven to 325°F.

Simmer the cream, cinnamon, and vanilla in a small saucepan over medium-low heat.

In a large bowl, whisk together the whole eggs and egg yolks with the remaining 1/2 cup of sugar; add a pinch of salt. Whisk until the mixture is pale yellow and thick. Temper the egg mixture by gradually whisking in the hot cream mixture. Pour the mixture through a mesh strainer. Pour the custard into the caramel-coated mold.

Place pour hot water into the roasting pan coming halfway up the side of the mold being careful not get water into the custard. Carefully transfer to the middle oven rack and bake for 30–45 minutes or until the custard is barely set and just jiggles slightly. Let the flan cool in the water bath. Refrigerate for at least 4 hours or overnight before serving.

When ready to serve, run a knife around the inside of the mold to loosen the flan. Place a dessert plate on top of the flan and invert to allow the flan to come out and the caramel sauce to run down the sides.

Clafoutis
Yield: One 9-inch pie

- 1 1/4 cups whole milk
- 2/3 cup granulated sugar, divided
- 3 large eggs
- 1 tablespoon vanilla extract
- 1/8 teaspoon salt
- 1 cup flour
- 1 pint fresh blueberries, blackberries, or cherries (pitted), rinsed and well drained
- powdered sugar for sprinkling

Heat oven to 350°F. Lightly butter 9-inch pie plate at least 1 1/2 inches deep. Set aside.

Whisk together the milk, 1/3 cup granulated sugar, eggs, vanilla, salt, and flour in a medium bowl.

Spread berries over the batter and sprinkle with the remaining 1/3 cup granulated sugar. Pour the batter over the berries. Place in the center of the oven and bake for 50–60 minutes, until top is puffed and browned. Cool to barely warm. Sprinkle with powdered sugar just before serving.

Meringue Cookies

Yield: about 1–2 dozen

- 4 egg whites, at room temperature
- 1/2 teaspoon cream of tartar
- 1 cup sugar
- 1 teaspoon vanilla or almond extract
- food coloring (optional)
- 1–2 cups mini chocolate chips (optional)

Preheat oven to 225ºF. Line sheet pan with parchment paper. Set aside.

With electric mixer, beat egg whites until frothy. Add cream of tartar and beat until soft peaks form. Gradually add sugar until it is fully incorporated and dissolved and stiff peaks form. Beat in the extract and food coloring (if using). Fold in chocolate chips, if desired.

Pipe or drop by rounded spoonfuls onto the sheet pan. Bake for 45 minutes. Turn off oven and leave in the oven for 1 hour.

Coconut Macaroons

Yield: 10–12 macaroons

- 4 large egg whites
- 1/2 cup sugar
- 1 teaspoon vanilla extract
- 1/4 teaspoon salt
- 3 cups sweetened shredded coconut, lightly toasted
- 4 ounces semi-sweet or bittersweet chocolate

Preheat oven to 350ºF. Line a sheet pan with parchment paper. Set aside.

In a large bowl, whisk together the egg whites, sugar, vanilla, and salt until frothy. Add the coconut and stir to combine well.

Scoop the mixture onto the baking sheet into 1–2-inch mounds. Bake for 15–20 minutes or until golden brown. Cool on a wire rack.

Melt the chocolate in a double boiler. Dip the bottom of the macaroons in the chocolate and place on a baking sheet lined with parchment. Drizzle remaining chocolate over the top of the macaroons. Allow to dry completely.

Keep in an airtight container for up to one week.

Chocolate Soufflé

Serves 4–6

- 1/2 cup (1 stick), softened, plus more for coating dish
- 4 tablespoons sugar, plus more for coating dish
- 8 ounces bittersweet chocolate, finely chopped
- 6 eggs, separated, at room temperature
- pinch fine sea salt
- 1/2 teaspoon cream of tartar

Remove wire racks from oven and place a baking sheet directly on oven floor. Heat oven to 400°F. Generously butter a 1 1/2-quart soufflé dish. Coat the bottom and sides thoroughly with sugar, tapping out excess.

In a double boiler, melt chocolate and butter over simmering water. Let cool only slightly. Whisk in egg yolks and salt.

Using an electric mixer, whip the egg whites and cream of tartar at medium speed until the mixture is fluffy and holds very soft peaks. Add sugar, 1 tablespoon at a time, beating until whites hold stiff peaks and look glossy.

Gently whisk a quarter of the egg whites into the chocolate mixture to lighten it. Fold in remaining whites in two additions, and then transfer batter to prepared dish. Rub your thumb around the inside edge of the dish to create about a 1/4-inch space between the dish and the soufflé mixture.

Transfer dish to baking sheet in the oven and reduce oven temperature to 375°F. Bake until soufflé is puffed and center moves only slightly when dish is shaken gently, about 25–35 minutes. Serve immediately.

Cheese Soufflé

Serves 4–6

- 2 tablespoons grated parmesan cheese
- 2 tablespoons unsalted butter plus more for buttering the pan
- 3 tablespoons flour
- 1 cup whole milk, warmed
- 1/2 teaspoon paprika
- Pinch of nutmeg
- 1/2 teaspoon salt
- 1/2 teaspoon pepper
- 4 egg yolks
- 5 egg whites at room temperature
- 1/2 teaspoon cream of tartar
- 1 cup grated gruyere cheese

Preheat oven to 400°F. Butter the bottom and sides of a 1-quart round baking dish. Coat the bottom and sides with parmesan cheese. Set aside.

Melt the 2 tablespoons butter in a saucepan set over medium heat. Add the flour and stir to make a roux. Cook for 1–2 minutes. While whisking, add the milk. Cook for 3–4 minutes to thicken. Stir occasionally to prevent burning. Add the paprika, nutmeg, salt, and pepper. Turn off the heat and stir in the egg yolks, one at a time until well incorporated. Pour mixture into a large mixing bowl.

In a mixing bowl, whip the egg whites with the cream of tartar until stiff peaks form. Scoop about 1/4 of the egg white mixture into the egg yolks mixture. Stir to mix well. This helps lighten the base. Working in 1–2 batches, gently fold in the egg whites. Fold in the cheese.

Pour the mixture into the prepared dish. Run your thumb around the edge of the soufflé. Place in the oven and lower the temperature to 375°F. Bake until the soufflé has puffed 2–3 inches above the rim of the pan and the top has browned nicely. Remove from the oven and serve immediately.

Macarons
Yield: about 30

- 1 3/4 cups powdered sugar
- 1 cup almond flour, finely ground
- 1 teaspoon salt, divided
- 3 egg whites, at room temperature
- 1/4 cup granulated sugar
- 1/2 teaspoon vanilla extract (or flavoring of choice)
- 2 drops food coloring of choice
- vanilla buttercream
- 1 cup unsalted butter, at room temperature
- 3 cups powdered sugar
- 1 teaspoon vanilla extract
- 2–3 tablespoons whole milk

Make the macarons: In the bowl of a food processor, combine the powdered sugar, almond flour, and 1/2 teaspoon of salt, and process on low speed, until extra fine. Sift the almond flour mixture through a fine-mesh sieve into a large bowl.

In a separate large bowl, beat the egg whites and the remaining 1/2 teaspoon of salt with an electric hand mixer until soft peaks form. Gradually add the granulated sugar until fully incorporated. Continue to beat until stiff peaks form.

Add the vanilla and beat until incorporated. Add the food coloring and beat until just combined.

Add about 1/3 of the sifted almond flour mixture at a time to the beaten egg whites and use a spatula to gently fold until combined. After the last addition of almond flour, continue to fold slowly until the batter falls into ribbons and you can make a figure eight while holding the spatula up.

Transfer the macaron batter into a piping bag fitted with a round tip.

Place 4 dots of the batter in each corner of a rimmed baking sheet, and place a piece of parchment paper over it, using the batter to help adhere the parchment to the baking sheet.

Pipe the macarons onto the parchment paper in 1 1/2-inch (3-cm) circles, spacing at least 1-inch (2-cm) apart. Tap the baking sheet on a flat surface five times to release any air bubbles.

Let the macarons sit at room temperature for 30 minutes to 1 hour, until dry to the touch.

Preheat the oven to 300°F.

Bake the macarons for 17 minutes, until the feet are well risen and the macarons don't stick to the parchment paper. Transfer the macarons to a wire rack to cool completely before filling.

Make the buttercream: In a large bowl, add the butter and beat with a mixer for 1 minute until light and fluffy. Sift in the powdered sugar and beat until fully incorporated. Add the vanilla and beat to combine. Add the cream, 1 tablespoon at a time, and beat to combine, until the buttercream is the desired consistency.

Transfer the buttercream to a piping bag fitted with a round tip. Add a dollop of buttercream to one macaron shell. Top it with another macaron shell to create a sandwich. Repeat with remaining macaron shells and buttercream.

Place in an airtight container for 24 hours to "bloom" before eating.

Mayonnaise
Yield: 1–2 cups

- 2 large egg yolks
- 1/2 teaspoon dijon mustard
- 1 teaspoon lemon juice or vinegar
- 1–2 cups oil (canola, olive oil, avocado, safflower, or grapeseed)
- salt and pepper, to taste

In a bowl, whisk together the yolks, mustard, and the lemon juice. Slowly drizzle in the oil while whisking constantly. Depending on the size of the egg yolks, it may take 1 1/2 cups oil. Add enough oil until the mixture is very thick. Season to taste with salt and pepper. Keep refrigerated for up to seven days.

Classic Aioli
Yield: 1–2 cups

- 8 garlic cloves, roughly chopped
- 1 teaspoon Kosher salt
- 3 large egg yolks
- 1 1/2 cups extra-virgin olive oil, canola, avocado, grapeseed, or safflower oil
- 2 tablespoons fresh lemon juice
- black pepper, to taste

Mince the garlic with the salt. Use the side of the knife to smash the garlic and create a paste. Scrape the mixture into a bowl, stir in the egg yolks, and let stand for 5 minutes.

To hold the bowl steady, place the bowl on a damp kitchen towel and begin whisking in 1/2 cup olive oil in a slow drizzle, whisking constantly. Once an emulsion has formed, continue adding the oil in a thin stream. When the aioli is very thick, add 2 teaspoons of the lemon juice. Gradually whisk in another 1/4 cup of the olive oil, then 2 more teaspoons of the lemon juice. Whisk in the remaining 1/4 cup of olive oil, add the 2 remaining teaspoons of lemon juice, and then whisk in the remaining oil. When all of the oil has been incorporated, adjust seasonings to taste.

Note: This recipe can also be made in an immersion blender or a regular blender.

Classic Chocolate Mousse
Yield: about 4 cups

- 6 ounces bittersweet chocolate, chopped
- 4 large eggs, separated, at room temperature
- 1 tablespoon sugar
- 1/4 cup espresso
- 2 tablespoons kahlúa or rum (optional)
- 2/3 cup heavy cream

Make a double boiler and bring the water to a simmer. Place a glass or metal bowl over the simmering water. Add the chocolate. Stir until melted. Set aside.

Whip the egg yolks and sugar until pale yellow and thick. Add the chocolate mixture and mix well to combine. Add the espresso and liqueur, if using. Set aside.

In a mixing bowl, whip the cream to stiff peaks (be careful not to over-whip). Fold the cream into the chocolate mixture and gently fold until just combined.
Whip the egg whites until they form stiff peaks. Fold into the chocolate mixture. Scoop mousse into serving glasses or cups. Chill for 2–6 hours.

Zabaglione
Yield: 2–3 cups

- 8 large egg yolks
- 3/4 cup marsala wine
- 1/2 cup sugar
- berries, if desired

Put the egg yolks, the marsala, and then the sugar into a large stainless-steel bowl. Set the bowl over a large saucepan filled with 1 inch of barely simmering water. Using a hand-held electric mixer on low speed or a whisk, beat the egg-yolk mixture until it is hot and the mixture forms a ribbon when the beaters are lifted, 5–8 minutes. Do not cook the zabaglione for too long, or it will curdle. Fold in fresh berries. Serve immediately or chill for up to 1–2 hours.

If you are going to store the zabaglione for longer, whip 1 cup cream to stiff peaks and fold into the zabaglione. Chill until ready to use, no longer than one day.

AQUAFABA RECIPES

Chocolate Vegan Macarons
Yield: 24–30 macarons

Macarons

- 1 cup chickpea liquid, aquafaba
- 1 cup powdered sugar
- 1 1/2 cups almond meal
- 1 tablespoon dark cocoa powder
- 1/2 tablespoon cream of tartar
- 1/2 cup sugar

Vegan Buttercream

- 1 cup vegan butter, at room temperature
- 3 cups powdered sugar
- 2 teaspoons non-dairy milk of choice
- 3/4 teaspoon vanilla extract

Pour 1 cup aquafaba into a pot and reduce to about 1/3 cup over low heat. Cool to room temperature. Aquafaba can be refrigerated overnight.

Preheat oven to 250°F.

In a bowl, whisk together the powdered sugar, almond meal, and dark cocoa powder.

Add the chilled aquafaba to another bowl and beat until soft peaks begin to form.

Add the cream of tartar and sugar to the whipped aquafaba and beat until soft peaks form.

Sift powdered sugar, almond meal, and dark cocoa powder into the whipped aquafaba, and gently fold ingredients together. Transfer the batter to a piping bag and pipe directly onto a parchment paper-lined baking sheet.

Let the tray rest at room temperature for 1–2 hours or until the surface does not stick to fingertips.

Bake for 30 minutes. Let the macarons cool for 15 minutes.

Make the buttercream by creaming together the butter and powdered sugar together. Add enough milk to desired consistency. Add the vanilla. Stir to combine.

Pipe a dollop of buttercream to one macaron shell. Top it with another macaron shell to create a sandwich. Repeat with remaining macaron shells and buttercream.

Refrigerate macarons for another 2 hours before serving. The macarons will taste even better the next day after they have fully "bloomed."

Chocolate Mousse (Aquafaba)
Yield: about 3 cups

- 3 1/2 ounces dark chocolate
- 1 teaspoon vanilla extract
- 1 teaspoon strong coffee or espresso (cooled)
- liquid of 1 14-ounce can chickpeas (drain the chickpeas, reserving the liquid)
- 2 teaspoons powdered sugar
- 1/2 cup coconut cream, chilled

Melt the chocolate in a double boiler set over medium low heat. Set aside to cool slightly.

Place the chickpea liquid in a bowl. Using an electric mixer, whip the liquid until soft peaks form. Add the powdered sugar. Whip until stiff peaks form.

Place the chocolate mixture in a large bowl. Stir in the vanilla and espresso. Stir in a 1/3 of the whipped aquafaba. This helps lighten the chocolate. Gently fold in the rest of the aquafaba mixture. Fold until combined.

Whisk the coconut cream until smooth. Fold into the mousse.

Scoop mixture into serving bowl(s). Chill until set, about 1–2 hours.

Vegan Aioli
Yield: 1 cup

- 1 teaspoon apple cider vinegar
- 1/2 teaspoon dijon mustard
- 1/2 teaspoon salt
- 3 tablespoons chickpea liquid (from canned chickpeas)
- 2 cloves garlic, minced
- 1 cup oil (olive oil, grapeseed, canola, etc.)

In a small bowl, combine the vinegar, mustard, salt, chickpea liquid, and garlic. Mix with an immersion blender until foamy. With the blender running, slowly drizzle in the oil. As you add the oil, the mixture will become very thick. Once it is the consistency of mayo, stop blending. Refrigerate until ready to use, up to one week. Use this to replace any mayo in a recipe.

Aquafaba Butter
Yield: about 1 cup

- 1/2 cup coconut oil, melted
- 2 teaspoons olive or avocado oil
- 3 tablespoons aquafaba
- 1 teaspoon apple cider vinegar
- salt and pepper, to taste

In a liquid measuring cup, mix together the coconut and olive oils.

Place the aquafaba, vinegar, salt, and pepper tall container for an immersion blender or in a blender or Vitamix. Start blending the mixture. Slowly add the oil mixture to create a thick mayo-like consistency. Pour into a container. Refrigerate until firm like butter.

Unit 6 Questions

1. Did the aquafaba whip up the same as the egg whites?
2. How does the flavor differ between the recipes made with eggs and ones made with aquafaba? Which one do you prefer and why?
3. In the hard-boiled egg experiment, which one had the most ferrous sulfide ring? Why is this?
4. Which scrambled egg method resulted in the creamiest scrambled eggs? Which one was your favorite?
5. What makes soufflés rise?
6. In experiment 3, which egg substitute resulted in the best texture compared to the control? Which egg substitute had the best flavor compared to the control? Were there any noticeable differences in appearance between the muffins? If so, what were they?

NOTES

1. Harold McGee, *On Food and Cooking: The Science and Lore of the Kitchen* (New York: Scribner, 2004), 75–77.
2. McGee, *On Food and Cooking*, 84–85.
3. McGee, 86.
4. "Shell Eggs from Farm to Table," USDA Food Safety and Inspection Service, "Shell Eggs from Farm to Table," accessed May 14, 2019, https://tinyurl.com/yaepwlj7.
5. "Shell Eggs from Farm to Table," USDA.
6. "Egg size conversion chart and tips," The Incredible Egg, accessed May 14, 2019, https://www.incredibleegg.org/cookingschool/tips-tricks/egg-sizes-equivalents-and-substitutions/.

7. "Guide to Egg Carton Labels," Egg Nutrition Center, accessed May 14, 2019, https://www.aeb.org/images/PDFs/Retail/enc-egg-labeling-guide.pdf.

8. "Guide to Egg Carton Labels," Egg Nutrition Center.

BIBLIOGRAPHY

Egg Nutrition Center. "Guide to Egg Carton Labels." Accessed 5/14/19. https://www.aeb.org/images/PDFs/Retail/enc-egg-labeling-guide.pdf.

The Incredible Egg. "Egg size conversion chart and tips." Accessed May 14, 2019. https://www.incredibleegg.org/cooking-school/tips-tricks/egg-sizes-equivalents-and-substitutions/.

McGee, Harold. *On Food and Cooking: The Science and Lore of the Kitchen*. New York: Scribner, 2004.

USDA Food Safety and Inspection Service. "Shell Eggs from Farm to Table." Accessed May 14, 2019. https://tinyurl.com/yaepwlj7.

IMAGE CREDITS

Fats and Oils

OBJECTIVES

- Describe differences in fat molecular structure
- Evaluate fat substitutes in baking
- Evaluate different olive oils
- Discuss effect of frying time on biscuits
- Use basic cooking skills to prepare recipes

FATS AND OILS

Nutritionally, fats are one of the three macronutrients and are found as solid or liquid (oil) at room temperature. Fats are split into three categories of fatty acids: saturated, monounsaturated, and polyunsaturated. Even though many fats and oils contain a percentage of all three fatty acids, they each generally consist of one main fatty acid. Fats and oils come from either animal or plant sources.

Sources of fats:

- tree nuts
- peanuts
- fatty fish: salmon, tuna, sardines, anchovies
- mammals and poultry
- avocados
- coconut
- olives

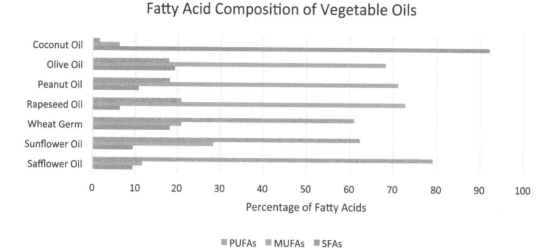

FIGURE 7.1 Fatty Acid Composition of Vegetable Oils[1]

Solid at room temperature, saturated fatty acids (SFAs) include butter, lard, and coconut oil. Contributing to their solid state is the molecular structure, which does not contain double bonds in the fatty acid chain.

Due to a double bond in the molecular structure, monounsaturated fatty acids (MUFAs) are liquid at room temperature. Examples include canola and olive oil.

Polyunsaturated fatty acids (PUFAs) are also liquid at room temperature and contain two or more double bonds on their molecular structure. An example of polyunsaturated oil is sunflower oil.

Smoke Point

Fats and oils each have a particular smoke point, the temperature at which oil breaks down. At this point, the oil starts to smoke and acquire an acrid or burnt flavor. Typically, the more refined the oil, the higher the smoke point.

TABLE 7.1 **Smoke Points of Common Cooking Oils and Fats**[2]

Oil / Fat	Smoke Point
Safflower Oil	510°F
Light/Refined Olive Oil	465°F
Peanut Oil	450°F
Clarified Butter	450°F
Sunflower Oil	440°F
Lard	370°F
Avocado Oil (Virgin)	375–400°F

(Continued)

TABLE 7.1 *(Continued)*

Butter	350°F
Coconut Oil	350°F
Extra Virgin Olive Oil	325–375°F
Canola Oil	400°F

Because fats are hydrophobic, an emulsifier is needed when mixing fats and oils with a water-like substance. When making vinaigrettes, egg yolks, mustard, and honey can be used to help emulsify the mixture.

EVALUATION

Olive Oil Tasting

Determine the flavor differences between several types of olive oils.

Olive Oil	Appearance	Flavor	Fat Content
Extra Virgin			
Olive Oil (Virgin)			
Extra Light			

EXPERIMENTS

Experiment 1: Fat Substitutes in Baking

Basic Recipe: Brownies (control)

- 1/2 cup unsalted butter, melted
- 2 large eggs
- 1 cup sugar
- 1 teaspoon vanilla
- 1/2 cup AP flour
- 1/2 cup cocoa powder
- 1/2 teaspoon salt
- 1/2 teaspoon baking powder

Preheat oven to 350°F. Grease bottom and sides of an 8- or 9-inch square baking pan. Set aside.

In a bowl, combine the butter, eggs, sugar, and vanilla. Add the flour, cocoa powder, salt, and baking powder. Mix well. Pour batter into the pan. Bake for 25 minutes. Cool in the pan. Cut into squares. Serve.

Variations:

In place of the butter, add:

- 1/3 cup applesauce
- 1/3 cup baby food carrots
- 1/3 cup plain non-fat yogurt

Brownies	Appearance	Flavor	Texture
Butter (Control)			
Applesauce			
Carrots			
Yogurt			

Experiment 2: Mayonnaise

Make mayonnaise with different types of oils.

Basic Recipe: Mayonnaise (Control)

- 1 large egg yolk, at room temperature
- 1/2 teaspoon lemon juice
- 1 teaspoon dijon mustard
- 1/4 teaspoon kosher salt
- 1 teaspoon cold water
- 3/4 to 1 cup canola oil

In a medium bowl, whisk together the egg yolk, lemon juice, mustard, salt, and 1 teaspoon cold water until frothy. Whisking constantly, slowly dribble in the oil until mayonnaise is thick and oil is incorporated. When the mayonnaise emulsifies and starts to thicken, you can add the oil in a thin stream, instead of drop by drop.

Variations

In place of the canola oil, substitute:

- extra virgin olive oil
- avocado oil
- melted coconut oil

Oil	Color of the Mayo	Flavor
Canola (control)		
Olive oil		
Avocado oil		
Coconut oil		

Experiment 3: Potato Chips

Determine the best method for frying potato chips

Method 1: Vinegar Soak

- 1 pound russet potatoes, sliced 1/8-inch thick
- 1/3 cup distilled white vinegar
- 5 cups water
- 2 quarts safflower or canola oil
- kosher salt

Cover the potatoes in cold water. Stir to release starch; drain. Repeat until water runs clear. Return potatoes to the bowl; cover with the vinegar and water. Allow the potatoes to sit in the vinegar water for 40 minutes. Drain well and pat dry.

Pour the oil in a large pot. Heat over medium high until temperature of the oil reaches 325°F.

Working in batches, fry the potatoes until golden brown and crisp, about 7–9 minutes. After removing the chips from the oil, season with salt.

Method 2: Boil in Vinegar

- 1 pound russet potatoes, sliced 1/8-inch thick
- 2 tablespoons distilled white vinegar
- 2 quarts water
- 2 quarts safflower or canola oil
- kosher salt

Rinse the potatoes under cold water. Drain well. Bring the vinegar and water to a boil in large saucepan. Add the potatoes; cook for 3 minutes. Drain and spread on sheet pan lined with paper towels. Allow to dry for five minutes.

Heat oil in large pot or dutch oven to 325°F. Working in batches, add the potatoes and fry, 10–20 minutes. Transfer chips to a large platter lined with paper towels and sprinkle with salt

Repeat until all the potatoes are fried.

Method 3: Water Soak

- 1 pound russet potatoes, cut into 1/8-inch slices
- 1 quart ice water
- 1-2 tablespoons kosher salt
- 2 quarts safflower or canola oil

Place the potatoes in a large bowl; add ice water and 1 tablespoon salt. Soak for 30 minutes. Drain potatoes; place on paper towels and pat dry.

In a large pot or Dutch oven, heat about 6-7 cups of oil to 325°F. Fry potatoes in batches until golden brown, about 3-4 minutes.

Remove with a slotted spoon and drain on paper towels. Immediately sprinkle salt.

Potato Chip	Color	Texture	Flavor
Vinegar soak			
Boiled in vinegar			
Water soak			

RECIPES

Basic Vinaigrette
Yield: 1/3 cup

The basic ratio for vinaigrette is 3 parts oil to 1 part vinegar. However, the ratio can be changed according to preferred tastes. A basic vinaigrette includes oil, vinegar, and seasonings. Here is a basic recipe with many different options.

- 1-2 tablespoons vinegar of choice*
- 1 clove garlic, minced (optional)
- 1 teaspoon dijon mustard
- 1 teaspoon honey, agave, or maple syrup (optional)**
- 1/4 cup oil of choice
- salt and pepper, to taste
- fresh herbs of choice (optional)
- spices of choice (optional)

In place of vinegar, substitute fresh citrus juice.
**Pomegranate molasses could be used as an additional sweetener.*

In a small bowl, whisk together the vinegar, garlic, mustard, and sweetener (if using). Slowly whisk in the oil. Whisk vigorously until you create an emulsion. Season to taste with salt and pepper. Add fresh herbs or spices if desired.

Beet Salad with Honey Apple Vinaigrette

Serves 4

Salad

- 1 pound medium-sized fresh beets, peeled and cut into wedges
- 2 tablespoons canola oil
- 4 ounces arugula
- 1 honeycrisp apple, sliced thin
- 2 ounces goat cheese
- 2 tablespoons chopped walnuts, lightly toasted
- salt and pepper, to taste

Vinaigrette

- 2 tablespoons honey
- 2 tablespoons apple cider vinegar
- 1 clove garlic, minced
- 1 teaspoon dijon mustard
- 3–4 tablespoons extra virgin olive oil
- 1 tablespoon chopped fresh sage leaves
- salt and pepper, to taste

Preheat oven to 375°F. Line a sheet pan with parchment paper.

In a bowl, toss together the beets and oil. Season lightly with salt and pepper. Spread onto the sheet pan. Roast until fork tender, about 20–25 minutes. Set aside to cool.

In a large bowl, toss together the beets, arugula, apple, goat cheese, and walnuts. In a small bowl, whisk together the honey, vinegar, garlic, and dijon mustard. Season with salt and pepper. While whisking, drizzle in the olive oil. Add the sage and adjust seasonings to taste.

Pour vinaigrette over the salad mixture. Toss to coat well. Serve immediately.

The beets and vinaigrette can be made up to two days ahead of time.

Mixed Greens with Raspberry Vinaigrette

Serves 4

Salad

- 5 ounces mixed greens
- 2 ounces crumbled feta cheese
- 1/4 cup lightly toasted pumpkin seeds

Vinaigrette

- 1/4 cup fresh or frozen raspberries (thawed if frozen)
- 2 tablespoons red wine vinegar
- 2 tablespoons lemon juice
- 1 tablespoon honey
- 1/3 to 1/2 cup extra virgin olive oil
- salt and pepper, to taste

In a large bowl, toss together the greens, cheese, and pumpkin seeds. Set aside.

In a blender, combine the raspberries, vinegar, lemon juice, and honey. Puree mixture. With the motor running, drizzle in the olive oil to desired flavor and consistency. Season to taste with salt and pepper.

Pour vinaigrette over the greens and toss to coat well. Serve immediately.

Vinaigrette can be made two to three days ahead of time.

Caesar Salad
Serves 4–6

Caesar Dressing

- 4 anchovy filets
- 2 large egg yolks
- 2 garlic cloves
- zest and juice of 1 lemon
- 1/4 cup grated parmesan cheese
- 1/2 cup extra virgin olive oil
- salt and pepper, to taste

Croutons

- 1/2 loaf day-old bread, cut into cubes
- 3–4 tablespoons canola, olive, or safflower oil
- 1 tablespoon dried herbs: basil, oregano, or Italian seasoning
- 1 teaspoon garlic powder
- 1 teaspoon onion powder
- 1 teaspoon salt
- 1/2 teaspoon pepper

Salad

- 1–2 heads Romaine lettuce, washed and cut into pieces
- 1/2 cup parmesan cheese
- croutons
- dressing

Make the dressing: In a blender, combine the anchovies, egg yolks, and garlic. Blend to chop up mixture. Add the lemon zest, lemon juice, and parmesan. With the motor running, slowly drizzle in the olive oil. Season to taste with salt and pepper. Refrigerate until ready to use.

Make the croutons: Preheat oven to 375°F. Toss the bread with the oil, dried herbs, garlic powder, onion powder, salt, and pepper. Spread mixture onto a sheet pan. Bake until golden brown and crispy, about 10–20 minutes. Set aside to cool.

Make the salad: In a large bowl, toss together the Romaine, parmesan, and 1–2 cups croutons. Add enough dressing to just coat the leaves. Serve immediately.

California Chop Salad
Serves 4

Vinaigrette

- 2 tablespoons lemon juice
- 2 tablespoons champagne vinegar or white wine vinegar
- 1 teaspoon dijon mustard
- 1 clove garlic, minced
- 1/2 teaspoon turmeric
- 1/2 teaspoon pepper
- Salt, to taste
- 1/2 cup avocado oil

Salad

- 1 head bib lettuce, washed and torn into bite-sized pieces
- 4 radishes, sliced thinly
- 1 carrot, shredded
- 1 cup sliced cucumbers
- 1 (15-ounce) can chickpeas, drained and rinsed well
- 1/4 cup sliced almonds, lightly toasted
- shaved parmesan for garnish

In a bowl, whisk together the lemon juice, vinegar, dijon, garlic, turmeric, pepper, and salt. While whisking, drizzle in the oil. Season to taste with salt and pepper.

In a large bowl, toss together the lettuce, radishes, carrot, cucumbers, chickpeas, and almonds. Add the vinaigrette. Toss to coat the salad well. Garnish with shaved parmesan. Serve.

Vinaigrette can be made two to three days ahead of time.

Greens with Asian Vinaigrette
Serves 4

Vinaigrette

- 2 tablespoons unseasoned rice vinegar
- 1 tablespoon soy sauce
- 1 tablespoon honey or maple syrup
- 1 clove garlic, minced
- 1 teaspoon freshly grated ginger
- 1 tablespoon sesame oil
- 2–3 tablespoons canola, safflower, or grapeseed oil
- pepper, to taste

Salad

- 3–5 ounces baby greens of choice
- 1 red bell pepper, julienned
- 1 bunch scallions, sliced thin
- 1–2 mandarin oranges, segmented
- 1/4 cup peanuts

In a bowl, whisk together the vinegar, soy sauce, honey, garlic, and ginger. While whisking, drizzle in the sesame oil and canola oil. Season to taste with pepper.

In a large bowl, toss together the greens, pepper, scallions, oranges, and peanuts. Add the vinaigrette, tossing to coat well. Serve immediately.

Vinaigrette can be made two to three days ahead of time.

Fruit Salad
Serves 6

Vinaigrette

- 3 tablespoons fresh lemon juice
- 1 tablespoon white wine vinegar
- 1 tablespoon honey
- 1 tablespoon minced fresh chives
- 1/2 cup extra virgin olive oil
- salt and pepper, to taste

Salad

- 2 cups fresh pineapple chunks (or 1 15-ounce can pineapple chunks, drained)
- 1 orange, segmented
- 1 gala, braeburn, or fuji apple, diced
- 1 cup blueberries or red grapes
- 1 cup green grapes
- 3–4 cups arugula

Make the vinaigrette by whisking together the lemon juice, vinegar, honey, and chives. Add the olive oil in a steady stream until well incorporated. Season to taste with salt and pepper. Set aside.

In a large bowl, gently mix together the pineapple, orange, apple, blueberries, and grapes. Toss in the arugula. Add the vinaigrette. Toss gently to combine well. Serve.

Optional additions/substitutions:

- melon: watermelon, cantaloupe, honey dew can be added or substituted for the pineapple
- a substitution for arugula is thinly sliced fennel
- strawberries and raspberries could be added for additional color
- peaches, nectarines, and plums can be substituted for the apple

Spinach Salad with Candied Walnuts
Serves 4

Candied Walnuts

- 1 cup walnuts halves (or pecans)
- 1/4 cup sugar
- 2 tablespoons unsalted butter

Vinaigrette

- 3 tablespoons fresh orange juice
- 2 tablespoons cider vinegar
- 1 teaspoon Dijon mustard
- 1 teaspoon honey
- 1/2 cup extra virgin olive oil
- salt and pepper, to taste

Salad

- 5 ounces baby spinach
- 1/2 cup dried cranberries
- 2–4 ounces gorgonzola cheese crumbles (or goat cheese)

Make the walnuts by heating the walnuts, sugar, and butter in a skillet set over medium heat. Cook for 5 minutes, stirring frequently until sugar melts completely. Transfer to a sheet pan lined with parchment paper. Allow to cool. Set aside.

Make the vinaigrette by whisking together the orange juice, vinegar, mustard, and honey. Slowly whisk in the olive oil until well combined. Season to taste with salt and pepper.

In a bowl, toss together the spinach, cranberries, cheese, and walnuts. Drizzle on the vinaigrette, tossing to coat well. Serve.

Fish and Chips
Serves 6

Fries/Chips

- 1 gallon safflower or canola oil
- 4 large russet potatoes, sliced and rinsed in cold water
- kosher salt

Fish

- 2 cups flour
- 1 tablespoon baking powder
- 1 teaspoon kosher salt
- 1/2 teaspoon paprika
- 1/4 teaspoon cayenne pepper
- 1/4 teaspoon garlic powder
- 1/4 teaspoon onion powder
- 1 bottle brown beer
- 1 1/2 pounds firm-fleshed whitefish (tilapia, pollock, cod), cut into 1-ounce strips
- cornstarch, for dredging

Preheat oven to 200°F.

Heat the safflower oil in a large pot or dutch oven over high heat until it reaches 320°F.

In a bowl, whisk together the flour, baking powder, salt, paprika, cayenne pepper, garlic powder, and onion powder. Whisk in the beer until the batter is completely smooth and free of any lumps. Refrigerate for at least 15 minutes or up to 1 hour.

Drain potatoes well. Pat dry to remove excess water. When oil reaches 320°F, fry the potatoes in batches for 2–3 minutes. This is called "blanching" the potatoes. Remove from oil, drain, and cool to room temperature.

Increase the temperature of the oil to 375°F. Fry the potatoes again until crisp and golden brown, about 3 minutes. Remove from the oil and immediately season with salt while hot.

To fry the fish, allow oil to return to 350°F. Lightly dredge fish strips in cornstarch. Working in small batches, dip the fish into batter and then fry in the hot oil. When the batter is set on one side, turn the pieces of fish over and cook until golden brown, about 2–3 minutes. Remove and drain on paper towels. Season lightly with salt. Serve with the chips.

Fried Chicken
Serves 6–8

- 1 whole chicken, cut into 8 pieces
- 2 cups buttermilk
- 4 cups flour
- 2 teaspoons salt
- 2 teaspoons paprika
- 1 teaspoon pepper
- 1 teaspoon garlic powder
- oil for frying

Place the chicken pieces in a deep bowl or container. Add the buttermilk. Allow to sit at room temperature for 30 minutes or up to 2 hours in the refrigerator.

Heat the oil in a heavy, large pan (cast iron skillet or dutch oven work great) to 325°F.

In a bowl or large shallow pan, mix together the flour, salt, paprika, pepper, and garlic powder. Remove the chicken from the buttermilk and allow the excess to fall off. Dredge the chicken in the flour mixture until coated well. Shake off excess flour.

Fry the chicken in the hot oil for 15 minutes, flipping halfway through. Check the internal temperature of the chicken. Legs and thighs should be at 180°F when done, and the breast and wings need to read 165°F when done. Cook in the oil until the chicken is cooked through to the proper temperature.

Remove from the oil and drain on a wire rack set over a sheet pan or on paper towels. Serve.

Andouille Sausage and Corn Fritters with Creole Mayo
Yield: about 2 dozen fritters

- 2 cups flour
- 1/4 cup sugar
- 1 tablespoon baking powder
- 1 teaspoon smoked paprika
- 1 teaspoon salt
- 1/2 teaspoon pepper
- 1/2 teaspoon cayenne pepper
- 1/2 cup finely diced andouille sausage
- 1 1/2 cups frozen corn kernels, thawed
- 2 large eggs
- 1 cup milk
- 1 tablespoon fresh thyme
- 1/2 cup unsalted butter, melted
- 3–4 tablespoons canola oil

In a large bowl, whisk together the flour, sugar, baking powder, paprika, salt, pepper, and cayenne. Add the andouille, corn, eggs, milk, and thyme. Mix well. Stir in the melted butter and combine well.

Heat the oil in a nonstick skillet set over medium heat. Ladle about 2 ounces of batter into the hot oil and shape into a mini-pancake. Cook fritters for 2–3 minutes before flipping and cooking on the other side. Repeat until batter is used up. Transfer to a platter. Serve with creole mayo (recipe below).

Creole Mayo

- 1 cup mayonnaise
- 1/4 red onion, minced
- 1 clove garlic, minced
- 2 tablespoons minced red bell pepper
- 1 tablespoon minced jalapeno pepper
- cayenne pepper, to taste
- tabasco to taste
- salt to taste

Mix ingredients together. Refrigerate until ready to serve. Can be made 1–2 days ahead of time.

Fried Zucchini
Serves 4–6

- 1 3/4 cup grated parmesan cheese
- 1 1/2 cups bread crumbs
- 1 teaspoon salt
- 1/2 teaspoon pepper
- 2 large eggs
- canola oil for frying
- 3 medium zucchini, cut into 1/2-inch rounds

In a bowl, combine the parmesan cheese, bread crumbs, salt, and pepper. In another bowl, whisk the eggs and season lightly with salt and pepper.

Pour enough oil into a large skillet to reach a depth of 2 inches. Heat the oil to 350°F.

Working in batches, dip the zucchini in the eggs to coat completely and allow excess to fall off. Place the zucchini into the bread crumb mixture. Place on a sheet pan. Repeat process for the rest of the zucchini.

When the oil is hot, fry the zucchini until golden brown on both sides. Remove from the oil and place on paper towels. Serve hot with pizza sauce.

Tempura
Serves 4

Batter

- 1 1/2 cups sweet rice flour (glutinous rice flour)
- 1 1/4 to 1 1/2 cups club soda
- 1/2 teaspoon baking powder

Vegetables of Choice

- 1 cup green beans
- 1 cup broccoli florets

Peanut or canola oil for frying

Make the batter by mixing together the rice flour, club soda, and baking powder. The batter should be thick and able to coat the vegetables. Let sit for 10 minutes.

Heat the oil in a deep fryer or stock pot to 375°F.

Drop the vegetables into the batter until well coated. Fry in the hot oil until lightly golden brown and crispy. Remove from oil and drain on paper towels. Serve with dipping sauce (see below).

Dipping Sauce

- 1/2 cup soy sauce
- 1/4 cup rice vinegar
- 2 tablespoons minced fresh ginger
- 1 clove garlic, minced
- 2 teaspoons sugar
- 1 teaspoon sesame oil

Mix ingredients together. Refrigerate until ready to use.

Apple Fritters
Yield: about 2 dozen

- 2 cups flour
- 1/3 cup sugar
- 2 1/4 teaspoons baking powder
- 1 teaspoon salt
- 1/2 teaspoon ground cinnamon
- 3/4 cup whole milk
- 2 large eggs, at room temperature
- 2 tablespoons unsalted butter, melted
- 1/2 teaspoon vanilla extract
- 2 apples peeled and diced small (gala, braeburn, or MacIntosh)
- canola or safflower oil for frying
- powdered sugar for dusting

In a large bowl, whisk together flour, granulated sugar, baking powder, salt, and cinnamon. In another bowl, whisk together milk, eggs, butter, and vanilla. Gently fold milk mixture into flour mixture until just combined. Fold in apples.

Meanwhile, heat 2 inches of oil in a heavy-bottomed pot over medium-high heat until a thermometer registers 350°F. Set a wire rack in a rimmed baking sheet.

Working in batches, drop heaping tablespoons of dough into the oil. Cook, turning once, until puffed and golden, about 3–4 minutes. Transfer to rack with a slotted spoon. Cool slightly and then dust with powdered sugar. Serve warm.

Coconut Oil Blondies

Yield: 1 8-inch pan

- 1/2 cup nut butter of choice (almond, peanut butter)
- 1/4 cup coconut oil, melted
- 3/4 cup sugar
- 1 large egg
- 1 tablespoon vanilla extract
- 1 cup almond flour (almond meal)
- 1/2 cup rolled oats
- 1 teaspoon baking soda
- 1/4 teaspoon salt
- 4 ounces semi-sweet or bittersweet chocolate chips

Preheat oven to 350°F. Grease and line an 8-inch square baking pan with parchment paper Set aside.

In a bowl, whisk together the nut butter, coconut oil, sugar, egg, and vanilla extract until smooth. Stir in the almond flour, oats, baking soda, and salt. Fold in the chocolate chips.

Spread in prepared pan and bake for 20 minutes, or until golden brown.

Cool completely, and then cut into squares.

Optional addition: nuts, flaked coconut

Rosemary Olive Oil Cookies

Yield: 2 dozen cookies

- 2 cups all-purpose flour
- 1/2 teaspoon baking soda
- 1/2 teaspoon baking powder
- 1/4 teaspoon salt
- 1 cup sugar
- 1/3 cup extra virgin olive oil
- 1 1/2 teaspoons lemon zest
- 1 teaspoon finely chopped fresh rosemary
- 2 large eggs

Preheat oven to 350°F. Line a sheet pan with parchment paper.

In a medium bowl, whisk together the flour, baking soda, baking powder, and salt. Set aside.

In a mixing bowl, cream together the sugar, olive oil, lemon zest and rosemary until smooth. Add the eggs one at a time, mixing well after each addition. Stir in the dry ingredients. Mix until combined.

Roll cookies into 1-inch size balls. Place on sheet pan and sprinkle each cookie with sugar. Bake for 11–13 minutes, or until golden brown. Remove from oven. Cool on the baking sheet for 10 minutes before cooling completely on a wire rack.

Optional: Drizzle each cookie with a glaze made from powdered sugar and fresh lemon juice.

Beet Chips

Yield: 2–3 cups

- 3 medium sized beets, sliced very thin (1/16-inch)
- 1–2 tablespoons canola or safflower oil
- 2 teaspoons salt (kosher or sea salt)
- 2 teaspoons dried herbs or spices of choice

Preheat the oven to 400°F. Rub a sheet pan with the oil (it should be a thin layer of oil). Layer the sliced beets onto the pan being careful not to overlap.

Bake the chips on the bottom rack of the oven for 10–15 minutes, depending on how thin the beets are cut and how large they are.

While the beets are baking, mix together the salt and herbs.

Remove the rack from the oven and sprinkle with the herb salt. Allow the beets to cool on the pan. Once cool, transfer to a cooling rack to continue to dry and crisp. Repeat with the remaining slices of beets.

Parsnip Chips

Yield: 2–3 cups

- 2 medium sized parsnips, sliced thinly
- 1–2 tablespoons canola or safflower oil
- 1 teaspoon salt
- 1/2 teaspoon pepper
- 1/2 teaspoon garlic powder

Preheat the oven to 425°F. Line a sheet pan with parchment paper.

Place the parsnip slices in a bowl and drizzle with the oil. In a small bowl, mix together the salt, pepper, and garlic powder. Season the parsnips with the salt mixture.

Spread the chips in a single layer on the baking sheet. Bake for 10 minutes. Flip and bake for another 10 minutes, or until browned and crisp.

Remove and allow to cool.

Unit 7 Questions

1. In Experiment 1, describe the differences in texture and flavor between the brownies. Which one produced a good, moist brownie?

2. What can cause an emulsion like mayonnaise to break? Describe some ways to fix it.

3. Describe the differences in flavor and color between the olive oils tasted. Name appropriate uses or recipes for each one.

4. What are some nutritional concerns of hydrogenated vegetable oils?

5. Which countries around the world produce olive oil?

6. In Experiment 2, which oil made the best-tasting mayonnaise? Describe the flavor differences between the different types?

7. In Experiment 3, which potato chip method resulted in the crispiest chip? Why do you think this is?

8. In Experiment 3, why are the potatoes rinsed with water first? What is an advantage of doing this?

NOTES

1. Jana Orsavova, Ladislava Misurcova, Jarmila V. Ambrozova, Robert Vicha, and Jiri Mlcek, "Fatty Acids Composition of Vegetable Oils and Its Contribution to Dietary Energy Intake and Dependence of Cardiovascular Mortality on Dietary Intake of Fatty Acids," *International Journal of Molecular Sciences*. 16, no. 6 (2015): 12871–90.

2. MasterClass, "Cooking Oils and Smoke Points: What to Know and How to Choose the Right Cooking Oil," updated September 25, 2019, accessed May 14, 2019, https://www.masterclass.com/articles/cooking-oils-and-smoke-points-what-to-know-and-how-to-choose#chart-of-oil-smoke-points.

BIBLIOGRAPHY

MasterClass. "Cooking Oils and Smoke Points: What to Know and How to Choose the Right Cooking Oil." Updated September 25, 2019. Accessed May 14, 2019. https://www.masterclass.com/articles/cooking-oils-and-smoke-points-what-to-know-and-how-to-choose#oil-smoke-point-chart.

Orsavova, Jana, Ladislava Misurcova, Jarmila V.Ambrozova, Robert Vicha, and Jiri Mlcek. "Fatty Acids Composition of Vegetable Oils and Its Contribution to Dietary Energy Intake and Dependence of Cardiovascular Mortality on Dietary Intake of Fatty Acids." *International Journal of Molecular Sciences*. 16, no. 6 (2015): 12871–90. doi: 10.3390/ijms160612871.

IMAGE CREDITS

Grains, Nuts, and Seeds

- Identify different cereals and grains
- Evaluate different types of rice
- Evaluate variations in oatmeal
- Use basic cooking skills to prepare recipes

CEREALS AND GRAINS

Named for the Roman goddess, Cerees, the goddess of agriculture and grain, cereals were first domesticated about 10,000–15,000 years ago in an area known as the Fertile Crescent.[1] Situated along the Tigris and Euphrates Rivers, the Fertile Crescent is now home to the nations of Iran and Iraq. During the time when cereals were domesticated, great strides were made in agriculture production as humans evolved from hunter gatherers to settling communities.

While there are many different varieties of cereals, the most common ones found today are wheat, corn (maize), rice, barley, oats, rye, sorghum, millet, and amaranth. Cereals and grains can be purchased in whole form or processed into groats or flour.

Parts of a Grain Kernel[2]

All kernels of grain consist of the three edible parts: bran, germ, and endosperm.

Bran

Outer skin of the wheat kernel that contains antioxidants, B vitamins, and fiber.

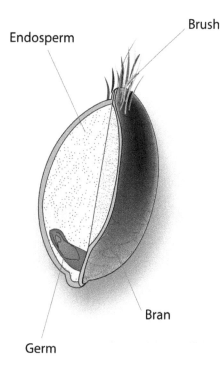

Endosperm

Brush

Bran

Germ

FIGURE 8.1 Parts of a wheat kernel.

Germ
Embryo of the kernel containing the DNA to sprout a new plant. Nutritionally, it contains B vitamins, protein, minerals, and healthy fats.

Endosperm
Food supply for the germ. It is comprised mainly of starches and proteins.

Hulled and Pearled Grains
Sometimes grains can be purchased as hulled, pearled, or semi-pearled. Hulled grains have the inedible hull removed from the kernel, leaving the bran intact. Pearled and semi-pearled are similar. Pearled grains have the bran removed from the grain whereas semi-pearled grains have only part of the bran removed.

Grains that are hulled typically require soaking for 8–10 hours prior to cooking or they may have a long cooking time, 1–2 hours depending on the grain. Grains that are pearled or semi-pearled have a much shorter cooking time and do not need to be soaked ahead of time.

Gluten
In Latin, gluten means "glue." In baking, gluten is responsible for the structure and elastic texture of dough, hence acting as glue. Stored in the endosperm of the wheat kernel, gluten is primarily comprised of gliadin and glutenin proteins.[3] When water is added to flour, it activates the proteins which form a complex structure. Gluten is found in all derivatives of wheat including wheat, rye, triticale, and ancient grains such as spelt, farro, and Kamut.

Wheat Flour[4]
When sold commercially, flours made from wheat are processed or refined. In the refining process, the bran and germ is removed, decreasing the fiber and micronutrient content. Because flour has been stripped of its nutrients, bread made from white flour is typically enriched with iron and B vitamins.

Wheat flour is made from certain types of wheat that are characterized by their protein content, the season they are grown, and the color of the kernel.

Protein Content: Hard or Soft Wheat
Hard wheat has a higher protein content and more gluten than soft wheat. Hard wheat varieties are made into bread flour. Soft wheat is used for cake and pastry flours because of the lower protein content.

Season: Winter or Spring Wheat

Winter wheat is planted in the fall. After it partially grows, it goes dormant in the winter months and resumes growing in the spring. It's harvested in early summer. On the other hand, spring wheat is planted in April or May and harvested in August and September.

Color: Red or White

Wheat kernels can be red or white in color. Nutritionally, the two varieties are the same. White wheat may have less bitterness due to the lack of tannins in its bran.

Types of Wheat Flour[5]

Whole Wheat Flour

The kernel is left intact and ground into flour. Regular grinding of the kernel is done with steel rollers. Stone ground whole wheat flour is slowly ground using stones and leaves the germ more intact.

White Whole Wheat Flour

White whole wheat flour is from a particular variety of wheat that does not have color. It can be used in place of whole wheat flour. It is lighter in flavor and color.

All Purpose (AP) Flour

Blend of hard and soft flours with a protein content of 8–11%. Good for general use.

Bread Flour

High protein content of 12–14%. It is the preferred flour for baking high-quality bread products because it forms strong elastic gluten structures.

Cake Flour

Soft wheat with 8% protein content; it is used for delicate cakes and pastries.

Pastry Flour

Soft wheat with slightly higher protein content than cake flour, at 9–10%. Good for pastries requiring a stronger flour for good gluten formation that will not produce a tough product.

00 Flour (Italian)

Superfine flour with high protein content typically used for making pasta and pizza dough.

Semolina

Made from durum wheat, semolina is a coarser, darker (more yellow) flour compared to AP flour. It is used for making pasta in Italy.

Other Cereals[6]

Farro/Emmer

Farro is an ancient grain used in Italian cuisine. Specifically, it is classified as three different grains: farro piccolo (einkorn), farro medio (emmer), and farro grande (spelt). Emmer is the most common form of farro found in the United States.

Bulgur

Quick cooking, bulgur are the groats (the bran, germ, and endosperm) of a wheat kernel.

Spelt

Spelt is an ancient grain that has increased in popularity since it is a good alternative for those with wheat intolerances. It is more water-soluble than regular flour. If using as a substitution, decrease the amount of liquid in the recipe by three-quarters (3/4).

Kamut

Another ancient grain with a very high protein content compared to wheat flour. It contains gluten but those with wheat intolerances may be able to tolerate it.

Barley

Popular grain that has been cultivated for several centuries. The most common type of barley found is pearled barley. However, there are several varieties of barley available, including bronze and purple barley for food consumption and many types of barley for brewing beer.

Millet

Tiny, round grain grown in arid regions. It is very popular in Northern Africa and is used to make porridge. Very high protein and fiber content.

Teff

Tiny grain from Northern Africa. It is a staple in Ethiopia where it used in the flat bread *injera*. It is high in protein and iron.

Amaranth

Ancient grain originating in the Americas. It can be ground into flour to use in breads, cooked in porridge, or popped. It has a very high protein content of 17% and is high in the essential amino acid, lysine.

Oats

Found in several forms in the market: rolled oats (old fashioned), quick oats, and steel-cut oats. Rolled oats are the groats that have been flattened. Rolled oats that have been processed even further and parcooked become quick oats. Steel cut oats are groats that are chopped smaller.

Corn (Maize)

Maize is a cereal cultivated by the indigenous peoples of North and Central America. A whole grain form of corn is polenta, a type of coarsely ground cornmeal popular in Italian cuisine. Polenta may also be known as gruel or mush. Today, byproducts of corn are found in many processed foods.

Sorghum

One of the top five grains in the world, sorghum can be grown as a grain, forage for livestock, or sweet crop for sorghum syrup.

Quinoa

Technically a seed, not a grain, quinoa originated in the Andes region in South America about 5000 years ago. It has a much higher protein content than other cereals.

Rice[7]

A staple around the world, rice has been cultivated for thousands of years. Because of its importance in many food cultures around the world, there are hundreds of varieties of rice from short grain to long grain rice.

Rice Types

Converted Rice
Rice that has been parcooked, helping to retain nutrients.

Long Grain Rice
Longer than it is wide. Cooks up light and fluffy. High in amylose.

Long Grain Rice
Standard type of rice.

Long Grain Brown Rice
Long grain rice with the bran still in tact.

Jasmine
Named after the jasmine flower, jasmine rice is native to Thailand and has a slightly floral scent and flavor.

Basmati
Fragrant and nutty, basmati is cultivated in India and Pakistan.

Medium Grain Rice
Shorter and wider than long grain. Cooks up moist and tender with a slightly sticky texture. Lower in amylose than long grain.

Forbidden Rice or Black Rice
Originating from Japan and cultivated in parts of China, Forbidden rice is a whole grain rice with a nutty flavor. High amounts of anthocyanins contribute to its deep, dark color.

Bhutan Red Rice
Native to the Kingdom of Bhutan in the Eastern Himalayas, this rice has a slight red color and nutty flavor.

Short Grain Rice
Even shorter and wider than medium grain. Cooks up very sticky and clumps together. Very low in amylose compared to long grain rice.

Arborio
Short grain rice used in Italian cuisine to make risotto.

Sushi
Short grain rice used in many Asian cuisines.

Bomba Rice
Cultivated in Spain, Bomba rice is typically used to make Paella.

Other Rice

Wild Rice

Wild rice is not a rice but rather the seed of a type of grass; wild rice is native to North America.

NUTS AND SEEDS[8]

All nuts are seeds but not all seeds are nuts. There are many varieties of edible nuts and seeds, most of which are good sources of dietary fiber and healthy fats. Nuts can be categorized as botanical nuts, drupes, or gymnosperms.

Botanical nuts

Dry, hard-shelled fruit

Drupe

Fleshy fruit around a pit

Gymnosperm

Seed without an enclosure to protect it

Types of Nuts and Seeds

Seeds

Chia

Once a major crop in Central America and cultivated 3500 years ago by the Aztecs, chia seeds are high in fiber, omega-3 fatty acids and micronutrients such as calcium, magnesium, and iron.

Flax

First cultivated in ancient Egypt and China, flax seeds are high in fiber and omega 3 fatty acids.

Sunflower

Sunflower seeds are the fruit of the sunflower plant, Helianthus annuus. They are a good source of folate and vitamin E.

Pumpkin (Pepitas)

Pumpkin seeds or pepitas in Spanish are the seeds of the pumpkin or similar winter squash. They are high in B vitamins, iron, and magnesium.

Hemp

Hemp seeds come from the cannabis sativa plant and are high in omega-3 and omega-6 fatty acids.

Sesame

From the flowering plant, Sesamum. This is an ancient food grown in Asia and is the base for tahini.

Nuts

Almonds (Drupe)
Native to the Mediterranean region, almonds are the seed from a type of fruit called a drupe. They are an excellent source of Vitamin E, fiber, and monounsaturated fat.

Walnuts (Drupe)
Black walnut trees are native to North America and found in the Midwest and Northeastern parts of the United States. More commonly found, the English walnut variety has been grown in California since the late 1700s. Today, California grows 99% of the world's English walnuts. Walnuts are a great source of fiber, omega-3 fatty acids, and mono- and polyunsaturated fatty acids.

Chestnuts (Nut)
Chestnut trees are native to regions in the Northern Hemisphere. It is the only nut to contain Vitamin C.

Hazelnuts (Nut)
Grown on the Corylus tree that is cultivated around the Mediterranean in countries such as Turkey, Spain, and Italy, hazelnuts are high in manganese, Vitamin E, and many antioxidants.

Pecans (Drupe)
The pecan tree is a member of the hickory family and is native to North America. Pecans are high in flavonoids, monounsaturated fatty acids, and B vitamins.

Macadamia Nuts (Legume)
Originating in the rainforests of North Eastern Australia, macadamia nuts are high in calcium, selenium, vitamins A and E, and monounsaturated fatty acids.

Pistachios (Drupe)
Pistachios are a member of the cashew family originating in the Middle East. They are high in vitamin B6 and antioxidants.

Cashews (Drupe)
Originating in Brazil, cashews have a softer, buttery texture and are high in Vitamin C, folate, magnesium, and mono- and polyunsaturated fatty acids.

Brazil Nuts
Grown on the Brazil nut tree, brazil nuts are high in selenium and monounsaturated fatty acids.

Coconut (Drupe)
From the coconut palm tree grown in tropical regions. Most of the coconut is used in a variety of applications from making cosmetics to cooking.

Pine Nut (Gymnosperm)
Pine nuts come from one of eighteen species of pine trees grown in Asia, Europe, and North America. The pine nut is found in the pinecone of the tree and it is difficult to harvest.

EXPERIMENTS

Experiment 1: Rice Variations

Discuss the differences between varieties of rice when cooked.

<u>Basic Recipe</u>

- 1 cup water
- 1/2 cup long grain rice
- 1/4 teaspoon salt

Rinse rice under cold running water until the water runs clear.

In a saucepot, combine the water, rice, and salt. Place over medium-high heat. Bring to a boil. Cover and reduce heat to low. Simmer for 15 minutes. Turn off heat and steam until the rice is cooked through.

<u>Variations</u>

Substitute the following for the long grain rice and make adjustments where noted.

- Long grain brown rice
  - increase water to 1 1/4 cups
  - do not rinse prior to cooking
  - simmer for 30 minutes
- Sushi rice
- Jasmine rice
- Basmati rice
- Forbidden rice
  - do not rinse prior to cooking

Rice	Appearance	Flavor	Texture
Long grain			
Brown			
Sushi			
Jasmine			
Basmati			
Forbidden			

Experiment 2: Oatmeal Variations

Test and evaluate different types of oatmeal.

Quick Cooking Oats

- 1/2 cup quick cooking oats
- 1/2 cup water
- 1/4 cup milk
- sugar to taste

Combine the oats, water, and milk in a saucepan. Bring to a simmer. Cover and cook for 2–3 minutes. Add sugar to taste. Serve warm.

Old Fashioned (Rolled) Oats

- 1/2 cup old fashioned rolled oats
- 1/2 cup water
- 1/4 cup milk
- sugar to taste

Combine the oats, water, and milk in a saucepan. Bring to a simmer. Cover and cook for 5–6 minutes. Add sugar to taste. Serve warm.

Steel Cut Oats

- 1/2 cup steel cut oats
- 3/4 cup water
- 1/2 cup milk
- sugar to taste

Combine the oats, water, and milk in a saucepan. Bring to a simmer. Cover and cook for 30–40 minutes. Add sugar to taste. Serve warm.

Instant Oats

Cook instant oats according to package directions.

Oatmeal	Appearance	Flavor	Texture
Quick cooking			
Old fashioned			
Steel cut			
Instant			

RECIPES

Nut Butter
Yield: 2 cups

- 1 pound raw nut of choice (almonds, walnuts, pecans, hazelnuts, cashews, peanuts)
- 1/4 teaspoon salt

Preheat oven to 350°F. Spread the nuts on a sheet pan. Bake until lightly toasted, about 10 minutes. Allow the nuts to cool for 10 minutes.

Place the nuts in a food processor. Blend until creamy, scraping down the sides of the bowl as necessary. Blend until the mixture is very creamy, about 10–12 minutes. Add the salt.

Transfer mixture to a glass jar. Store in the refrigerator for up to one month.

Creamy Polenta with Tomato Sauce
Serves 2

Polenta

- 2 1/2 cups chicken or vegetable stock
- 3/4 cup polenta (not quick cooking)
- 2 tablespoons grated parmesan cheese
- 2 tablespoons unsalted butter
- salt and pepper, to taste

In a large saucepan, bring the stock to a simmer over medium heat. Sprinkle in the polenta. Reduce heat to low and stir until it thickens, about 15–20 minutes. Add the cheese, butter, and season to taste with salt and pepper. Keep warm until ready to serve.

Tomato Sauce

- 1 tablespoon olive oil
- 1 clove garlic, minced
- Pinch red pepper flakes
- 1 tablespoon tomato paste
- 1 (15-ounce) can crushed tomatoes
- salt and pepper, to taste
- fresh basil and/oregano for garnish (or used dried herbs)

Heat oil, garlic, and red pepper flakes in a saucepan set over medium heat. Cook until the garlic starts to sizzle. Add the tomato paste. Cook for 1–2 minutes. Add the tomatoes and season with salt and pepper. Reduce heat to low. If using dried herbs, add them now. Cook for 10 minutes. If using, add fresh herbs right before serving. Adjust seasonings to taste. Serve with the polenta.

Risotto
Serves 2–3

- 3 cups chicken or vegetable stock
- 1 teaspoon olive oil
- 1/4 cup onion, minced
- 1/2 cup Arborio rice
- 1/4 cup white wine
- 1/4 cup grated parmesan cheese
- salt and pepper, to taste

In a small saucepot, bring the stock to a boil. Reduce heat to low and keep warm.

Heat the oil in a sauté pan set over medium heat. Add the onion and sauté until translucent, about 2–3 minutes. Add the rice and coat to mix in the hot oil. Cook for 1–2 minutes. Stir in the wine and allow to reduce down to about 1 tablespoon.

Add the stock, one ladle at a time. Stir the rice constantly and only add a ladle of stock when the liquid has been absorbed in the pan. Add enough stock until the rice is al dente. When the rice is done, add the parmesan cheese and season to taste with salt and pepper. Serve immediately.

Granola Bars
Yield: 16 bars (9 × 13-inch pan)

- 2 1/2 cups old-fashioned rolled oats
- 1 cup nuts of choice: almonds, pecans, walnuts, cashews, macadamia, hazelnuts
- 1 cup shredded coconut
- 1/2 cup toasted wheat germ, ground flax, or ground chia
- 2/3 cup honey
- 1/4 cup nut butter of choice
- 1/4 cup light brown sugar
- 3 tablespoons unsalted butter
- 2 teaspoons vanilla extract
- 1/4 teaspoon salt
- 1 1/2 cups dried fruit of choice

Preheat oven to 350ºF. Lightly grease a 9 × 13-inch baking dish. Line with parchment paper. Set aside.

On a sheet pan, toss together the oatmeal, nuts, and coconut. Bake for 10–12 minutes or until lightly golden brown. Remove and pour mixture into a large mixing bowl. Stir in the wheat germ.

Reduce oven temperature to 300ºF. Place the honey, nut butter, brown sugar, butter, vanilla, and salt. Bring to a boil over medium heat. Pour mixture over the oatmeal mixture. Add the dried fruit. Pour mixture into the prepared pan. Wet your fingers with water and gently press the mixture into the pan. Bake for 25–30 minutes or until lightly golden brown. Cool at least 2–3 hours before cutting into squares. Serve at room temperature.

Granola

Yield: 5 cups

- 1/2 cup oil of choice: canola, coconut (melted), or safflower
- 1/2 cup honey or maple syrup
- 1 teaspoon vanilla extract
- 1/2 teaspoon salt
- 3 cups old-fashioned rolled oats
- 1 cup nuts and/or seeds of choice: almonds, pecans, walnuts, cashews, macadamia, hazelnuts, sunflower seeds, pumpkin seeds (roughly chopped if large)
- 1 cup dried fruit of choice

Preheat oven to 300°F. Line a baking sheet with parchment paper. Set aside.

In a large bowl, whisk together the oil, honey/maple syrup, vanilla, and salt. Add the oats and nuts/seeds. Stir to coat well. Spread onto the baking sheet into a single layer. Bake for 20–25 minutes or until golden brown.

Stir in the dried fruit. Allow to cool to room temperature. Store in airtight container for one to two weeks.

Optional additions: shredded coconut, chocolate chips (add after baking), flax seeds, chia seeds, ground cinnamon.

Kamut Pancakes

Yield: 8–12 pancakes

- 2 1/4 cups Kamut flour
- 2 tablespoons sugar
- 1 tablespoons baking powder
- 1 teaspoon baking soda
- 1 teaspoon salt
- 1 1/4 cups buttermilk
- 2 large eggs
- 3 tablespoons canola oil

Mix together the flour, sugar, baking powder, baking soda, and salt. In another bowl, whisk together the milk, eggs, and oil. Add the wet ingredients to the dry ingredients and mix until just combined. Add more milk if it seems too thick.

Preheat griddle. Pour batter onto hot griddle to make pancakes. Cook 2–3 minutes per side. Serve warm with maple syrup.

Cauliflower and Barley Salad
Serves 6

- 1/2 cup bronze or purple barley, soaked overnight if not semi-pearled
- zest and juice of 1 lemon
- 1 tablespoon mayonnaise
- 2 teaspoons dijon mustard
- 6 tablespoons extra virgin olive oil
- 1/2 teaspoon red pepper flakes
- 1 medium-sized head cauliflower, cut into florets
- 1 (15-ounce) can chickpeas, drained and rinsed
- 1/2 cup flat-leaf parsley, chopped
- salt and pepper, to taste

Drain the barley and place in a saucepan. Cover by 2 inches with water. Season lightly with salt and pepper. Bring to a boil over medium heat. Reduce heat to medium low and cover. Cook until tender, about 30–45 minutes. Drain off excess water. Set aside.

Whisk together the lemon zest and juice, mayonnaise, and dijon mustard in a bowl. Whisk in 5 tablespoons oil. Season to taste with salt and pepper. Set aside.

Heat the remaining 1 tablespoon of olive oil in a large skillet set over medium heat. Add the red pepper flakes and cauliflower florets. Stir occasionally until lightly golden brown. Reduce heat to medium low and add 3–4 tablespoons water. Cover and cook until the cauliflower is tender, about 5 minutes. Season lightly with salt and pepper.

Place the cauliflower in a large bowl. Add the chickpeas, parsley, and barley. Toss well. Pour in the dressing and toss to coat the vegetables and barley well. Serve.

Salad can be made 2–3 days ahead of time if kept in the refrigerator.

Farro with Roasted Broccoli
Serves 6

Salad

- 2 tablespoons olive oil
- 2 cups broccoli florets
- 1/2 pound semi-pearled farro
- 3–4 cups vegetable stock
- 4 ounces pancetta, diced
- pinch of red pepper flakes
- salt and pepper, to taste

Dressing

- 1/4 cup extra virgin olive oil
- 2 tablespoons lemon juice
- 2 tablespoons chopped parsley
- salt and pepper, to taste

Preheat oven to 375°F.

Toss the broccoli with 1 tablespoon oil. Season lightly with salt and pepper. Place on a baking sheet. Bake for 25–30 minutes.

Meanwhile, add the farro to a 2-quart saucepan. Pour enough stock in the pan to cover the farro by 1 inch. Bring to a boil. Cover and reduce heat to low. Simmer until the farro is cooked, about 20–25 minutes. Drain off excess liquid. Toss with olive oil.

Heat the remaining 1 tablespoon oil over medium heat in a large sauté pan. Add the pancetta and cook until crispy. Remove from the heat and add the farro and crushed red pepper flakes. Season lightly with salt and pepper.

Combine the farro mixture and the cooked broccoli in a large bowl. In a small bowl, whisk together the dressing ingredients. Pour dressing over the farro and broccoli, mixing well. Serve slightly warm or at room temperature.

Spicy Bulgur Salad
Serves 6

Salad

- 1 1/2 cups bulgur
- 1/2 cup chopped walnuts
- 1/2 cup chopped almonds
- 1/2 cup flat leaf parsley
- 1/2 cup red onion, sliced thin
- 1/2 cup feta cheese
- 1 head romaine lettuce, chopped

Dressing

- 2 tablespoons lemon juice
- 2 tablespoons tomato paste
- 1 clove garlic, minced
- 1 tablespoon ground coriander
- 1 teaspoon ground cumin
- 1/2 teaspoon cayenne
- 1/4 cup extra virgin olive oil
- salt and pepper, to taste

Place the bulgur in a bowl. Pour 3–4 cups hot tap water over the bulgur. Let sit for 30 minutes. Drain bulgur and dry off on paper towels.

Pour the bulgur into a bowl. Add the walnuts, almonds, and parsley.

In a small bowl, whisk together the lemon juice, tomato paste, garlic, coriander, cumin, and cayenne. Whisk in the oil. Season to taste with salt and pepper.

Pour dressing over the bulgur mixture. Toss to combine. Add the onions, feta, and lettuce.

Popped Amaranth Bars
Yield: 8 bars (8-inch pan)

- 2 cups popped amaranth (see below)*
- 1/4 cup dried fruit of choice
- 1/4 cup nuts and/or seeds of choice
- 1/2 cup nut butter of choice: peanut or almond butter
- 1/2 cup honey
- 1/2 teaspoon fine sea salt
- Optional: a few drops vanilla or almond extract, 1/2 teaspoon ground cinnamon, ginger, or allspice

Spray an 8-inch square baking pan with nonstick cooking spray and line with parchment paper, allowing an overhang on opposite sides.

In a large bowl, combine the popped amaranth, dried fruit, and nuts.

In a small saucepan, combine the nut butter, honey, and salt. Cook and stir over medium-low heat until bubbly. Remove from heat and stir in optional flavorings, if desired, then immediately pour over amaranth mixture, stirring to coat. Scrape mixture into prepared pan and tamp down mixture.

Cover loosely and refrigerate for 2–4 hours. Use the parchment overhang to remove bars from pan. Cut into 8 bars.

Popping Amaranth or Sorghum
Heat a large pot over high heat. When a bead of water dropped on the bottom immediately sizzles, stir in half of the grain. Lower the heat to medium. Stir constantly until the grains turn a shade or two darker and most of the grains have popped. Repeat with remaining grain.

Amaranth Fritters
Yield: 8–10 fritters

- 1 1/2 cups low-sodium chicken or vegetable stock
- 1 cup dry amaranth
- 1 teaspoon salt
- 1 large egg
- 2–3 tablespoons AP flour (or GF AP flour)
- 1 tablespoon curry powder
- 1 teaspoon garlic powder
- 1 teaspoon onion powder
- 1/2 teaspoon pepper
- 2–3 tablespoons canola or safflower oil

Combine the stock, amaranth, and 1/2 teaspoon salt in a saucepan set over medium high heat. Bring to a boil. Reduce heat to low, cover and simmer for 40 minutes. Drain off excess liquid if necessary. Cool slightly.

In a large bowl, combine the cooked amaranth, egg, 2 tablespoons flour, curry powder, 1/2 teaspoon salt, and pepper. Add additional flour if the mixture is too wet. Set aside.

Heat oil in a sauté pan set over medium heat. Drop the amaranth mixture by spoonfuls into the hot oil. Fry until golden brown on each side. Add more oil to pan as necessary.

Serve hot with yogurt dipping sauce.

Yogurt Dipping sauce: Combine 1/2 cup plain greek yogurt, 1 tablespoon olive oil, 2 teaspoons lemon juice, and 1 clove minced garlic in a small bowl. Season with salt and pepper to taste.

Rice Pilaf
Serves 4

- 1 tablespoon unsalted butter or canola oil
- 1/2 cup diced onion
- 1 cup long grain white rice
- 1 1/2 cups chicken or vegetable stock
- 1/2 cup fresh or frozen peas
- salt and pepper, to taste

Melt the butter in a saucepot set over medium heat. Add the onion and sauté until soft, about 5–6 minutes. Season lightly with salt and pepper. Add the rice. Cook for 1–2 minutes. Pour in the stock. Season with salt and pepper. Bring to a boil. Cover and reduce heat to low. Cook for 10–15 minutes or until the liquid is absorbed. Remove lid and add the peas to the top of the pilaf. Turn off the heat and keep the rice covered for 5 minutes. Fluff with a fork and serve.

Wild Rice Pilaf
Serves 6

- 5 cups water
- 1 1/3 cups wild rice
- 2 tablespoons maple syrup (or honey)
- 2 teaspoons fresh ginger
- 1 teaspoon salt
- 1 teaspoon cinnamon
- 1/4 teaspoon nutmeg
- 1 gala, fuji, or honeycrisp apple, diced small
- 1/2 cup lightly toasted pumpkin seeds or sliced almonds
- 1/4 cup chopped parsley
- 1/4 cup chopped scallions
- 1 tablespoon canola or safflower oil

Bring the water to a boil in a large pot set over medium heat. Add 1 cup of the wild rice, maple syrup, ginger, salt, cinnamon, and nutmeg. Bring back to a boil. Cover and reduce heat to low. Cook until the rice opens up, about 45 minutes. Drain off excess liquid from the rice.

Place rice in a large bowl. Add the apples, seeds/almonds, parsley, and scallions. Stir to mix well.

Heat the oil in a skillet set over medium high heat. Add the remaining 1/3 cup rice to the oil. Cook until the wild rice pops open, about 2–4 minutes. Stir the popped rice into the other rice mixture.

Serve warm.

Quinoa Chickpea Burgers
Yield: 8–10 burgers

- 1/2 cup dry quinoa
- 1 cup water
- 1 (15-ounce) can chickpeas, drained and rinsed
- 1/2 cup onion, chopped
- 1/2 cup dark leafy greens, chopped
- 1/2 cup carrot, chopped
- 1 garlic clove
- 1/2 cup wheat or gluten free flour of choice (gluten free options: garbanzo bean or quinoa flour)
- 1 teaspoon curry powder
- 1/2 teaspoon cumin
- 1/2 teaspoon cayenne pepper
- salt and pepper to taste
- 2–3 tablespoons canola or safflower oil
- burger toppings as desired

Cook the quinoa: Place the quinoa and water in a saucepan. Bring to a boil over medium high heat. Cover and reduce heat to low. Cook until the liquid is absorbed, about 15 minutes.

Place the chickpeas, onion, greens, carrot, and garlic in a food processor. Pulse several types to chop the mixture into small pieces.

In a large bowl, combine the quinoa, chickpea and vegetable mixture, flour, curry powder, cumin, cayenne, salt, and pepper. Form into 6–8 patties.

Heat the oil in a nonstick skillet set over medium heat. Cook the quinoa burgers until golden brown on each side. Serve with burger toppings.

Teff and Oatmeal Pancakes (Gluten Free)
Yield: 10 pancakes

- 1 cup teff flour
- 1 cup millet flour (or quinoa or chickpea flour)
- 3/4 cup rolled oats
- 1 1/2 teaspoons baking powder
- 1 teaspoon baking soda
- 1/2 teaspoon salt
- 1 1/2 cups buttermilk
- 2 large eggs
- 2 tablespoons honey, warmed for 10 seconds in the microwave
- 2 tablespoons canola or safflower oil
- 1 cup fresh or frozen blueberries (thaw if frozen)

In a bowl, stir together the teff, millet, oats, baking powder, baking soda, and salt. Set aside. In another bowl, whisk together the buttermilk, eggs, honey, and oil. Whisk in the flour mixture. Stir until just combined.

Heat a nonstick griddle to moderate temperature. Ladle batter onto the hot griddle. Dot each pancake with blueberries. Cook until sides are set and the bottom is brown, about 2–3 minutes. Flip and finish cooking on the other side. Serve hot with maple syrup.

Millet Oatmeal Bars
Yield: 16 bars (9 × 13-inch pan)

- 1 1/2 cups water
- 1/2 teaspoon salt
- 3/4 cup dry millet
- 2 cups rolled oats
- 1 cup dried fruit of choice
- 1/2 cup shredded coconut
- 2/3 cup mix of pumpkin seeds, sunflower seeds, or nuts of choice
- 1 teaspoon cinnamon

- 1 teaspoon baking powder
- 2 large eggs, beaten
- 1/2 cup nut or seed butter of choice
- 1/3 cup honey
- 1 teaspoon vanilla extract

Bring the water and salt to a boil in a medium saucepot set over medium high heat. Add the millet. Cook until tender, about 20 minutes. Drain off any excess liquid. Pour millet into a large bowl. Allow to cool.

Preheat oven to 350°F. Line a 9 × 13-inch baking pan with parchment, leaving a 1-inch overhang.

To the millet, add the oats, dried fruit, coconut, seeds/nuts, cinnamon, and baking powder. Mix well. Add the eggs and stir in to incorporate well.

Combine the peanut butter, honey, and vanilla in a small, microwave safe bowl. Microwave on high for 30–45 seconds. Pour peanut butter mixture over the millet mixture. Stir to coat evenly.

Spread mixture in the prepared baking pan, pressing in create an even layer. Bake for 15–20 minutes.

Cut and serve.

Optional Topping: Melted chocolate spread on top and sprinkled with chopped nuts. Melted chocolate and peanut butter, spread on top.

Millet Burgers
Yield: 8 burgers

- 1 1/2 cups water
- 3/4 cup dry millet
- 1/2 cup grated carrots (or zucchini)
- 2 tablespoons minced shallot or onion
- 1 clove garlic, minced
- 2 tablespoons chopped parsley
- 1 large egg, lightly beaten
- 1 1/2 teaspoons salt
- 1/2 teaspoon black pepper
- optional seasonings, to taste: garam masala, curry powder, chili powder
- 2 tablespoons oil of choice: canola, olive, grapeseed, or safflower

Place the millet and the water in a saucepot set over medium high heat. Bring to a boil. Cover and reduce heat to low. Simmer until millet is tender and water is absorbed, about 15–20 minutes. Remove from heat. Drain off any excess water if necessary.

Place the millet in a medium bowl. Add the carrots, shallot, garlic, and parsley. Stir to mix well. Add the egg, salt, pepper, and optional seasonings. Mix well to combine. Form the mixture into patties.

Heat the oil in a skillet set over medium heat. Sauté the patties on each side until golden brown. Serve hot with burger toppings.

Vegan Chocolate Tart
Yield: 1 8-inch tart

Crust

- 2/3 cup hazelnuts or almonds
- 1/2 cup unsweetened shredded coconut
- 3 tablespoons cocoa powder
- 1 teaspoon salt
- 1 cup pitted dates

Filling

- 12 ounces pitted dates
- 1 1/2 cups water
- 1 2/3 cup cashews, walnuts, or pecans, soaked for 6–8 hours
- 1 teaspoon vanilla extract
- 1 1/4 cups cocoa powder
- 1/2 cup coconut oil
- fruit chia jam, recipe follows

To make the crust

Place the nuts, coconut, cocoa powder, salt, and dates in a food processor. Blend until well combined and the mixture holds together when formed into a ball. If too dry, add more dates or 1–2 tablespoons water.

Press the mixture into an 8-inch tart pan (or onto the bottom of a springform pan). Refrigerate while making the filling.

Place the dates and 1/2 cup water in a food processor. Blend until very smooth. Add the nuts and vanilla. Blend until smooth. Add the cocoa powder and coconut oil. Pulse until incorporated. Pour mixture into the crust. Refrigerate for up to 6 hours. It can also be placed in the freezer for 1 hour to set. Top with chia jam.

Fruit Chia Jam

- 1 cup chopped berries of choice
- 1–2 tablespoons fresh lemon juice
- 1–2 tablespoons honey, agave, or maple syrup
- 1 tablespoon ground chia seeds

Place the berries in a saucepan. Cook over medium heat for 5–10 minutes or until they soften. Mash with a potato masher. Add the lemon juice and honey. Cook for 2–3 minutes. Add the chia seeds. Turn off the heat. Let sit for 10 minutes or until thickened. Refrigerate until ready to use. Keep jam refrigerated for up to 1 week.

Homemade Wheat Crackers
Yield: 4–5 dozen

- 1 1/4 cups whole wheat flour
- 1 1/2 tablespoons sugar
- 1/2 teaspoon salt
- 1/4 teaspoon paprika
- 4 tablespoons unsalted butter, cut into cubes
- 1/3 cup water

Preheat oven to 400°F. Line sheet pan with parchment paper.

Combine the flour, sugar, salt, and paprika. Using a pastry blender, cut the butter into the flour mixture until it looks like coarse crumbs. Add the water to the mixture. Mix until a smooth dough forms.

Divide the dough into 4 pieces. Working with one piece at a time, roll the dough on a lightly floured surface. Roll into a rectangle until about 1/16-inch thick. Trim the edges and cut into squares. Transfer squares to the sheet pan. Sprinkle with coarse sea salt. Repeat process with remaining dough.

Bake crackers until crisp and browned, about 5–10 minutes. Check the crackers at 5 minutes and remove the ones that are browning too quickly. Cool on a rack.

Unit 8 Questions

1. Describe the differences in flavor and texture between the different types of rice in experiment 1.
2. Describe the differences in texture and flavor between the different types of oatmeal cooked in experiment 2.
3. Why do you rinse some rice prior to cooking?
4. Why does risotto need to be stirred constantly while cooking?
5. Why is it important to consume whole grains as opposed to refined grains?

NOTES

1. "Cereal Grains," Dictionary of American History, accessed May 14, 2019, https://www.encyclopedia.com/history/dictionaries-thesauruses-pictures-and-press-releases/cereal-grains.
2. "What's a whole grain? A refined grain?" Whole Grains Council, accessed May 14, 2019, https://wholegrainscouncil.org/whole-grains-101/whats-whole-grain-refined-grain.
3. Vickie A. Vaclavik and Elizabeth W. Christian, *Essentials of Food Science*, 4th ed. (New York: Springer, 2014), 66.

4. Vaclavik and Christian, *Essentials of Food Science*, 67–68.
5. Vaclavik and Christian, 70.
6. "Whole Grains A–Z," Whole Grains Council, accessed May 14, 2019, https://wholegrainscouncil.org/whole-grains-101/whole-grains-z.
7. Vaclavik and Christian, 71–72.
8. "Are you nuts?" Spices, Inc., accessed May 14, 2019, https://www.spicesinc.com/p-5922-are-you-nuts.aspx.

BIBLIOGRAPHY

Dictionary of American History. "Cereal Grains." Accessed May 14, 2019. https://www.encyclopedia.com/history/dictionaries-thesauruses-pictures-and-press-releases/cereal-grains.

Spices, Inc. "Are you nuts?" Accessed May 14, 2019. https://www.spicesinc.com/p-5922-are-you-nuts.aspx.

Vaclavik, Vickie A., and Elizabeth W. Christian. *Essentials of Food Science*, 4th ed. New York: Springer, 2014.

Whole Grains Council. "What's a whole grain? A refined grain?" Accessed May 14, 2019. https://wholegrainscouncil.org/whole-grains-101/whats-whole-grain-refined-grain.

Whole Grains Council. "Whole Grains A–Z." Accessed May 14, 2019. https://wholegrainscouncil.org/whole-grains-101/whole-grains-z.

IMAGE CREDITS

Pasta and Starch

OBJECTIVES

- Discuss different pastas from around the world
- Explain different types of starches used as thickening agents
- Explain uses of roux
- Evaluate effect of thickening agents in pudding
- Use basic cooking techniques to prepare recipes

NOODLES AND PASTA[1]

The terms *noodles* and *pasta* refer to the same thing. However, noodles are typically associated with Asian cuisine and pasta is from the Italian for paste and therefore pasta is often used in Italian cuisine.

While the origin of pasta and noodles is not known, it is believed that China was the first to develop noodles. Italian merchant and adventurer, Marco Polo, traveled to Asia on his many travels and is thought to have brought noodles back to Italy. Since that time, Italians have developed many types of pasta, all differing in shapes and sizes.

TABLE 9.1

Common Italian Pasta	Common Asian Noodles	Other Pasta
Angel hair or capellini	Cellophane or glass noodles	Spätzle (Germany)
Cavatappi	Chow mein	Couscous (Middle East)
Chiocciole (resemble snails)	Lo mein	Israeli couscous (Israel)
Farfalle (bowties)	Ramen	
Fettuccine	Rice noodles (come in many sizes)	
Fusilli, Rotini	Soba	
Linguine	Udon	
Orecchiette		
Orzo		
Pappardelle		
Penne		
Rigatoni		
Shells		
Spaghetti		
Tagliatelle		
Ziti		

STARCH

In cooking, starches are used for thickening sauces, soups, and stews. Because of their properties for absorbing liquid, starches can also be used as a replacement for eggs in baking, providing binding, and act as stabilizing agents in a variety of recipes.

Common Starches[2]

Grain Starches: Starches from grains are better for longer cooking times. Contain 26–28% amylose.

- Cornstarch—from the endosperm of corn kernels
- Flour—white flour is from the endosperm of wheat kernel

Root/Tuber Starches: Comprised of 99% amylopectin and 17–23% amylose, root and tuber starches are best for shorter cooking times.

- Arrowroot—from the rhizomes of tropical plants
- Potato—from potatoes; most refined starch
- Tapioca—from the cassava or yucca root

Thickening Agents

To utilize starches as thickening agents, fat or water is mixed with the starch prior to adding to the recipe. Most starches will not come to their full thickening power until they come to a boil. As they cool, the thickening will continue as the starches begin to relax and absorb more liquid. All starches have a saturation point: the point at which it cannot take in more liquid. At this point, the thickening stops, and some starches may begin to weep or expel liquid.

Slurry—starch plus water

- Most common starch used in a slurry is cornstarch, although any starch can be used in slurries.

Roux—Equal parts of flour plus fat (butter or oil). Roux is cooked.

- A roux can be white, blond, dark/brown.
- Sauces that use roux as a base include Bechamel, a sauce made with white roux plus milk, and velouté, a sauce made with stock plus blond roux.

Beurre manie—equal parts flour plus room temperature butter kneaded together.

- A beurre manie is added at the end of cooking and is used in some soups and stews. In addition to thickening, this also adds a sheen to the finished dish.

EXPERIMENTS

Experiment 1: Different Thickening Agents

Evaluate the differences between different starches in a basic pudding recipe.

Basic Recipe (Control)

- 1 1/2 tablespoons cornstarch*
- 3 tablespoons sugar
- 1 cup whole milk
- pinch of salt
- 1/2 teaspoon vanilla extract

1 1/2 tablespoons = 1 tablespoon + 1 1/2 teaspoons

Mix together the cornstarch and sugar in a saucepan. Add the milk and salt. Whisk until combined. Cook over medium-low heat, stirring constantly. Cook until the mixture comes to a boil and boil for 1 minute. Remove from the heat and stir in the vanilla. Pour pudding into a bowl and cover with plastic wrap (place directly on the surface of the pudding to prevent a skin from forming). Refrigerate until cold, about 1 hour.

Variations:

In place of the cornstarch, use:

- quick cooking tapioca
- tapioca starch
- potato starch
- arrowroot

Pudding	Appearance	Flavor	Texture
Cornstarch (control)			
Quick cooking tapioca			
Tapioca starch			
Potato starch			
Arrowroot			

Experiment 2: Roux Variations

Explain the differences in different types of roux.

Ingredients:

- 2 tablespoons unsalted butter
- 2 tablespoons flour
- 1 cup white chicken stock
- salt and pepper, to taste

White Roux

In a saucepan, melt the butter over medium heat. Add the flour. Stir to make a paste. Cook for 1 minute. Pour in the chicken stock while whisking constantly. Cook for, stirring occasionally, over medium low heat for 10–15 minutes or until the sauce coats the back of a spoon. Season to taste with salt and pepper.

Blond Roux

In a saucepan, melt the butter over medium heat. Add the flour. Stir to make a paste. Cook for 3 minutes. Pour in the chicken stock while whisking constantly. Cook for, stirring occasionally, over medium low heat for 10–15 minutes or until the sauce coats the back of a spoon. Season to taste with salt and pepper.

Brown Roux

In a saucepan, melt the butter over medium heat. Add the flour. Stir to make a paste. Cook for 9–10 minutes or until the roux turns amber or brown in color. Pour in the chicken stock while whisking constantly. Cook for, stirring occasionally, over medium low heat for 10–15 minutes or until the sauce coats the back of a spoon. Season to taste with salt and pepper.

Beurre Manie

In a small bowl, knead together the butter and flour to form a paste. Set aside. In a saucepan, bring the stock to a boil over medium high heat. Add the beurre manie and whisk until smooth. Allow the sauce to thicken and boil for about 5 minutes, whisking occasionally. Season to taste with salt and pepper.

Roux	Appearance	Flavor	Sauce thickness	Mouthfeel
White roux				
Blond roux				
Brown roux				
Beurre manie				

RECIPES

Stovetop Macaroni and Cheese

Serves 6

- 1 pound elbow macaroni
- 4 tablespoons unsalted butter
- 1/4 cup all-purpose flour
- 2 cups whole milk
- salt and pepper, to taste
- 8 ounces shredded cheese of choice
  - cheddar
  - fontina (6 ounces) + parmesan (2 ounces)
  - pepper jack
  - white cheddar (5 ounces) + gruyere (3 ounces)
  - goat cheese (3 ounces) + white cheddar (6 ounces)
- paprika or cayenne, to taste

Cook macaroni according to package directions. When done, toss with 1–2 tablespoon oil to keep from sticking.

In a large saucepan, melt the butter over medium heat. Stir in the flour. Cook for 1–2 minutes. Whisk in the milk until smooth. Cook for 5–10 minutes or until thickened. Season with salt and pepper. Stir in the cheese. Season with cayenne or paprika. Adjust seasonings to taste. Stir in the cooked pasta. Serve.

Cream of Chicken Soup
Serves 6

- 8 tablespoons (4 ounces) unsalted butter
- 1 medium yellow or white onion, diced small
- 2 stalks celery, diced small
- 3 medium carrots, diced small
- 1/2 cup AP flour
- 7 cups low sodium chicken stock
- 1 tablespoon fresh thyme
- 1 bay leaf
- 2 3/4 cups cooked, diced chicken
- 1/2 cup heavy cream
- salt and pepper, to taste
- 2 tablespoons chopped flat-leaf parsley

Melt the butter in a large soup pot over medium heat. Add the onion, celery, and carrots and cook, covered, stirring occasionally, until soft, about 10–12 minutes. Season lightly with salt and pepper. Add the flour and cook, stirring with a wooden spoon, for 2 minutes more.

Pour in the stock and bring to a boil while whisking constantly. Add the thyme and bay leaf. Reduce heat to low; simmer for 15 minutes.

Stir in the chicken and bring to a boil. Remove from the heat.

Whisk the heavy cream and wine into the soup. Season to taste with salt and pepper. Remove the bay leaf. Stir in the parsley.

Roast Chicken with Pan Gravy
Serves 6

- 4 ounces (or 8 tablespoons or 1 stick) unsalted butter, at room temperature
- 1 clove garlic, minced
- 1 tablespoon finely chopped rosemary
- 1 tablespoon fresh lemon zest
- 2 teaspoons salt
- 2 teaspoons pepper
- 1 (3–4 pound) whole chicken
- 1–2 tablespoons olive oil
- 1 medium onion, cut into quarters
- 3 tablespoons AP flour
- 1–2 cups unsalted or low-sodium chicken stock

In a small bowl, stir together 7 tablespoons butter, garlic, rosemary, lemon zest, 1 teaspoon salt, and 1 teaspoon pepper. Set aside.

Preheat oven to 400°F. Pat chicken dry with paper towels. Place chicken on a cast iron or roasting pan. Stuff the butter under the skin of the breast and thigh/leg of the chicken. Rub the outside of the chicken with olive oil and season with the remaining salt and pepper. Place onion quarters around the chicken.

Roast the chicken for 15 minutes. Reduce heat to 350°F. Roast until the internal temperature of the chicken in the thigh is 170°F (165°F for the breast), about 1 hour and 15 minutes to 1 hour and 30 minutes.

Remove chicken from the pan and allow to rest on a cutting board or platter.

Make the pan gravy by draining the liquid from the pan into a measuring cup. Add enough stock to make 2 cups. Discard the onion. The fat and liquid should separate. Pour 1–2 tablespoons of the fat back into the pan. Place pan over medium heat. Add the remaining 1 tablespoon butter. Stir until melted. Add the flour and cook for 3–4 minutes or until light brown in color. Whisk in the stock. Bring to a boil and reduce heat to low. Simmer for 10–15 minutes or until thickened to sauce consistency. Adjust seasonings to taste. Serve with the chicken.

Fresh Pasta
Yield: 1 pound

- 6 ounces AP flour
- 2 ounces semolina flour
- 1 teaspoon salt
- 2 large eggs
- 1 large egg yolk
- 2 tablespoons olive oil
- 1 tablespoon water

Mix together the AP flour, semolina, and salt. Place on the counter and make a well in the center. Add the eggs, oil, and water to the center of the flour. With a fork, whisk the wet ingredients and add little bit of the flour. Mix in a small amount of flour at a time, being careful not to break the wall of flour. Once a dough forms (not too sticky or too dry; adjust flour and moisture as needed), knead by hand for 10 minutes. Wrap in plastic wrap and allow to rest for 45–60 minutes.

When you're ready to roll it out, cut the dough into quarters and roll out and cut into shapes with a pasta roller. Toss the pasta in semolina to prevent from sticking. Pasta can be also rolled into sheets to make lasagna or ravioli. If using for lasagna or ravioli, do not cook beforehand.

To cook the pasta, bring a pot of water to a boil. Season with salt. Boil pasta for 2–3 minutes. Drain and toss with olive oil until ready to serve.

Spinach Pasta
Yield: about 1 pound

- 6 ounces fresh spinach
- 2 large eggs
- 1 large egg yolk
- 2 tablespoons olive oil
- 2 2/3 cups flour
- 1 teaspoon salt

Steam the spinach over simmering water until soft and wilted. Let cool slightly. Squeeze out liquid using a clean kitchen towel or paper towels. Puree spinach in a food processor.

Add eggs, yolk, and oil to the puree in food processor, and process until combined. Add flour and 1 heaping teaspoon salt, and process until dough just comes together, about 20 seconds. If the dough is dry, add 1–2 tablespoons water.

Transfer dough to a floured surface. Knead until smooth and elastic, 5–10 minutes, adding up to 2 tablespoons flour if dough is too sticky. Place on a piece of parchment, and cover with an inverted bowl, or wrap tightly in plastic; let rest for 1 hour

Cut dough into 8 pieces. Working with 1 piece at a time (keep the remaining pieces covered with the inverted bowl), flatten dough into an oblong shape slightly thinner than the pasta machine's widest setting (number 1). Dust dough very lightly with flour, and feed through machine. Fold lengthwise into thirds and rotate 90 degrees. Repeat twice on same setting to smooth dough and increase its elasticity.

Turn the dial to next narrower setting. Pass dough through twice, gently supporting it with your palm. Continue to press dough, passing it through ever-finer settings, two passes on each setting, until sheet is almost translucent and very thin but still intact (number 5 of 8 on a KitchenAid pasta roller). The dough will stretch to about 16 inches long. If dough bubbles or tears, pass it through again, and dust with flour if the dough is sticking.

Ravioli Filling: Cheese Ravioli
Yield: 2 cups

- 15 ounces whole milk ricotta cheese
- 4 ounces grated parmesan cheese
- 2 large eggs
- 3 tablespoons chopped fresh parsley
- salt and pepper, to taste

Mix ingredients together and use to make ravioli.

Ravioli Filling: Squash
Yield: 2–3 cups

- 1/2 of a whole butternut or acorn squash, cut in half and seeded
- olive oil
- salt and pepper, to taste
- whole bulb of garlic
- 1/4 cup parmesan cheese
- 1 pound fresh pasta dough, rolled into sheets
- egg wash (1 egg mixed with 1 tablespoon water)

Preheat oven to 375°F. Lightly oil the squash and season with salt and pepper. Place on a sheet pan. Bake for 20–25 minutes or until tender. Cut the garlic bulb in half to expose the garlic cloves. Place garlic in the center for a piece of foil. Drizzle both halves with olive oil. Wrap the garlic up in the foil and bake in the hot oven for 25 minutes.

Peel off the skin of the squash and place the flesh into a food processor. Squeeze the roasted garlic from its skin and place in the food processor with the squash. Season with salt and pepper. Add the parmesan cheese. Puree until smooth.

Ravioli

Roll out a quarter of the dough and cut in half, so that you have two pieces of dough roughly 15 inches long and five inches across. Cover one sheet of pasta with a towel or plastic wrap to keep it from drying out.

Fold the first sheet along its midline to make a light crease and then re-open it. Working so that your filling is approximately 1 1/2 inches in diameter and 1/2 inch apart, place 6 even heaping tablespoons along the lower half of the dough.

Moisten the dough lightly with water. And then fold it over along the crease, pressing from the folded point outward to remove excess air.

Gently pat the dough down around each lump of filling to create a seal.

Use the fluted side of the ravioli cutter or a stamp to slice your ravioli into even squares. Place on a sheet pan dusted with semolina.

To cook ravioli, bring a pot of water to a boil. Season with salt. Boil the ravioli for 2–3 minutes. Immediately place in sauce.

Pesto Sauce
Yield: about 1 cup

- 2 cups basil leaves
- 2 tablespoons pine nuts (or walnuts or almonds)
- 3 tablespoons lemon juice
- 1 clove garlic
- 1/4 cup parmesan cheese
- 1/4 cup extra virgin olive oil
- salt and pepper, to taste

Using a food processor, blend the basil, pine nuts, lemon juice, garlic, and parmesan cheese. While the moto is running, drizzle in the olive oil. Blend to desired consistency. Season to taste with salt and pepper. Toss in hot cooked pasta.

Alfredo Sauce
Yield: about 1 1/2 cups

- 1 tablespoon olive oil
- 1 tablespoon unsalted butter
- 1 clove garlic, minced
- 2 tablespoons flour
- 2 cups whole milk
- 1/2 cup grated parmesan cheese
- salt and pepper to taste

Heat the oil and butter in a sauté pan set over medium heat. Add the garlic and sauté for 1 minute. Add the flour to make a roux. Cook for 1 minute. Whisk in the milk, making sure to whisk out flour clumps. Reduce heat to medium low. Whisk in the cheese. Cook for 2–3 minutes. Season to taste with salt and pepper. Toss in hot pasta. Serve immediately.

Tomato Sauce
Yield: about 2–3 cups

- 1 tablespoon olive oil
- 1/2 cup diced onion
- 2 cloves garlic, minced
- pinch red pepper flakes
- 2 tablespoons tomato paste
- 1 (28-ounce) can whole peeled tomatoes, San Marzano preferred
- 1 tablespoon dried oregano and/or dried basil
- salt and pepper, to taste

In a saucepot, heat the oil over medium heat. Add the onions and sauté until softened, about 5–6 minutes. Add the garlic, red pepper flakes, and tomato paste. Sauté for 1–2 minutes.

Season lightly with salt and pepper. Pour the canned tomatoes into a bowl and crush with your hands. Pour tomatoes into the pan. Season with salt and pepper and add the dried herbs. Reduce heat to low. Simmer for 15 minutes. Serve warm with pasta.

Pancetta Sage Sauce
Yield: 1 cup

- 1 tablespoon olive oil
- 4 ounces pancetta
- 3 ounces unsalted butter
- 3 tablespoons chopped fresh sage
- 2 garlic cloves, minced
- 1/4 cup chicken stock
- 1/4 cup cream
- salt and pepper to taste

Heat the olive oil in a sauté pan set over medium heat. Add the pancetta and cook until crispy. Remove from pan. Add the butter and melt. Add the sage and garlic. Cook for 1–2 minutes. Pour in the stock and cream. Bring to a boil. Reduce slightly. Season to taste with salt and pepper. Add the pancetta just before serving.

Classic Lasagna Bolognese
Serves 6–8

- 4 tablespoons unsalted butter
- 4 tablespoons all-purpose flour
- 3 cups whole milk
- salt and pepper, to taste
- pinch freshly grated nutmeg
- 2 pounds fresh homemade pasta, cut into pasta sheets that fit the length of the pan
- 1 1/2 quarts warm ragù Bolognese (choose from recipes follow)
- 3 ounces Parmigiano-Reggiano cheese

In a small saucepan, melt butter over medium-high heat (do not allow it to brown). Add flour and whisk to form a roux. Continue to cook, stirring for about 1 minute. Whisking constantly, gradually pour in the milk. Cook for 5–10 minutes, stirring occasionally to prevent burning. The sauce should thicken and coat the back of a spoon. Season with salt and pepper and add the nutmeg. Set aside.

To assemble and bake lasagna, preheat oven to 375°F. Grease a 9 × 13-inch baking dish with butter. Spoon a thin, even layer of ragù on bottom of baking dish, then lay down a layer of lasagna noodles; it's fine if they overlap somewhat, but you can cut any sheets that are too large to avoid excessive doubling up.

Top pasta with another thin layer of ragù (thin enough that you can see the pasta through it in some spots). Drizzle a small amount of béchamel all over ragù, then top with a showering of grated Parmigiano-Reggiano. Repeat this layering process with pasta, ragù, béchamel, and grated cheese until baking dish is full; this should be about 6 layers. Finish with a top layer of pasta, then coat that with an even layer of the remaining béchamel sauce. Grate a final generous amount of cheese on top.

Cover with foil and bake lasagna until bubbling, about 40 minutes. Remove foil and bake for another 10 minutes. Remove from oven and allow to rest for 10 minutes before serving.

Traditional Bolognese Sauce
Yield: 1 1/2 quarts

- 1 tablespoon olive oil
- 6 ounces ground beef
- 6 ounces ground veal or ground pork
- 3 ounces thinly sliced pancetta or bacon, chopped
- 1 large white or yellow onion, diced small
- 2 celery stalks, diced small
- 2 medium carrots, diced small
- 2 cloves garlic, minced
- 3 tablespoons tomato paste
- 1/2 cup dry red wine
- 3 cups low-sodium beef stock or chicken stock
- salt and pepper, to taste

Heat oil in a large heavy pot over medium-high heat. Add beef, veal, and pancetta. Cook until brown, about 10 minutes. Add the onions, celery, and carrots. Sauté until soft, about 5–8 minutes. Season lightly with salt and pepper. Stir in the tomato paste. Cook for 1 minute. Pour in the wine and bring to a boil for 1 minute. Add 2 1/2 cups stock. Reduce heat to low and simmer for 1 1/2 hours. Season to taste with salt and pepper. Add additional 1/2 cup stock to loosen the sauce if desired.

Chicken and Mushroom Bolognese
Serves 4–6

- 1 tablespoon olive oil
- 1 pound boneless, skinless chicken thighs, cut into 1-inch pieces
- 1/2 white or yellow onion, roughly chopped
- 2 garlic cloves, chopped
- 10 ounces crimini mushrooms, cleaned and quartered
- 2 tablespoons tomato paste
- 1/2 cup red wine
- 1 28-ounce can whole peel tomatoes, crushed by hand
- 1 bay leaf
- kosher salt and freshly ground black pepper, to taste
- 12 ounces pasta, any shape you desire

Put the chicken thighs into the bowl of a food processor, pulse several times until the chicken is finely ground. Heat the olive oil in a large pot over medium heat. Add the ground chicken to the oil and begin to brown. Chop the onions and garlic in the food processor until chopped fine, about 15–20 pulses. Add the onions and garlic to the meat. Sauté for 3–5 minutes. Season lightly with salt and pepper. Finely chop the mushrooms in the food processor. Add the mushrooms to the meat mixture. Sauté for another 3–5 minutes. Add the tomato paste; cook for 1–2 minutes. Add the red wine, tomatoes, and bay leaf. Season lightly with salt and pepper. Reduce heat to medium low and cook for about 3 hours.

Taste the sauce and season to taste with salt and pepper.

Potato Gnocchi with Sage Butter Sauce
Serves 4–6

Gnocchi

- 1 1/2 pounds russet potatoes, washed
- 1 cup flour
- 1 large egg
- pinch of salt
- 1 teaspoon olive oil

Place the potatoes in a saucepan and cover by 1–2 inches with water. Cover and bring to a boil. Reduce heat to simmer and cook until tender, about 45 minutes. Remove from the water and peel the skins off the potatoes. Run the potato flesh through a food mill or potato ricer. Place in a bowl.

Bring 4–6 quarts of water to a boil.

Mix the flour in the potatoes. Make a well in the center of the potatoes. Break an egg in the center of the potatoes and add the salt. Using a fork, whisk the egg into to potato mixture. Once the egg is mixed into the potato mixture, knead it gently to form a dough. Knead for 3–4 minutes or until the dough is dry to the touch but still soft.

Divide the dough into 3 balls. Roll each piece into a 3/4-inch diameter rope. Cut the ropes into 1-inch pieces. Flick the pieces off a fork to score the sides. Cook the gnocchi in batches in the boiling water. Cook until they float, about 2–3 minutes. Remove with a slotted spoon and toss with olive oil or directly into the sage sauce. Repeat process until the gnocchi are all cooked.

Sage Butter Sauce

- 4–5 tablespoons unsalted butter
- 8 whole sage leaves
- salt and pepper, to taste
- parmesan cheese for garnish

Melt the butter in a large sauté pan set over medium heat. Cook until the butter starts to brown and turn a light brown color. Add the sage and season with salt and pepper. Add the cooked gnocchi and garnish with the cheese. Serve.

Ricotta Cheese Gnocchi
Serves 4

- 1–2 tablespoons salt
- One 15-ounce container whole milk ricotta cheese
- 2 large eggs, lightly beaten
- 1 1/4 cups grated parmesan, plus more for serving
- black pepper, to taste
- 3/4–1 cup flour
- 3 tablespoons unsalted butter
- 10 or more sage leaves

Bring a large pot of water to a boil and add 1 tablespoon salt. Combine the ricotta, eggs and parmesan in a large bowl, along with some salt and pepper. Add about 1/2 cup flour and stir; add more flour until the mixture forms a very sticky dough. Scoop up a spoonful of dough and boil it to make sure it will hold its shape; if it does not, stir in a bit more flour.

Melt the butter in a large sauté pan set over medium heat. Brown the butter until it turns amber in color. Add the sage; fry in the butter for 1–2 minutes. Reduce heat and keep warm. Boil the gnocchi in the hot water until they float, about 3–4 minutes. Remove with a slotted spoon and transfer to the sage butter mixture. Adjust seasonings to taste. Serve with parmesan cheese.

Carbonara
Serves 6

- 1–2 tablespoons salt
- 1 pound spaghetti
- 3 large eggs
- 2 large yolks
- 1 cup grated parmesan cheese, plus more for serving
- 1 teaspoon black pepper
- 1 tablespoon olive oil
- 6 ounces pancetta or bacon, diced
- 2 cloves garlic, minced

In a mixing bowl, whisk together the eggs, yolks and pecorino and parmesan. Season with a pinch of salt and black pepper. Set aside.

Place a large pot of lightly salted water (no more than 1 tablespoon salt) over high heat and bring to a boil.

Heat oil in a large skillet over medium heat, add the pancetta. Sauté until the fat just renders and gets crispy. Add the garlic. Cook for 30 seconds. Remove from heat and set aside.

Add pasta to the water cook to al dente. Reserve 1 cup of pasta water, then drain pasta and add to the skillet set over low heat. Toss to combine the pasta with the bacon. Turn off the heat and stir in the egg mixture. Add the reserved pasta water to make the sauce creamy. Serve immediately, dressing it with a bit of additional parmesan and pepper.

Spaetzle
Serves 4

- 2 large eggs
- 1/2 cup milk
- 1 1/2 cups flour
- 1 teaspoon salt
- 2–3 tablespoons extra virgin olive oil or melted butter
- 1/4 cup mixed chopped herbs: parsley, chives, oregano, sage, and/or chives

Bring a large pot of water to a boil over high heat. Add a hefty pinch of salt to the water.

In a small bowl, whisk together the eggs and milk. In a large bowl, whisk together the flour and salt. Gradually mix the flour into the egg mixture. Mix until combined.

Place a colander with big holes or a spaetzle maker over the pot of boiling water. Pour the batter into the colander or spaetzle maker and push batter through into the boiling water. Boil the spaetzle for 2–3 minutes. Drain and place in a medium bowl. Toss with olive oil (or melted butter) and the fresh herbs. Serve immediately.

Stir-Fried Udon
Serves 4

- 2 8-ounce packages udon noodles[i]
- 2–3 teaspoons sesame oil
- 1/2 cup mirin
- 1/2 cup soy sauce
- 1–2 teaspoons sambal
- 2 tablespoons canola or safflower oil
- 8 ounces ground pork or ground turkey
- 1 tablespoon fresh ginger, minced
- 1 clove garlic, minced
- 1 savoy cabbage, shredded
- 1 bunch scallions, sliced

---

i For a gluten free version, use rice noodles in place of the udon and tamari as a substitute for the soy sauce.

Cook the udon according to package directions. When done, toss with the sesame oil and set aside.

In a small bowl, stir together the mirin, soy sauce, and sambal. Set aside.

Heat the oil in a large sauté pan or wok. Add the pork. Cook until golden brown on all sides and no pink remains, about 10 minutes. Push the pork to the side of the pan. Add a little more oil as needed. Add the ginger and garlic; sauté for 1–2 minutes. Add the cabbage. Toss to combine well. Sauté until the cabbage starts to wilt, about 5 minutes. Pour in half of the mirin mixture. Stir to coat. Add the udon noodles. Pour in the remaining mirin mixture. Toss to coat well. Toss in the scallions. Serve.

Ramen Bowls
Serves 4

Ramen Base

- 1 teaspoon sesame oil
- 1 teaspoon canola or safflower oil
- 2 cloves garlic, minced
- 1 tablespoon fresh ginger, minced
- 1/2 cup shredded carrots
- 1/2 cup shiitake mushrooms, sliced
- 1 quart unsalted (or low sodium) chicken or vegetable stock
- 1 tablespoon rice vinegar
- 3 tablespoons soy sauce
- 1 tablespoon sriracha or sambal
- 2 (3-ounce) packages ramen noodles (discard flavor packets)

Toppings, as Desired

- Sliced scallions
- Dark leafy greens of choice (kale, chard, savoy cabbage, cabbage, or bok choy), chopped
- Sliced radish
- Sesame seeds
- Soft boiled eggs or over-easy fried eggs

Heat the sesame and canola oil in a medium sized pot set over medium heat. Add the garlic and ginger. Cook for 1–2 minutes. Add the carrots and mushrooms. Cook until soft, about 5 minutes. Add the stock, vinegar, soy sauce, and sriracha. Stir to combine. Add the ramen and cook until soft, about 3–4 minutes.

Ladle in to soup bowls. Top with desired toppings.

Soba Noodle Bowls
Serves 4

Noodle Base

- 1 cup low-sodium or unsalted chicken or vegetable stock
- 1/4 cup soy sauce
- 1 1/2 tablespoons fresh ginger, minced
- 3 tablespoons honey
- 2 tablespoons canola or safflower oil
- 1 (8-ounce) package tempeh, sliced
- 1 pound soba noodles

Toppings, as Desired

- dark leafy greens (kale, chard, spinach), chopped
- bok choy or savoy cabbage, thinly sliced
- radishes, sliced
- carrots, shredded
- sliced jalapenos
- sliced avocado
- scallions, sliced
- toasted almonds
- sesame seeds

In a small saucepan, combine the stock, soy sauce, and ginger. Bring to a simmer over medium heat. Cook for 2–3 minutes. Remove from heat and stir in the honey.

Heat 1 tablespoon oil in a sauté pan set over medium heat. Add the tempeh and sauté on both sides until brown. Add 1/2 cup of the soy sauce mixture. Remove from heat. Set aside.

Cook the soba according to package directions. When done, drain well. Heat remaining tablespoon oil in a sauté pan. Add the noodles and 1/2 cup of the soy sauce mixture. Cook for 2–3 minutes. Remove from heat.

To serve, add a serving of noodles to a bowl. Add a serving of the tempeh and toppings as desired. Serve remaining soy sauce mixture on the side.

Unit 9 Questions

1. In experiment 1, describe the differences between the puddings. Which pudding had the best flavor? Which had the best texture? Which starch thickened the best?
2. In experiment 2, describe the differences between the sauces. Which sauce had the best mouthfeel? Which sauce had the nuttiest flavor? Which sauce did you prefer?
3. Why are you warned on the package of Jell-O not to add pineapple?

4. Why does pasta dough need to rest for 45–60 minutes before rolling out?
5. Why do you salt the boiling water before cooking pasta?
6. Why are russet potatoes used in making gnocchi (as opposed to using red potatoes)?

NOTES

1. Alfonzo Lopez, "The Twisted History of Pasta," National Geographic, accessed May 14, 2019, https://www.nationalgeographic.com/archaeology-and-history/magazine/2016/07-08/daily-life-pasta-italy-neapolitan-diet/.
2. Vickie A. Vaclavik and Elizabeth W. Christian, *Essentials of Food Science,* 4th ed. (New York: Springer, 2014), 41.

BIBLIOGRAPHY

Lopez, Alfonzo. "The Twisted History of Pasta." National Geographic. Accessed May 14, 2019. https://www.nationalgeographic.com/archaeology-and-history/magazine/2016/07-08/daily-life-pasta-italy-neapolitan-diet/.

Vaclavik, Vickie A., and Elizabeth W. Christian. *Essentials of Food Science*, 4th ed. New York: Springer, 2014.

Quick Breads and Gluten-Free Baking

OBJECTIVES

■ Describe the differences between chemical leavening agents
■ Explain the impact of steam and air in baking
■ Demonstrate proper mixing techniques
■ Describe the Maillard reaction
■ Evaluate effect of chemical leavening agents in baking
■ Explain effect of gluten in baking
■ Define gluten-free baking
■ Use basic cooking techniques to prepare recipes

QUICK BREADS[1]

Quick breads get their name because they are quickly made compared to yeast breads. To facilitate the rising, quick breads are made using chemical leavening agents like baking soda and baking powder, which produce carbon dioxide that help baked goods rise.

The technical term for baking soda is sodium bicarbonate, an alkaline substance. When combined with an acidic substance (lemon juice, buttermilk, yogurt, or chocolate), it creates carbon dioxide, causing rising to occur.

Baking powder consists of baking soda, along with an acidic component such as cream of tartar. Baking powder is either single acting or double acting. Single acting baking powder only has one reaction which occurs when moisture is added to the batter. Batters using single-acting baking powder need to be baked right after mixing. Conversely, double-acting baking powder has two reactions. The first reaction occurs when moisture is added to the batter and the second reaction happens when heat is applied. Most baking powder sold in the United States is double acting.

Quick breads also utilize air and steam to facilitate the rising action. In biscuits, cold butter is cut into the dry ingredients dispersing it throughout the dough. During baking, the butter melts creating flaky layers because of the steam produced by the cold butter. In the case of popovers, the batter rises due to steam created as it heats up.

High-Altitude Baking[2]

Baking at high altitudes poses a few challenges due to the decrease in air pressure the further in elevation you go. As altitude increases, the air pressure decreases. As a result, some recipes for quick breads need to be adjusted based on the elevation you are at.

Use these basic guidelines for high-altitude baking.

- Increase oven temperature by 15–25ºF. Use the lower number for cakes.
- Decrease baking time by 5–10 minutes per 30 minutes of baking.
- Decrease sugar by 1 tablespoon per cup.
- Increase liquid by 1–2 tablespoons at 3000 feet. Increase it an additional 1 1/2 teaspoons per 1000 above 3000 feet.
- Increase flour 1 tablespoon per recipe at 3000–4000 feet. Per 1500 feet above 4000 feet, increase flour an additional 1 tablespoon.

TABLE 10.1 Chemical Leavening Agents (baking soda and baking powder)

Amount of baking powder and baking soda	3000–5000 feet	5000–6500 feet	6500–8000 feet
1 teaspoon to 2 1/2 teaspoons	Decrease by 10%	Decrease by 50%	Decrease by 75%
1 tablespoon	Use 2 teaspoons	Use 1 1/4 teaspoons	Use 1 teaspoon
4 teaspoons	Use 2 1/2 teaspoons	Use 1 1/2 teaspoons	Use 1 teaspoon

Muffin Method

To produce optimal results in baking, muffins are made with a particular method.

First, the dry ingredients are sifted or whisked together. In a separate bowl, the wet ingredients are mixed together. Create a well in the dry ingredients and pour the wet ingredients in the center. Gradually stir the dry ingredients into the wet ingredients. Mix just until the batter is semi-smooth. It's important not to overmix the batter and there should be some small clumps of batter present.

Overmixing the batter results in tunneling of the muffins where an air pocket has formed in the muffin and the muffins have a pointed top.

Maillard Reaction

The maillard reaction is a French term referring to the browning of the breads, quick breads, cakes, and cookies. The browning is a reaction between amino acids and sugar in the presence of heat.

GLUTEN-FREE BAKING

Gluten serves an important role in baking by providing structure for quick breads, cakes, and yeast breads. Found in wheat flour, gluten is comprised of many proteins that create a complex network of interlinking chains to provide the structure needed in baking.

However, due to various dietary restrictions including wheat allergies or celiac disease, some people need to avoid consuming gluten products. The challenge posed for gluten-free baking is mimicking the structure gluten provides in baked goods. Some ways to provide structure to gluten-free baked goods is to utilize binders and gums.

Xanthan Gum and Guar Gum

Both xanthan and guar gum can be used interchangeably using a ratio of 1/2 teaspoon gum per 1 cup gluten-free flour.

Eggs

As mentioned previously in unit 6, eggs serve as binders in baked goods, while also providing moisture.

Ground Chia and Ground Flax Seeds

Both ground chia and flax seeds work as binders. To use as a binder, soak 1 tablespoon ground seeds in 3 tablespoons water for about 5 minutes.

Psyllium Husk

Psyllium works as a binder by creating a gel.

Lentils

Cooked or soaked red split lentils can act as a binder and also provide structure to gluten-free baked goods. Cook the lentils until soft and puree until smooth before using. Alternately, soak the lentils in water for 6 hours, drain, and grind into a paste.

Tips for Successful Gluten-Free Baking[3]

- Use a variety of GF flours and starches for best results.
- Mix batters longer than you would for regular quick breads.
- Allow batters to rest for 30 minutes to allow starches to absorb the moisture. This helps reduce grittiness and improves the quality of the end product.
- May need to bake longer, by about 10 minutes to reduce gumminess.

Troubleshooting[4]

Here are ways to troubleshoot issues that may arise from GF baking.

Common Problem	Solution
Greasy mouthfeel	Reduce fat and substitute with sour cream, plain yogurt, or cream cheese
Dense crumb	Reduce fat and increase liquid, baking powder, and/or egg
Gummy	Decrease oven temperature Increase baking time
Excessive spreading in cookies	Add binder Allow dough to rest for 30 minutes before baking
Gritty texture	Rest batter/dough for 30 minutes before baking
Too crispy	Increase brown sugar Decrease white sugar
Crumbly texture	Add extra egg and binder
Dry texture	Add additional moisture (sour cream, plain yogurt)

EXPERIMENTS

Experiment 1: Effect of Chemical Leavening Agent on Muffins
Evaluate differences between chemical leavening agents.

Basic Recipe (Control)

Yield: 6 muffins

- 1 cup flour
- 1/3 cup sugar
- 1 1/2 teaspoons baking powder
- 1/4 teaspoon salt
- 1 large egg
- 1/2 cup milk
- 2 tablespoons canola oil

Preheat oven to 400°F. Lightly grease muffin tins or line with muffin papers. Set aside.

In a mixing bowl, sift together the flour, sugar, baking powder, and salt. In another bowl, whisk together the egg, milk, and oil. Make a well in the center of the flour mixture and pour the wet ingredients into the well. Mix together until the flour is mostly incorporated. Be careful not to overmix.

Fill muffin tins about 3/4 of the way. Bake for 15–20 minutes or until lightly browned. Remove from pan and cool on a wire rack.

Variations:

In place of the baking powder, use:

- 1 1/2 teaspoons baking soda
- 1 1/2 teaspoons cream of tartar
- no chemical leavening agent

Muffin	Appearance	Flavor	Texture
Baking powder (control)			
Baking soda			
Cream of tartar			
No chemical leavening agent			

Experiment 2: Mixing Muffins

Determine which method produces the best results.

Basic Recipe (Control)

- 1 cup flour
- 1/3 cup sugar
- 1 1/2 teaspoons baking powder
- 1/4 teaspoon salt
- 1 large egg
- 1/2 cup milk
- 2 tablespoons canola oil

Preheat oven to 400°F. Lightly grease muffin tins or line with muffin papers. Set aside.

In a mixing bowl, sift together the flour, sugar, baking powder, and salt. In another bowl, whisk together the egg, milk, and oil. Make a well in the center of the flour mixture and pour the wet ingredients into the well. Mix together using 15 strokes around the bowl. Be careful not to overmix.

Fill muffin tins about 3/4 of the way. Bake for 15–20 minutes or until lightly browned. Remove from pan and cool on a wire rack.

Variations:

Increase mixing strokes or speed:

- 30 strokes
- hand mixer: mix batter until smooth

Muffin	Appearance	Flavor	Texture
Control: 15 strokes			
30 strokes			
Hand mixer			

Experiment 3: Biscuits
Evaluate the differences in fats used to make biscuits

Basic Recipe (Control)

Yield: 6 biscuits

- 1 cup flour
- 1 teaspoon sugar
- 1 teaspoon baking powder
- 1/4 teaspoon baking soda
- 1/2 teaspoon salt
- 1/4 cup shortening
- 1/3 cup buttermilk

Preheat oven to 425°F. Line a sheet pan with parchment paper.

In a bowl, mix together the flour, sugar, baking powder, baking soda, and salt. Cut in the shortening with a pastry blender or with two forks until the mixture is crumbly. Stir in the buttermilk to make a slightly sticky dough. Don't overmix the dough.

Dust the counter with flour and knead the dough about 5 times. Roll it out to about 1/2-inch thickness. With a round biscuit cutter, cut the dough into shapes. Place the biscuits on a baking sheet. Bake until golden brown, about 15 minutes.

Variations:

In place of the shortening, add:

- butter (cold, unsalted)
- lard
- coconut oil (solid, not melted)
- room temperature butter

Biscuit	Appearance	Flavor	Texture
Control – shortening			
Butter (cold)			
Lard			
Coconut oil			
Room temperature butter			

Experiment 4: Effect of Resting GF Pancake Batter

Determine if resting GF pancake batter makes a difference in texture and rise.

Basic GF Pancake (control)

Yield: 7 pancakes

- 1 cup GF AP Flour
- 1 1/2 teaspoons baking powder
- 1 teaspoon sugar
- 1/2 teaspoon salt
- 1/2 teaspoon xanthan gum (omit if the GF AP flour contains it)
- 1 cup milk, at room temperature
- 1 large egg, at room temperature
- 2 tablespoons canola oil

Preheat griddle over medium heat.

In a medium bowl, whisk together the flour, baking powder, sugar, salt, and xanthan gum. In a small bowl, whisk together the milk, eggs, and oil. Add the milk mixture to the flour mixture. Mix well to combine.

Ladle batter onto the hot griddle, using grease if necessary. Cook until golden brown on both sides, about 3–4 minutes per side.

Serve warm with maple syrup.

Variations:

- Allow batter to rest at room temperature for 30 minutes before cooking pancakes.
- Allow batter to rest in the refrigerator for 4 hours before cooking pancakes.

Variation	Overall flavor	Texture	Appearance
Control (no resting)			
30-minute rest			
4-hour rest			

RECIPES

Quick Bread Recipes

Dried Fruit Scones

Yield: 1 dozen

- 2 cups AP flour
- 1/2 cup sugar, plus more for sprinkling the top
- 2 teaspoons baking powder
- 1/4 teaspoon salt
- 1/3 cup chilled unsalted butter, cut into cubes
- 2/3 cup whipping cream
- 1 large egg
- 1 teaspoon vanilla
- 1 cup dried fruit of choice
  - cranberries
  - raisins
  - cherries
  - currants
  - blueberries
  - apricots
  - dates, chopped
- egg wash (1 egg mixed with 1 tablespoon water)

Preheat oven to 325°F. Line a sheet pan with parchment paper. Set aside.

In a bowl, combine the flour, 1/2 cup sugar, baking powder, and salt. Cut the butter into the flour mixture using a pastry blender until the mixture resembles coarse meal. In a small bowl, whisk together the cream, egg, and vanilla. Stir the wet ingredients into the dry ingredients. Mix until the dough starts to come together. Fold in the dried fruit.

Place the dough on a lightly floured surface. Knead 4–5 times to form a smoother dough. Roll the dough into a 1/2-inch thick rectangle. Use a pastry cutter or knife to cut the dough into circles, squares, or triangles. Place on the baking sheet. Brush the top of the scones with egg wash and sprinkle with sugar. Bake for 15–18 minutes or until golden brown. Remove from the pan and place on a wire rack to cool.

Banana Bread

Yield: 1 9 × 5 loaf or 12 muffins

- 1 1/2 cups AP flour
- 1 teaspoon cinnamon
- 1/2 teaspoon baking soda
- 1/2 teaspoon baking powder
- 1/2 teaspoon salt
- 2 medium-sized ripe bananas
- 2 tablespoons orange juice
- Zest of 1 orange
- 1/2 cup butter, at room temperature
- 3/4 cup sugar
- 2 large eggs
- 1 teaspoon vanilla extract
- 1 cup chopped walnuts (optional)

Preheat oven to 350°F. Generously grease and flour a 9 × 5-inch loaf pan. Set aside.

In a small bowl, whisk together the flour, cinnamon, baking soda, baking powder, and salt. Set aside. In another small bowl, mash together the bananas, orange juice, and zest. Set aside.

In a mixing bowl, cream together the butter and sugar until light and fluffy. Add the eggs and vanilla. Mix well to combine.

Stir in 1/3 of the flour mixture and mix well. Add 1/2 of the banana mixture and mix well. Mix in another 1/3 of the flour mixture and add remaining bananas, mixing well after each addition. Stir in remaining flour mixture and fold in the walnuts.

Pour into greased loaf pan. Bake for 50–60 minutes or until a toothpick inserted in the center comes out clean.

Cool for 10 minutes. Remove from pan and cool completely on a wire rack.

For muffins: line muffin tin with paper liners. Decrease baking time to 20–30 minutes.

Popovers

Yield: 6 popovers

- 3/4 cup AP flour
- 1/2 teaspoon salt
- 2 large eggs, at room temperature
- 3/4 cup whole milk, at room temperature
- 1 tablespoon unsalted butter, melted

Preheat oven to 425ºF. Grease popover pans with butter. Set aside.

Place the popover pan in the oven for 2 minutes to preheat. As the pans are heating, whisk together the flour, salt, eggs, milk, and melted butter until smooth. The batter will be thin. Remove the pan from the oven and fill each one less than half full. Bake for 30 minutes. The popovers should be nicely golden brown and have risen above the top of the pan.

Remove from oven and cool before serving.

Cornbread

Yield: 1 8-inch pan; about 6–7 muffins

- 1 1/2 cups cornmeal
- 1/2 cup AP flour
- 1/3 cup sugar
- 2 teaspoons baking powder
- 1 teaspoon salt
- 1/2 teaspoon baking soda
- 1 1/2 cups buttermilk
- 1/4 cup canola oil
- 2 large eggs

Preheat oven to 425ºF. Grease and flour an 8-inch baking pan. In a medium bowl, whisk together the cornmeal, flour, sugar, baking powder, salt, and baking soda. In a small bowl, whisk together the buttermilk, oil, and eggs. Add the buttermilk mixture into the dry ingredients. Mix until just combine. Pour into the pan. Bake until golden brown, about 25–30 minutes.

Cool slightly before serving.

To make muffins, line muffin tin with paper liners (or grease with butter). Fill 3/4 of the way up. Bake for 13–18 minutes or until a toothpick inserted in the center comes out clean.

Cheddar and Chive Biscuits

Yield: 1–2 dozen

- 2 cups AP flour
- 2 teaspoons baking powder
- 1 teaspoon baking soda
- 1 teaspoon sugar
- 1 teaspoon salt
- 1/2 cup (4 ounces) cold unsalted butter, cut into cubes
- 1 cup cold buttermilk
- 1/2 cup shredded cheddar cheese
- 2 tablespoons finely chopped fresh chives (or 2 teaspoons dried chives)

Preheat oven to 425ºF. Line a sheet pan with parchment paper. Set aside.

In a bowl, whisk together the flour, baking powder, baking soda, sugar, and salt. Add the cubed butter to the flour mixture. With a pastry blender, cut the butter into the flour mixture until it resembles coarse meal. Stir in the buttermilk. Mix until a dough starts to form. Add the cheese and chives. Fold to combine.

Place the dough on a lightly floured surface. Knead 4–5 times. Roll the dough to about 1/2-inch thick. Using a biscuit cutter, cut the dough into shapes and place a baking sheet. Reroll dough to make more biscuits.

Bake for 10–15 minutes or until golden brown. Cool slightly on a wire rack. Biscuits are best served slightly warm.

Zucchini Bread

Yield: 1 9 × 5-inch loaf

- 2 1/2 cups AP flour
- 1 1/2 teaspoons baking powder
- 1 1/2 teaspoons cinnamon
- 1/2 teaspoon salt
- 1 cup sugar
- 2/3 cup butter, melted (or canola oil)
- 2 large eggs
- 1 teaspoon vanilla
- 2 cups shredded zucchini
- 3/4 cup chopped walnuts or pecans

Preheat oven to 350ºF. Generously grease and flour a 9 × 5 loaf pan. Set aside.

In a large bowl, whisk together the flour, baking powder, cinnamon, and salt. Set aside.

In a medium sized bowl, whisk together the sugar, butter, eggs, and vanilla. Add the zucchini. Pour the mixture into the flour mixture. Stir until just combined. Fold in the chopped nuts.

Pour batter into prepared pan. Bake for 45–60 minutes or until a toothpick inserted comes out clean. Cool for 20 minutes in the pan. Loosen the edges of the bread with a knife. Remove bread from pan. Cool completely on a wire rack.

Zucchini Bread with Lentils

Yield: 1 9 × 5-inch loaf

Lentil Puree

- 1/2 cup green lentils
- 1 cup water

Zucchini Bread

- 1 1/2 cups whole wheat flour
- 1 teaspoon baking soda
- 1/2 teaspoon salt
- 1/4 teaspoon baking powder
- 1/2 teaspoon ground cinnamon
- 1 cup sugar
- 1/2 cup canola or safflower oil
- 2 large eggs
- 1 cup lentil puree
- 1 cup shredded zucchini
- 1/3 cup chopped walnuts or pecans

Preheat oven to 350ºF. Generously grease and flour a 9 × 5-inch loaf pan. Set aside.

Combine the lentils and water in a saucepan. Bring to a boil over medium high heat. Cover and reduce heat to simmer. Cook until the lentils are tender, about 25–30 minutes. Transfer lentils and the remaining water to a food processor. Pulse until smooth. The mixture should resemble canned pumpkin. Set aside.

In a large bowl, whisk together the whole wheat flour, baking soda, salt, baking powder, and cinnamon. Set aside. In a medium sized bowl, whisk together the sugar, oil, eggs, and lentil puree. Stir in the zucchini. Pour the wet mixture into the flour mixture. Mix until just combined. Fold in the chopped nuts.

Pour mixture into the prepared pan. Bake for 60–75 minutes or until a toothpick inserted comes out clean. Cool for 20 minutes in the pan. Loosen the edges of the bread with a knife. Remove bread from pan. Cool completely on a wire rack.

Pumpkin Muffins

Yield: 1 dozen muffins

- 1 3/4 cup AP flour
- 1 1/2 teaspoons baking powder
- 1/2 teaspoon baking soda
- 1/2 teaspoon salt
- 1 teaspoon ground cinnamon
- 1/2 teaspoon ground ginger
- 1/4 teaspoon ground nutmeg
- 1/4 teaspoon ground cloves
- 1 cup pumpkin puree
- 1 cup packed brown sugar
- 1/2 cup buttermilk
- 2 large eggs
- 1/3 cup canola or safflower oil
- 1 teaspoon vanilla

Preheat oven to 375°F. Grease a muffin tin or line with muffin papers. Set aside.

In a large bowl, whisk together the flour, baking powder, baking soda, salt, cinnamon, ginger, nutmeg, and cloves.

In a medium sized bowl, stir together the pumpkin puree, sugar, buttermilk, eggs, oil, and vanilla. Add the wet ingredients to the dry ingredients. Mix until combined.

Fill muffin tins about 3/4 of the way up. Bake for 18–20 minutes. Remove from pan and cool on a wire rack.

Quinoa-Millet Blueberry Muffins

Yield: 12–16 muffins

- 1/2 cup dry quinoa
- 1/4 cup whole millet, lightly toasted
- 1 cup water
- 1 cup AP flour
- 1 cup whole wheat flour
- 2 teaspoons ground cardamom (or cinnamon)
- 1 teaspoon baking powder
- 1/2 teaspoon baking soda
- 1/2 teaspoon salt
- 1 cup packed brown sugar
- 6 tablespoons unsalted butter, melted
- 3 large eggs
- 1/3 cup whole milk
- 1 tablespoon lemon zest
- 2 tablespoons fresh lemon juice
- 1 cup fresh blueberries

Preheat oven to 375°F. Grease a muffin tin or line with muffin papers. Set aside.

In a small saucepan, combine the quinoa and water. Bring to a boil over medium high heat. Cover and reduce heat to low. Simmer until water is absorbed, about 15 minutes.

Soak the millet in warm tap water for 10 minutes. Drain off excess water.

In a large bowl, whisk together the flour, whole wheat flour, baking powder, baking soda, and salt. Stir in the quinoa and millet. Set aside.

In a medium sized bowl, stir together the sugar, butter, eggs, milk, lemon zest, and lemon juice. Add the wet ingredients to the dry ingredients. Mix until combined. Fold in the blueberries.

Fill muffin tins about 3/4 of the way up. Bake for 18-20 minutes. Remove from pan and cool on a wire rack.

Bran Muffins

Yield: about 12 muffins

- 3 ounces wheat bran, lightly toasted in a dry pan
- 6 ounces AP flour
- 2 ounces sugar
- 2 teaspoons baking powder
- 1/2 teaspoon salt
- 3/43/4 cup milk
- 4 tablespoons unsalted butter, melted
- 3 tablespoons honey
- 3 tablespoons molasses
- 1 large egg
- 1/2 teaspoon vanilla

Preheat oven to 350°F. Grease muffins tins (or line with muffin papers). Set aside.

In a large bowl, combine the wheat bran, flour, sugar, baking powder, and salt. In a medium bowl, whisk together the milk, butter, honey, molasses, egg, and vanilla. Stir the milk mixture into the flour mixture. Mix until just combined. Fill muffin tins about 3/4 of the way. Bake for 18-20 minutes. Remove from pan and cool on a wire rack.

Spiced Muffins

Yield: 1–2 dozen muffins

- 1 1/2 cups AP flour
- 1 cup brown sugar
- 1/2 cup quick oats
- 1 tablespoon baking powder
- 1/2 teaspoon baking soda
- 1/2 teaspoon salt
- 1 teaspoon ground cinnamon
- 1/2 teaspoon ground allspice
- 1/2 teaspoon ground cloves
- 1/4 teaspoon ground nutmeg
- 1 1/4 cups plain Greek yogurt (low or full fat)
- 1/2 cup canola or safflower oil
- 2 large eggs
- 1 tablespoon orange zest
- 1 teaspoon vanilla

Preheat oven to 350°F. Grease muffins tins (or line with muffin papers). Set aside.

In a large bowl, combine the flour, sugar, oats, baking powder, baking soda, salt, cinnamon, allspice, cloves, and nutmeg. In a medium bowl, whisk together the yogurt, oil, eggs, orange zest, and vanilla. Stir the yogurt mixture into the flour mixture. Mix until just combined. Fill muffin tins about 3/4 of the way. Bake for 18–20 minutes. Remove from pan and cool on a wire rack.

Biscuits with Coconut Oil

Yield: about 12 biscuits

- 2 cups AP flour
- 1 tablespoon baking powder
- 1 teaspoon sugar
- 3 tablespoons chopped fresh herbs of choice:
  - chives
  - parsley
  - thyme
  - rosemary
- 1/2 teaspoon salt
- 1/2 cup coconut oil
- 3/4 cup canned full fat coconut milk

Preheat oven to 425ºF. Line sheet pan with parchment paper. Set aside.

In a bowl, whisk together the flour, baking powder, sugar, herbs, and salt. Add the coconut to the flour mixture. With a pastry blender, cut the coconut oil into the flour mixture until it resembles coarse meal. Stir in the coconut milk. Mix until a dough starts to form.

Place the dough on a lightly floured surface. Knead 4–5 times. Roll the dough to about 1/2-inch thick. Using a biscuit cutter, cut the dough into shapes and place on a baking sheet. Reroll dough to make more biscuits.

Bake for 15–18 minutes or until golden brown. Cool slightly on a wire rack. Biscuits are best served slightly warm.

Gluten-Free Recipes
Gluten-Free Biscuits

Yield: 1 dozen biscuits

- 1 1/2 cups all-purpose gluten-free flour
- 1/2 cup millet flour
- 1/4 cup grated parmesan cheese
- 1 teaspoon xanthan gum (omit if GF flour mix contains it)
- 1 teaspoon salt
- 2 1/2 teaspoons baking powder
- 6 tablespoons cold unsalted butter, cubed
- 3/4 cup milk (dairy or non-dairy)
- 2 tablespoons chopped fresh herbs: chives, rosemary, or thyme

Preheat the oven to 425°F.

In a large bowl, whisk together the flour, parmesan cheese, xanthan gum, salt, and baking powder. Use a pastry cutter to cut the butter into the flour mixture until it resembles coarse cornmeal.

Stir in the milk until incorporated. You may need an additional 1–2 tablespoons of milk to insure all the flour is moistened. Fold in fresh herbs. Form the dough into a ball and knead about 10 times in the bowl.

Roll the dough out on a floured board to 1 1/2 to 2 inches thick. Gently re-roll dough as needed.

Place biscuits on an ungreased baking sheet and refrigerate for 30 minutes (uncovered) before baking. After 30 minutes chilling, bake 12–15 minutes or until done (cooking time will depend on thickness of the biscuit). Serve warm.

Gluten-Free Cornbread

Yield: 1 10-inch pan cornbread

- 1/2 cup split red lentils
- 1/2 cup unsalted butter
- 1/2 cup maple syrup
- 2 large eggs
- 1/2 cup sour cream
- 3/4 cup buttermilk
- 1 1/4 cups cornmeal
- 1 cup gluten-free flour mix
- 2 teaspoons baking powder
- 1/2 teaspoon baking soda
- 1 teaspoon salt

Soak the lentils: Place the lentils in a bowl and soak for 8 hours. Drain and finely grind the lentils into a paste in a food processor.

Preheat oven to 375°F.

Place the butter in a 10-inch cast iron pan. Melt it over medium heat. Cook until the butter browns (turns a dark amber color), about 4–5 minutes. Pour butter into a small bowl and allow it to cool slightly. Do not wipe out the pan.

In a small bowl, mix together the wet ingredients: butter, maple syrup, eggs, sour cream, buttermilk, and lentils. In a large bowl, mix together the dry ingredients: cornmeal, gluten-free flour, baking powder, baking soda, and salt. Add the wet ingredients to the dry and mix until just combined. Pour the batter into the cast iron pan.

Bake for 30–40 minutes or until lightly golden brown and a toothpick inserted in the center comes out clean. Serve warm.

Gluten-Free Pancakes

Yield: 6 pancakes

- 1/4 cup brown rice flour
- 1/4 cup oat flour
- 1/4 cup teff
- 2 tablespoons millet flour
- 2 tablespoons quinoa flour
- 1 tablespoon sugar
- 1/2 teaspoon baking powder
- 1/4 teaspoon baking soda
- 1/4 teaspoon xanthan gum
- 1/4 teaspoon salt
- 1/4 teaspoon cinnamon or cardamom
- 1 large egg
- 1 tablespoon butter, melted
- 1 1/2 cups buttermilk

Add all dry ingredients to a bowl and whisk until well combined. Add the egg, butter, and buttermilk. If mixture is too thick, then add more buttermilk.

Let batter rest for 5–10 minutes and preheat griddle to medium heat. Ladle batter onto the hot griddle. Cook for 3–4 minutes or until bubbles form on top and the edges appear dry. Flip and finish cooking on the other side. Serve hot with maple syrup.

Gluten-Free Coconut Chocolate Chip Cookies

Yield: about 20 small cookies

- 3/4 cup creamy nut butter of choice
- 1/2 cup coconut sugar
- 2 tablespoons coconut oil, melted and cooled
- 2 large eggs
- 1/4 cup coconut flour
- 1/2 teaspoon baking soda
- 1/4 teaspoon salt
- 1/3 cup chocolate chips

Preheat oven to 350°F. Line a cookie sheet with parchment paper.

Combine the almond butter, coconut sugar and coconut oil in a food processor; process until it comes together, about 1 minute. Add eggs and process again.

Next, add in coconut flour, baking soda and salt; process again until a dough forms. Gently fold in chocolate chips.

Use a cookie scoop to drop dough onto prepared cookie sheet. Flatten the cookies slightly.

Bake for 8–10 minutes or until cookies turn slightly golden brown around the edges. Allow them to cool on cookie sheet for at least 5 minutes, then transfer to a wire rack to finish cooling.

Gluten-Free Apple Cinnamon Muffins

Yield: 12 muffins

- 1/2 cup brown rice flour
- 1/2 cup oat flour
- 1/2 cup almond meal/flour
- 1/4 cup tapioca starch
- 1/4 cup cornstarch
- 2 teaspoons baking powder
- 1/4 teaspoon baking soda
- 1/2 teaspoon xanthan gum
- 1/2 teaspoon salt
- 1 teaspoon cinnamon
- 1/2 cup unsalted butter, melted
- 2 ripe bananas, mashed

- 2/3 cup sugar
- 2 tablespoons honey
- 2 large eggs
- 1 apple, shredded with skin on

Preheat oven to 375°F. Line a 12-cup muffin tin with cupcake liners.

In a bowl, whisk together the dry ingredients: brown rice flour, almond flour, tapioca starch, cornstarch, baking powder, baking soda, xanthan gum, salt, and cinnamon. Set aside.

In a mixing bowl, cream together the butter, bananas, sugar, and honey. Add the eggs. Mix well to combine. Add the wet ingredients to the dry and mix just until combined. Stir in the apple.

Fill the muffin cups. Bake for 20–25 minutes. Cool in pan for 5 minutes before removing. Cool completely on a wire rack.

Gluten-Free Blueberry Lemon Pound Cake

Yield: 1 9 × 5-inch loaf

Cake

- 1 cup GF AP flour
- 1 cup millet flour
- 1/2 cup almond meal
- 1/2 cup quinoa or coconut flour
- 2 teaspoons baking powder
- 1 teaspoon (omit if the GF AP flour contains it)
- 1/4 teaspoon baking soda
- 1/2 teaspoon salt
- 2 cups sugar
- 1 cup unsalted butter, melted
- 4 large eggs, at room temperature
- 1/2 cup milk, at room temperature
- 2 teaspoons lemon zest
- 1/4 cup fresh lemon juice
- 2 cups fresh blueberries

Glaze

- 1 cup powdered sugar
- 1 teaspoon lemon zest
- 1–2 tablespoons lemon juice

Preheat oven to 350°F. Generously grease a 9 × 5-inch loaf pan. Line with parchment paper. Set aside.

In a bowl, whisk together the flour, millet flour, almond meal, quinoa flour, baking powder, and salt. Set aside.

In a medium bowl, whisk together the sugar, butter, eggs, milk, lemon zest, and lemon juice. Stir in the dry ingredients. Mix until combined. Fold in the blueberries.

Pour batter into the prepared pan. Let the batter rest at room temperature for 10 minutes. Bake for 60–75 minutes or until a toothpick inserted in the center comes out clean. Cool in pan for 10 minutes. Remove from pan and cool on a wire rack.

Make the glaze by whisking together the powdered sugar, zest, and lemon juice. Add enough juice to make a glaze consistency.

Drizzle glaze over the cake. Serve.

Gluten-Free Scones

Yield: 8 scones

- 1 cup brown rice flour
- 1/2 cup cornstarch
- 1/2 cup quinoa flour
- 1/4 cup teff flour
- 1/4 cup sugar
- 2 teaspoons baking powder
- 1/2 teaspoon xanthan gum
- 1/2 teaspoon salt
- 1/4 teaspoon cinnamon or nutmeg
- 1/2 cup cold unsalted butter, cut into cubes
- 3/4 cup dried fruit of choice
- 2 large eggs
- 1/3 cup milk (dairy or non-dairy)
- 1 teaspoon vanilla

Preheat oven to 400°F. Line a baking sheet with parchment.

In a bowl, whisk together the flour or flour blend, sugar, baking powder, xanthan gum, salt, and nutmeg. Cut the cold butter into the mixture until it resembles coarse crumbs. Fold in the dried fruit. In a small bowl, whisk together the eggs, milk, and vanilla. Stir the wet ingredients into the dry ingredients. The dough will be sticky.

Drop the scones onto the baking sheet in about 1/4 to 1/3 cup mounds. Flatten slightly. Bake for 15–20 minutes or until golden brown. Remove from oven and cool on wire rack.

Gluten-Free Banana Bread

Yield: 1 9 × 5 loaf

- 1/2 cup brown rice flour
- 1/2 cup almond meal
- 1/4 cup cornstarch
- 1/4 cup quinoa or garbanzo bean flour
- 1 1/4 teaspoons baking powder
- 1/2 teaspoon baking soda
- 3/4 teaspoon salt
- 1 cup mashed ripe bananas
- 2 tablespoons orange juice
- 1 tablespoon orange zest
- 1/3 cup butter, at room temperature
- 2/3 cup sugar
- 2 large eggs
- 2 tablespoons milk
- 1/2 cup chopped walnuts or pecans (optional)

Preheat oven to 350°F. Generously grease a 9 × 5-inch loaf pan. Line with parchment paper. Set aside.

In a small bowl, whisk together the brown rice flour, almond meal, cornstarch, quinoa flour, baking powder, baking soda, and salt. Set aside. In another small bowl, mash together the bananas, orange juice, and zest. Set aside.

In a mixing bowl, cream together the butter and sugar until light and fluffy. Add the eggs and milk. Mix well to combine.

Stir in 1/3 of the flour mixture and mix well. Add 1/2 of the banana mixture and mix well. Mix in another 1/3 of the flour mixture and add remaining bananas, mixing well after each addition. Stir in remaining flour mixture and fold in the walnuts.

Pour into greased loaf pan. Bake for 50–60 minutes or until a toothpick inserted in the center comes out clean.

Cool for 10 minutes. Remove from pan and cool completely on a wire rack.

Gluten-Free Zucchini Bread

Yield: 1 9 × 5 loaf

- 1 cup GF AP flour
- 1/4 cup quinoa or garbanzo bean flour
- 1/4 cup almond meal
- 1 teaspoon ground cinnamon
- 3/4 teaspoon baking soda
- 1/2 teaspoon xanthan gum (omit if GF AP flour mix contains it)
- 1/2 teaspoon salt
- 1/2 teaspoon ground ginger
- 3/4 cup sugar
- 1/3 cup canola oil
- 2 large eggs
- 2 tablespoons maple syrup
- 2 cups grated/shredded zucchini
- 1/2 cup chopped walnuts or pecans (optional)

Preheat oven to 350°F. Generously grease a 9 × 5-inch loaf pan. Line with parchment paper. Set aside.

In a large bowl, whisk together the flour, quinoa flour, almond meal, cinnamon, baking soda, xanthan gum, salt, and ginger. Set aside.

In a medium bowl, whisk together the sugar, oil, eggs, and maple syrup. Stir in the zucchini. Stir the wet ingredients into the dry ingredients. Mix until just combined. Fold in nuts.

Pour into prepared loaf pan. Bake for 50–60 minutes or until a toothpick inserted in the center comes out clean.

Cool for 10 minutes. Remove from pan and cool completely on a wire rack.

Gluten-Free Pizza Crust

- 1 cup GF AP Flour
- 1/2 cup teff flour
- 2 tablespoons buttermilk powder
- 1 teaspoon baking powder
- 1 teaspoon salt
- 1 teaspoon xanthan gum (omit if the GF AP flour contains it)
- 1 cup warm water
- 1/4 cup olive oil, divided
- 1 1/2 teaspoons dry instant yeast
- Pizza toppings as desired

Whisk together the flour, teff flour, buttermilk powder, baking powder, salt, and xanthan gum in a mixing bowl. Set aside.

In a small bowl, whisk together the water, 2 tablespoons oil, and yeast. Add 1/2 cup of the flour mixture. Let sit at room temperature for 30 minutes. As it sits, it should get bubbly and resemble a sponge.

Add the wet sponge to the remaining flour mixture. Beat on medium speed with the paddle attachment for 4–5 minutes. It will be like a thick paste. Cover the bowl with plastic wrap. Let sit for 30 minutes at room temperature.

To make pizza, preheat the oven to 425°F. Brush the remaining 2 tablespoons oil on a sheet pan or cast iron skillet. Scrape the dough onto the pan. With wet fingers, press the dough in the shape of the pan, reaching the edges.

Let dough rest for 10–15 minutes. Bake crust for 8–10 minutes.

Remove from oven and top with desired pizza toppings. Bake for an additional 10–15 minutes.

Remove from oven. Cut and serve.

Unit 10 Questions

1. In experiment 1, describe the differences in the muffins baked with different chemical leavening agents.
2. In experiment 2, describe the differences between the muffins mixed for varying amounts of time. Did one have any tunneling issues? Why would this be?
3. What causes biscuits to rise aside from the baking powder?
4. What causes popovers to rise?
5. What functions do eggs serve in baking quick breads?
6. In experiment 3, what were the differences in texture and height between the biscuits made with the different fats? Which one had the flakiest texture? Why would this be?
7. Were there any differences in texture and flavor between the gluten-free and regular quick breads?
8. In experiment 4, describe differences in texture and appearance between the pancakes. Which pancake produced the best result? Why do you think this is?

NOTES

1. Vickie A. Vaclavik and Elizabeth W. Christian, *Essentials of Food Science*, 4th ed. (New York: Springer, 2014), 307–308.
2. "High-Altitude Baking," King Arthur Flour, accessed May 14, 2019, https://www.kingarthurflour.com/learn/high-altitude-baking.html.
3. "All About Gluten-Free Baking: Keys to Successful Gluten-Free Baking," America's Test Kitchen, accessed May 14, 2019, https://www.americastestkitchen.com/guides/gluten-free/keys-to-successful-gluten-free-baking.
4. "All About Gluten-Free Baking: Troubleshooting Gluten-Free Baked Goods," America's Test Kitchen, accessed March 19, 2020, https://www.americastestkitchen.com/guides/gluten-free/troubleshooting-gluten-free-baked-goods.

BIBLIOGRAPHY

America's Test Kitchen. "All About Gluten-Free Baking: Keys to Successful Gluten-Free Baking." Accessed March 19, 2020. https://www.americastestkitchen.com/guides/gluten-free/keys-to-successful-gluten-free-baking.

America's Test Kitchen. "All About Gluten-Free Baking: Troubleshooting Gluten-Free Baked Goods." Accessed March 19, 2020. https://www.americastestkitchen.com/guides/gluten-free/troubleshooting-gluten-free-baked-goods.

King Arthur Flour. "High-Altitude Baking." Accessed May 14, 2019. https://www.kingarthurflour.com/learn/high-altitude-baking.html.

Vaclavik, Vickie A., and Elizabeth W. Christian. *Essentials of Food Science*, 4th ed. New York: Springer, 2014.

Yeast Breads

OBJECTIVES

- Describe the differences in yeast
- Evaluate effects of salt in bread making
- Describe and describe importance of kneading in bread making
- Demonstrate proper technique for making breads
- Use basic cooking techniques to prepare recipes

YEAST BREADS[1]

Yeast bread is simply made with a combination of flour, water, salt, and yeast. Yeast serves as the leavening agent producing carbon dioxide from the fermentation of carbohydrates in the flour. Additional sugar can be added to facilitate this reaction but it is not necessary.

Most yeast used in bread baking is baker's yeast usually found in dry form. Baker's yeast needs to be "bloomed" prior to using in the recipe. Blooming yeast is a process where the yeast is placed in warm water with some sugar. This helps wake the yeast up and become alive.

Rapid rise or instant yeast is a common product found in stores. The dry yeast granules are smaller than baker's yeast and do not require the yeast to be bloomed prior to use.

Some professional bakers use fresh yeast or cake yeast which has a shorter shelf life and needs to be kept refrigerated. Most recipes call for dry yeast. If a recipe calls for cake or fresh yeast, use the following conversion:

1 (1/4 ounce) package dry yeast = 2 1/4 teaspoons = 1 ounce cake or fresh yeast

Once yeast is bloomed or in fresh form, it is a living organism. Because of this, yeast can be controlled or killed. Two ways to control yeast growth are with salt and extreme temperatures.

Salt: controls yeast growth by killing some yeast

Extreme temperatures: If the water in the recipe is above 135°F, this can kill off the yeast. On the contrary, if the water is below 85°F, the yeast will take a long time to grow.

The optimal conditions for yeast growth include warm water of 110°F, a food source rich in carbohydrates, and warm (70°F) air conditions.

Additional Components and Ingredients

Gluten

As discussed in chapter 10, gluten is a complex structure of several proteins in wheat flour. The primary proteins in gluten include long strands of amino acids of gliadin and glutelin. When water is added, this activates the proteins and gluten begins to form a cohesive mass. As it develops, it gives bread elasticity and structure. With protein content of 12–14%, bread flour has a high gluten content and is optimal for bread making.

Salt

In addition to controlling yeast growth, salt also plays a major role in facilitating the formation of gluten and improve its strength. Additionally, salt adds flavor.

Fat

A variety of fats can be added to bread dough providing both flavor and tenderness. Butter, olive oil, vegetable oil, or shortening can be added.

Milk

Either low fat or whole milk can be added to bread for additional flavor and tenderness.

Sourdough Starter

Sourdough starters are simply a mix of flour and water. When left at room temperature over a period of 5–6 days, natural yeasts and lactic acid bacteria, namely lactobacilli form to create a slightly acidic and sour mixture that can be used in place of active dry yeast in baking yeast breads.

High-Altitude Baking[2]

Baking at higher elevations poses some challenges to yeast breads.

According to the bakers at King Arthur Flour, yeast bread recipes need to be adjusted according to the elevation at which they are baked. Use these guidelines for high-altitude baking:

- Yeast: Decrease the amount in the recipe by 25%.
- Flour and water: Make water/flour adjustments as necessary to get a dough with the correct texture. Make sure your bowl has plenty of room for the dough to rise in. The air at higher elevations tend to be drier and you may need less flour or slightly more water than the recipe calls for.

- Rising/Fermentation: Cut the amount of time by 25%.
- Flavor: To improve the flavor of the bread since rising times are shortened, give the dough an extra rise by punching it down and allowing it to continue rising. The dough can also be placed in the refrigerator during the first rising. If using the refrigerator, double the rising time.
- Starters: Sourdough starters can also be used to improve the flavor of the recipe. Add it an addition to the yeast. Replace a portion of the water with sourdough starter. The starter will be best if made into a sponge first or it has been sitting at room temperature for 6–8 hours and is very active.

Steps of Yeast Bread

The steps to making yeast bread are straightforward. Some breads do not need a second rising, but most, if not all, require at least one rising, called "fermentation."

First the dough is mixed together by hand or with a mixer using the flat beater (paddle) attachment.

The dough is kneaded either by hand, using a pushing, turning motion, or by using a mixer fitted with a dough hook. Proper kneading has three purposes: distributing ingredients, developing gluten, and initiating fermentation.

Next the dough is set aside to rise or ferment. During this process, the yeast feeds off the carbohydrates in the dough and starts converting sugar to carbon dioxide, causing the dough to rise. Fermentation also allows flavors to develop in the bread.

After the dough has risen, it is necessary to punch it down to release any excess carbon dioxide.

Typically, the dough is divided, depending on the recipe and formed into shapes as described in the recipe. The dough may also require resting to relax the gluten prior to shaping or baking, especially if it springs back during shaping.

At this point, some yeast breads are ready to be baked. However, many others will need to continue with a few more steps to achieve desired results.

Some breads require a second rising or fermentation, called proofing. During proofing the flavors continue to develop and the yeast continues to grow. After the proofing stage, the loaves are then scored (marked) and baked.

For a typical loaf of bread, it should be baked to an internal temperature of 200°F. Allow the loaves to cool before slicing and serving, as this will help form the crust of the loaf.

EXPERIMENTS

Experiment 1: Effect of Salt on Bread

Evaluate the effect of salt in making yeast bread.

<u>Basic Recipe (Control)</u>[i]

- 1 3/4 cup AP flour
- 1 1/4 teaspoons instant dry yeast
- 1/2 teaspoon salt
- 1/2 cup warm water (110°F)
- 2 tablespoons canola oil

In a mixing bowl, combine the flour, yeast, and salt. Stir in the water and canola oil. Stir with a rubber spatula or wooden spoon just until a dough forms. Knead the dough with the dough hook or by hand for 10 minutes. Add sprinkles of flour if the dough is too sticky. Shape dough into a ball.

Lightly grease a bowl with oil or cooking spray. Place the dough into the bowl. Cover with plastic wrap. Place in a warm spot and allow to rise for 45 minutes. Punch down the dough and shape into a loaf. Place loaf in a small pan. Cover with a towel and allow to rise for another 30 minutes.

Preheat oven to 400°F. Bake for 25–30 minutes or until the internal temperature of the bread reaches 200°F. Cool on a wire rack. Slice and serve.

<u>Variations:</u>

Adjust the salt content:

- Increase amount of salt to 1 tablespoon
- Omit the salt

Loaf	Appearance	Flavor	Texture
Basic loaf (control)			
Extra salt			
No salt			

---

i   Adjust for high altitude

Experiment 2: Effect of Kneading on Bread

Evaluate the effect of over or under kneading in making yeast bread.

Basic Recipe (Control)[ii]

- 1 3/4 cup AP flour
- 1 1/4 teaspoons instant dry yeast
- 1/2 teaspoon salt
- 1/2 cup warm water (110°F)
- 2 tablespoons canola oil

In a mixing bowl, combine the flour, yeast, and salt. Stir in the water and canola oil. Stir with a rubber spatula or wooden spoon just until a dough forms. Knead the dough with the dough hook or by hand for 10 minutes. Add sprinkles of flour if the dough is too sticky. Shape dough into a ball.

Lightly grease a bowl with oil or cooking spray. Place the dough into the bowl. Cover with plastic wrap. Place in a warm spot and allow to rise for 45 minutes. Punch down the dough and shape into a loaf. Place loaf in a small pan. Cover with a towel and allow to rise for another 30 minutes.

Preheat oven to 400°F. Bake for 25–30 minutes or until the internal temperature of the bread reaches 200°F. Cool on a wire rack. Slice and serve.

Variations:

Adjust the kneading time:

- Knead for 3 minutes
- Knead for 30 minutes (use a mixer)

Loaf	Appearance	Flavor	Texture
Basic loaf (control)			
3 minute			
30 minute			

---

ii   Adjust for high altitude

Experiment 3: Effect of Different Flours on Yeast Bread

Evaluate the effect of gluten-free flour in making yeast bread.

Basic Recipe (Control)[iii]

- 1 3/4 cup AP flour
- 1 1/4 teaspoons instant dry yeast
- 1/2 teaspoon salt
- 2/3 cup warm water (110°F)
- 2 tablespoons canola oil

In a mixing bowl, combine the flour, yeast, and salt. Stir in the water and canola oil. Stir with a rubber spatula or wooden spoon just until a dough forms. Knead the dough with the dough hook or by hand for 10 minutes. Add sprinkles of flour if the dough is too sticky. Shape dough into a ball.

Lightly grease a bowl with oil or cooking spray. Place the dough into the bowl. Cover with plastic wrap. Place in a warm spot and allow to rise for 45 minutes. Punch down the dough and shape into a loaf. Place loaf in a small pan. Cover with a towel and allow to rise for another 30 minutes.

Preheat oven to 400°F. Bake for 25–30 minutes or until the internal temperature of the bread reaches 200°F. Cool on a wire rack. Slice and serve.

Variations:

Substitute the AP flour with:

- gluten-free AP flour
- whole wheat flour
- rye flour
- spelt or Kamut flour

Loaf	Appearance	Flavor	Texture
Basic loaf (control)			
Gluten-free AP flour			
Whole wheat			
Rye			
Spelt or Kamut			

iii   Adjust for high altitude

RECIPES

Cinnamon Rolls

Yield: about 1 dozen rolls

Dough

- 2/3 cup whole milk
- 1/3 cup water
- 6 tablespoons unsalted butter, at room temperature
- 2 large eggs, at room temperature
- 3–4 cups bread flour
- 1/3 cup sugar
- 2 1/4 teaspoons instant dry yeast
- 1/2 teaspoon salt

Filling

- 4 tablespoons unsalted butter, at room temperature
- 1/2 cup brown sugar
- 1/4 cup white sugar
- 1 teaspoon cinnamon

Glaze

- 1 cup powdered sugar
- 1/2 teaspoon vanilla
- Milk to desired consistency

In a small saucepan, combine the milk, water, and butter. Heat over low heat until milk warms up to 105°F. The butter will soften but not melt completely. Pour mixture into a mixing bowl. Add the eggs and mix to combine. Add 1 cup flour, sugar, yeast, and salt. Mix with the paddle attachment of the mixer. Add another cup of flour to the mixture. Mix well. Continuing adding the remaining flour until a soft dough forms. Switch to the dough hook. Knead for 10 minutes. If the dough is sticky, add sprinkles of flour. The dough should be soft and smooth.

Lightly grease a bowl with oil or cooking spray. Place the dough in the bowl. Cover with plastic wrap. Place in a warm spot. Rise for 45 minutes.

Take the dough out of the bowl and place on a lightly floured surface. Knead the dough to push out any air bubbles. Roll the dough into a rectangle about 1/4-inch thick. If the dough springs back while rolling it out, let it rest for 5–10 minutes to relax the gluten strands. In a bowl, combine the brown sugar, sugar, and cinnamon. Spread the butter on the dough, leaving a 1/2-inch border at the top edge. Sprinkle the sugar mixture over the butter. Press down slightly. Roll the dough up into a log. Cut into 1/2-inch thick slices. Place the slices in a lightly greased baking pan. Cover with a towel.

Rise in a warm spot for 30–45 minutes.

Preheat oven to 375ºF. Bake the rolls for 30–40 minutes or until golden brown. In a small bowl, whisk together the glaze ingredients.

When rolls are done, pour glaze over the rolls. Cool for 10–15 minutes before serving.

Pita
Yield: about 8 pitas

- 2–2 1/2 cups bread flour (AP flour may be substituted)
- 1 tablespoon sugar
- 2 1/2 teaspoons instant dry yeast
- 2 teaspoons salt
- 1 cup hot (120ºF) water
- 2 tablespoons olive oil
- 8 squares of aluminum foil

In a mixing bowl, combine 1 cup flour, sugar, yeast, and salt. Add the water and oil. Mix at low speed with the paddle attachment of the mixer for 1 minute. Increase speed to high and mix for 3 minutes. Reduce speed of the mixer and add remaining flour 1/2 cup at time. The dough will be a soft, shaggy mass that cleans the side of the bowl. If it's too wet, add a small amount of flour. Switch to the dough hook. Knead the dough on medium low speed for 6 minutes.

Preheat the oven to 475ºF. Divide the dough into 8 pieces. Roll into balls. Cover with a towel and allow to rest for 20 minutes.

With the palm of your hand, flatten the ball of dough into a disk. Using a rolling pin, roll the dough into a 6–inch disk (or close to it). The disk should be thin. Place each round of dough on a piece of foil. Carefully place 2–3 of the pitas in the hot oven. For best results place directly on the bottom floor of the oven or on the lowest shelf. Bake for 5–8 minutes or until they are lightly golden brown and puff up.

Remove from the oven. Keep wrapped in foil until service.

Pizza Dough
Yield: about 1 12-inch pizza

- 1 to 1 1/2 cups AP flour
- 1/2 cup whole wheat flour
- 2 1/4 teaspoons instant dry yeast
- 1/2 teaspoon salt
- 2/3 cup warm water
- 2 tablespoons olive oil

In a mixing bowl, combine 1 cup AP flour, whole wheat flour, yeast, and salt. Add the water and oil. Mix with the paddle attachment until dough forms. Switch to a dough hook. Knead for 4–5 minutes. Add the remaining AP flour as needed if the dough is too sticky.

Place the dough in a lightly greased bowl. Cover with plastic wrap. Rise in a warm spot for 1 hour.

Preheat oven to 425°F. Roll dough on a lightly floured surface to desired thickness. Place on a baking sheet or pizza pan that has been dusted with cornmeal. Top with desired toppings. Bake for 15 minutes or until golden brown.

Whole Wheat Pretzels

Yield: 8 pretzels

- 2 1/2 cups whole wheat flour
- 1–2 cups AP flour
- 2 1/4 teaspoons instant dry yeast
- 2 teaspoons salt
- 1 1/2 cups warm water
- 3 tablespoons canola or olive oil
- 2 tablespoons melted butter
- 1 tablespoon honey
- 3/4 cup baking soda
- egg wash: 1 egg yolk mixed with 1 tablespoon water
- kosher or pretzel salt for sprinkling

In a mixing bowl, combine the whole wheat flour, 1 cup AP flour, yeast, and salt. Add the water, oil, butter, and honey. Mix with the paddle attachment until dough forms. Switch to a dough hook. Knead for 4–5 minutes. Add the remaining AP flour as needed if the dough is too sticky. The dough should be soft but not overly sticky.

Place the dough in a lightly greased bowl. Cover with plastic wrap. Let dough rise in a warm spot for 1 hour.

Preheat oven to 450°F. Line a baking sheet with parchment paper. Set aside.

Heat 10–12 cups water in a stockpot set over medium high heat. Bring the water to a near boil (about 200°F). Sprinkle in the baking soda. Reduce heat to medium.

Remove dough from the bowl. Cut the dough into 8 pieces. On a dry (not floured) counter, roll each piece into a 24-inch rope. Form into a pretzel shape by making a U and while holding the ends of the rope, cross them over each other and press into the bottom of the U to form the pretzel.

Place the pretzels in the hot water one at a time for 30 seconds. Remove with a slotted spoon or spatula. Place on the baking sheet. Brush the top of the pretzels with egg wash and sprinkle with the salt. Bake the pretzels until dark golden brown, about 12–14 minutes. Transfer to a wire rack to cool. Serve with honey mustard.

Breadsticks

Makes 24 breadsticks

- 1 pound, 2 ounces bread flour
- 1 ounce sugar
- 5 teaspoons (1/2 ounce) instant dry yeast
- 3 teaspoons salt
- 1 1/4 cups warm water
- 1/2 cup olive oil
- Egg wash (1 egg yolk mixed with 1 tablespoon water)
- 1 teaspoon granulated garlic powder

Preheat oven to 375°F.

In a mixing bowl, combine 1 pound AP flour, sugar, yeast, and 2 teaspoons salt. Add the water and oil. Mix with the paddle attachment until dough forms. Switch to a dough hook. Knead for 4–5 minutes. Add the remaining AP flour as needed if the dough is too sticky. The dough should be soft but not overly sticky.

Remove from the bowl and allow to rest for 10–15 minutes. Line a baking sheet with parchment. Set aside.

Roll dough into rectangle about 1/4-inch thick. Cut the dough into 24 even pieces. Roll each piece into a rope and twist. Bring the ends together or tie into a knot. Place on the baking sheet.

Cover with a towel. Let the breadsticks rise for 20 minutes. In a small bowl, mix together the remaining teaspoon salt and garlic powder. Brush with egg wash and sprinkle with the garlic salt.

Bake for 12–15 minutes or until golden brown. Serve with pizza sauce.

Naan

Yield: 8 flat breads

- 3/4 cup warm water
- 1 teaspoon instant dry yeast
- 2 teaspoons honey
- 3 tablespoons plain Greek yogurt
- 2 tablespoons olive oil
- 1 cup AP flour
- 1 cup white whole wheat flour or whole wheat flour
- 1 teaspoon salt
- 1/8 teaspoon baking powder

In a mixing bowl, combine the water, honey, and yeast. Add the yogurt and olive oil. Stir to combine.

Stir in the AP flour, whole wheat flour, salt, and baking powder. Mix together with a spatula until the mixture forms a dough. Knead by hand to form a pliable and slightly sticky dough. Knead for 1–2 minutes.

Lightly grease a bowl. Place dough in the bowl. Cover with plastic wrap. Place in warm spot for 90 minutes.

Place a small bowl of flour and a small bowl of water on the counter near the stove. Divide the dough into 8 pieces. Toss the pieces in the flour to prevent them from sticking to each other.

Roll out each piece into a circle. Don't worry about perfection here; they should look oval and misshapen.

Heat a cast iron pan over medium-high heat. Have a lid nearby that fits the pan.

Dampen your hands with the water. Pick up a naan. Flip it back and forth between your hands. Lay the naan in the hot pan. Cook for 1 minute. Flip. Cover the pan for another minute or so or until the bread is cooked through. Remove from pan and repeat process with remaining naan.

English Muffins

Yield: about 8–10 muffins

- 1/2 cup non-fat dry milk
- 1 tablespoon sugar
- 1 teaspoon salt
- 1 1/3 cups hot water (120°F)
- 1 tablespoon unsalted butter
- 1 cup whole wheat flour
- 1 cup AP flour
- 2 1/4 teaspoons instant dry yeast
- non-stick spray
- 3-inch metal rings

In a bowl, combine the dry milk, sugar, 1/2 teaspoon salt, butter, and hot water. Stir until the sugar and salt are dissolved. Cool.

In a separate bowl, combine the whole wheat flour, AP flour, yeast and remaining 1/2 teaspoon salt. Stir in the dry milk mixture. Mix until well combined. Cover with plastic wrap and allow to rest for 30 minutes.

Place a non-stick skillet over medium-low heat. Place the metal rings in the pan and coat with the non-stick spray. Using a scoop, fill the rings with the batter, about 1/3 of the way full. Don't fill over 1/2 way up the ring, or the batter will overflow as it cooks. Cover with pan with a lid and cook for 5–6 minutes. Flip and cover. Cook for another 5–6 minutes. Place English muffins on a wire rack to cool. Repeat process until the batter is used up. Serve with butter and jam.

Sourdough Starter

- 1 cup whole wheat or AP flour + more for feeding
- 1/2 cup water + more for feeding

Day 1

Combine the flour and water in a 1-quart glass or stainless steel bowl. Stir until well combined. Cover with a towel. Let sit at room temperature (70°F is optimal) for 24 hours.

Day 2

Discard half the starter (about 1/2 cup). Add 1 cup AP flour and 1/2 cup lukewarm water. Mix well. Cover. Let sit for 24 hours.

Day 3

Remove 4 ounces of the starter and discard the rest. Add 1 cup AP flour and 1/2 cup water. Mix well. Cover and let sit for 24 hours. Repeat process.

Day 4

Remove 4 ounces of the starter and discard the rest. Add 1 cup AP flour and 1/2 cup water. Mix well. Cover and let sit for 24 hours. Repeat process.

Day 5

Remove 4 ounces of the starter and discard the rest. Add 1 cup AP flour and 1/2 cup water. Mix well. Cover and let sit for 24 hours. Repeat process. By the end of day 5, the starter should be bubbly and have a nice aroma. If the starter is not bubbly, repeat the process for 1–2 more days.

Day 6

Once the starter is ready, discard 1/2 cup of the starter and feed with 1 cup AP flour and 1/2 cup water. Let it rest at room temperature for 6–8 hours.

Use in a recipe.

To Keep the Starter

Place in glass container and store in the refrigerator. Feed once a week by discarding 1/2 cup starter and adding 1 cup AP flour and 1/2 cup water.

Rustic Sourdough

Yield: 1 large loaf or 2 medium loaves

- 1 cup "fed" sourdough starter
- 1 1/2 cups warm water
- 1 tablespoon honey
- 2 1/2 teaspoons salt
- 1 cup whole wheat flour
- 3 cups bread flour

Optional additions: 1/2 cup grated Parmesan cheese and/or 2 tablespoons finely chopped fresh rosemary

Combine all ingredients in a bowl of a stand mixer. Mix with the paddle attachment until the dough comes together. Switch to the dough hook. Knead with the dough hook until smooth and elastic, about 5–8 minutes. If the dough is too sticky, add a few sprinkles of bread flour.

Place the dough in a lightly greased bowl. Cover with plastic wrap. Rise in a warm spot for 90 minutes.

Divide the dough in two and shape the dough into rounds (boules) or ovals. Line a baking sheet with parchment paper. Place the bread on the baking sheet. Cover with a towel. Rise for 1 hour.

Preheat oven to 425°F. Spray loaves with water. Score the tops of each one with a sharp knife.

Bake for 25–30 minutes or until golden brown and the internal temperature reaches 200°F.

Alternatively, the bread can be baked in a dutch oven. If the dutch oven is big, one loaf can be made. If it's on the smaller side, divide the dough in two. Score the loaf.

To bake in a dutch oven, preheat the oven to 450°F. Place the dutch oven in the oven for 20 minutes to preheat the pan. When the pan is preheated, carefully place the loaf in the hot pan and cover with a lid. Bake for 30 minutes. The bread is done when the internal temperature of the loaf is 200°F. Remove from the pan and cool.

Flammkuchen
Yield: Serves 4–6

Dough

- 10 ounces AP flour
- 1 teaspoon salt
- 1 1/2 teaspoons instant dry yeast
- 3/4 cup warm water
- 1 tablespoon olive oil

Toppings

- 6 strips of bacon, chopped
- 1 medium yellow or white onion, julienned
- 8 ounces (by weight) crème fraiche
- 1/2 tsp nutmeg
- 1/2 tsp salt
- freshly ground black pepper

Combine all dough ingredients in a large bowl to form a rough dough. Knead the dough for 10 minutes until you have a smooth, elastic, stretchy and velvety dough. Place the dough in a lightly greased bowl and cover with plastic wrap; rise for 90 minutes in a warm spot.

Preheat the oven to 450ºF. Line a baking sheet with parchment paper. Set aside.

Shape the dough into a ball and allow to rest for 10 minutes.

In a bowl, combine the crème fraiche, the nutmeg, salt, and pepper and mix well. Set aside.

Roll the dough into a rectangle to fit the baking sheet. Place in the baking sheet.

Fry the bacon strips until nearly cooked but not crispy. Remove the bacon and drain paper towels. Sauté the onion in the same pan as the bacon until lightly browned, about 5 minutes.

Spread the crème fraiche mixture on the dough. Scatter the onions and bacon on top. Bake for about 12 minutes or until the edges are nicely browned and the bottom is crisp. Serve immediately.

Msemen – Rghaeif (Moroccan Flatbread)
Yield: 8 flatbreads

- 5 ounces AP Flour
- 5 ounces semolina flour
- 1/2 teaspoon salt
- 4–5 fluid ounces warm water
- 4 tablespoons canola or safflower oil
- 2 tablespoons melted butter

In large bowl, mix together the AP flour, semolina flour, and salt. Add the water and 2 tablespoons oil. Mix until a dough begins to form. If the dough is too dry, add more water as necessary. The dough should be soft, but not sticky.

Knead by hand for 15 minutes or with the mixer (using a dough hook) for 8 minutes.

Divide into 8 pieces. Lightly grease a baking sheet and place the dough on the sheet. Cover with plastic wrap and let rest to 30 minutes.

In a small bowl, mix together the melted butter and oil.

Place a piece of dough on the counter. Flatten it lightly and pour about 1/2 teaspoon of the butter mixture onto the dough. With your hands, flatten the dough as thin as you can, making a circle or square shape.

Fold each side of the dough towards the center to make a square shape. Place the flatbread on a lightly greased baking sheet and cover with plastic wrap. Repeat process for each piece of dough.

Place a non-stick skillet over medium high heat. Add 1 tablespoon oil.

Transfer one of the flatbreads to the counter and rub with 1/2 teaspoon of the butter mixture. Flatten it again to get as thin as possible.

Place the flatbread in the hot pan. Cook on each side until golden brown, about 2 minutes per side. If the flatbread is burning, turn down the heat.

Serve warm or at room temperature.

Sourdough Flatbread
Adapted from Edible Communities[3]

Yield: 8 flatbreads

- 2 1/2 cups AP flour
- 1 tablespoon sugar
- 1 teaspoon salt
- 1/2 teaspoon baking powder
- 1/2 cup sourdough starter
- 1/4 cup plain Greek yogurt
- 1/4 cup canola, olive, or safflower oil
- 1–2 tablespoons warm water
- 2 tablespoons unsalted butter, melted

In a large bowl, whisk together the flour, sugar, salt, and baking powder. Stir in the starter, yogurt, oil, and 1 tablespoon of water. Mix until a semi-smooth dough forms, about 2–3 minutes. It should feel soft but not sticky. Add additional flour or water to achieve the correct texture. Place in a lightly greased bowl and cover with plastic wrap. Allow to rise for 1 hour in a warm spot.

Place the dough on a lightly floured surface. Divide into 8 equal pieces. Cover with a towel.

Working with one piece at a time, roll the dough into a thin circle about 8 inches in diameter. The exact shape does not need to be perfect. As you roll the dough thinner, it will become more of a flatbread. If the dough is thicker, it will be similar to a puffy pita.

Warm a large cast-iron skillet over medium-low heat.

Cook the dough in the warm, dry pan for 2 to 3 minutes per side. When the dough puffs up and has a few bubbles on the surface, brush lightly with some of the melted butter and flip it over. Cook for 1 to 2 minutes on the other side. When finished, brush with more butter and transfer to a cutting board. Wrap in a towel to keep warm. Repeat process with the remaining flatbreads.

Rosemary Bread

Yield: 2 loaves

- 1 pound, 4 ounces bread flour
- 1 1/2 cups warm water
- 1/3 cup olive oil
- 1/2 ounce instant dry yeast
- 2 tablespoons finely chopped fresh rosemary
- 1 tablespoon salt
- egg wash (1 egg mixed with 1 tablespoon water)

Combine all ingredients in a bowl of a stand mixer. Mix with the paddle attachment until the dough comes together. Switch to the dough hook. Knead with the dough hook until smooth and elastic, about 5–8 minutes. If the dough is too sticky, add a few sprinkles of bread flour.

Place the dough in a lightly greased bowl. Cover with plastic wrap. Rise in a warm spot for 30 minutes. Punch down the dough and rise for another 30 minutes.

Divide the dough into 2 pieces and shape into round loaves. Sprinkle a baking sheet with cornmeal and place the loaves on the baking sheet. Cover with a towel. Rise for 1 hour.

Preheat oven to 400°F.

Score the loaves. Brush with egg wash. Bake for 20–30 minutes (depending on the size of the loaf) or until the internal temperature reaches 200°F. Cool before slicing.

Raisin Bread

Yield: 1 loaf

- 1 cup warm (110°F) whole milk
- 1/4 cup honey
- 1/2 ounce instant dry yeast
- 3 to 3 1/2 cups bread flour
- 3 tablespoons butter, softened
- 1 1/2 teaspoons salt
- 1 cup raisins
- 1/3 cup sugar
- 1/2 teaspoon ground cinnamon
- 1 tablespoon canola oil
- egg wash (1 egg mixed with 1 tablespoon water

In a mixing bowl, combine the milk, honey, and yeast. Add 3 cups of flour, butter, and salt. Knead with the dough hook for 8–10 minutes. Add more flour as necessary if the dough is too sticky. The dough should be soft but not overly sticky.

Lightly grease a large bowl. Place the dough in the bowl and cover with plastic wrap. Rise in a warm spot for 1 hour.

As the dough is rising, grease a 9 × 5-inch loaf pan. Set aside.

Remove dough from the bowl and place on a lightly floured surface. Knead the raisins into the dough. Let dough rest for 10 minutes. In a small bowl, mix together the sugar and cinnamon. Roll the dough out into a rectangle about 9 inches long. Brush with oil. Sprinkle with the sugar and cinnamon mixture. Roll the dough up into a log. Fold the ends under and place seam-side down in the pan.

Cover the loaf with a towel and proof until doubled in size about 1 hour.

Preheat oven to 375°F. Brush with the egg wash. Sprinkle with sugar. Bake for 40–45 minutes or until the internal temperature reaches 200°F. Cool for 15 minutes before removing from the pan. Cool before slicing.

White Sandwich Bread

Yield: 2 loaves

- 5–6 cups bread flour
- 1/4 cup non-fat dry milk
- 3 tablespoons sugar
- 2 teaspoons salt
- 2 1/4 teaspoons instant dry yeast
- 2 cups hot tap water (120°F)
- 3 tablespoons unsalted butter, at room temperature

In a large mixing bowl, combine 2 cups flour, dry milk, sugar, salt, and yeast. Pour in the hot water and mix with the flat beater until blended. Add the butter and mix well. Mix in 1 cup of flour.

Switch to the dough hook and add the remaining flour 1/4 cup at a time or until the dough forms a soft, elastic ball.

Place the dough in a lightly greased bowl and cover with plastic wrap. Rise in warm spot for 1 hour.

As the dough is rising, grease two 9 × 5-inch loaf pans. Set aside.

Turn the dough onto a lightly floured surface. Divide into 2 pieces. Shape into a ball. Let dough rest for 5 minutes. Shape into loaves. Place seam-side down in the loaf pans. Cover with a towel. Rise for 45 minutes.

Preheat oven to 400°F.

Bake loaves for 10 minutes. Reduce heat to 350°F. Bake for another 25–30 minutes or until internal temperature reaches 200°F.

Cool loaves for 15 minutes in the pan. Remove and cool before slicing.

Dinner Rolls
Yield: 15 rolls

- 3/4 cup warm whole milk (110°F)
- 1/4 cup unsalted butter, melted
- 1 large egg
- 2 tablespoons warm water
- 1/4 ounce instant dry yeast
- 1 tablespoon sugar
- 3 to 3 1/2 cups AP flour
- 1 teaspoon salt
- egg wash (1 egg mixed with 1 tablespoon water)

In a mixing bowl, combine the milk, butter, egg, water, yeast, and sugar. With the paddle attachment, mix in 3 cups of the flour and salt. Mix until it forms a dough. Switch to the dough hook and knead for 6–8 minutes, adding more flour as necessary to make a soft dough. The dough should not be overly sticky.
Lightly grease a bowl. Place the dough in the bowl and cover with plastic wrap. Rise in a warm spot for 1 hour.

Butter a 13 × 9-inch baking pan. Cut dough into 15 equal pieces. Shape into rolls. Arrange rolls in the greased baking pan. Cover with a towel. Rise for 1 hour.

Preheat oven to 375°F. Brush the tops of the rolls with egg wash. Bake until golden brown, about 20 minutes. Cool for 20 minutes before serving.

GF Parmesan Bread
Yield: 1 large loaf

- 1 1/4 cups AP gluten-free flour
- 1 cup arrowroot
- 1 cup millet flour
- 1 cup garbanzo bean or quinoa flour
- 1/4 cup buttermilk powder
- 1 tablespoon xanthan gum
- 5 teaspoons instant dry yeast
- 1 teaspoon salt
- 3 large eggs, at room temperature
- 1 1/3 cups club soda, at room temperature
- 1/2 cup olive oil plus more for pan
- 1 tablespoon honey
- 1 teaspoon apple cider vinegar
- 4 tablespoons finely chopped fresh rosemary
- 1/2 cup grated parmesan cheese

In a mixing bowl, whisk together the AP gluten-free flour, arrowroot, millet flour, garbanzo bean flour, buttermilk powder, xanthan gum, yeast, and salt. In another bowl, whisk together the eggs, 1 cup water, 1/2 cup oil, honey, and vinegar. Add the egg mixture to the dry ingredients. With a mixer, mix for 2 minutes on medium speed. If the batter is too stiff, add a little water until a thick, shaggy batter forms. Add the rosemary and parmesan cheese. Mix until well combined. Cover with a towel and rest for 30 minutes.

Preheat oven to 400°F. Pour 3 tablespoons oil in a 2-quart dutch oven or oven-proof baking dish with a lid. Place the pan or dish in the oven (without the lid) to preheat while the dough is resting.

Carefully scrape the batter/dough into the hot pan. Smooth out the top of the dough. Brush with 2 tablespoons oil. Cover with a lid. Bake for 35–45 minutes or until the internal temperature is 200°F.

Remove bread from pan and cool before serving.

Unit 11 Questions

1. In experiment 1, how did salt affect the dough? Note any differences in texture and flavor.
2. In experiment 2, how did the different kneading times affect the dough? Note differences in texture.
3. Based on the results in experiment 3, would you recommend using GF flour as a direct substitute in basic bread recipes? Why or why not?
4. If yeast is sitting in the cupboard for a long period of time, what might happen to it? How do you test to see if it's still active?
5. Kneading is an important step in making yeast breads. How do you know if you've kneaded the dough long enough?
6. How do you know if the dough has risen long enough?
7. Based on the area where you live, what are some challenges you may face when making yeast bread? How do you overcome these challenges?
8. What are the best ways to achieve a golden brown crust (maillard reaction) on yeast breads?

NOTES

1. Vickie A. Vaclavik and Elizabeth W. Christian, *Essentials of Food Science*, 4th ed. (New York: Springer, 2014), 309–10.
2. "High-Altitude Baking," King Arthur Flour, accessed May 14, 2019, https://www.kingarthurflour.com/learn/high-altitude-baking.html.
3. "Greek Yogurt Sourdough Flatbreads," Edible Communities, accessed June 28, 2019, https://www.ediblecommunities.com/recipes/skillet-greek-yogurt-sourdough-flatbreads/.

BIBLIOGRAPHY

Edible Communities. "Greek Yogurt Sourdough Flatbreads." Accessed June 28, 2019. https://www.edible-communities.com/recipes/skillet-greek-yogurt-sourdough-flatbreads/.

King Arthur Flour. "High-Altitude Baking." Accessed May 14, 2019. https://www.kingarthurflour.com/learn/high-altitude-baking.html.

Vaclavik, Vickie A., and Elizabeth W. Christian. *Essentials of Food Science*, 4th ed. New York: Springer, 2014.

Cakes and Cookies

OBJECTIVES

- Demonstrate proper mixing techniques for cakes and cookies
- Explain different types of cakes and cookies
- Explain different types of meringues and icings
- Evaluate effect of flour, sugar, and fat on cookies
- Evaluate effects of different flours in cakes
- Use basic cooking techniques to prepare recipes

CAKES AND COOKIES[1,2]

Cakes and cookies are simple in nature. Their creations involve a few basic ingredients, typically eggs, flour, sugar, butter (or other fat), and/or chemical leavening agents. However, as with most baking, cakes and cookies vary greatly in the ratio of ingredients, creating very different results.

The ubiquitous pound cake has been around for several centuries and its name derives from the ratio of ingredients used in the recipe: 1 pound flour, 1 pound sugar, 1 pound butter, and 1 pound eggs. These ingredients would have been staples in European and American kitchens, making this a perfect cake to throw together as a simple dessert.

Cookies, developed as small cakes, get their name from the Dutch, koekje, meaning "little cake." This type of confectionary dates back several centuries and has been part of cuisines around the world.

Notable to American cuisine is the chocolate chip cookie. Created in the late 1930s, this all-American cookie was invented by two female chefs working at the

Toll House Inn in Massachusetts. The cookie has remained one of the most popular cookies baked in home kitchens for several years.

Creaming

The creaming method is the most commonly used method for mixing cookie dough and cake batter. Creaming involves mixing together the fat and sugar, helping to incorporate air into the batter and create a tender cookie or cake as an end result. After initial creaming of the fat and sugar, additional wet ingredients, if being used, are added next. The flour and other dry ingredients are sifted together and added last.

Cake Method

In the cake method, the fat is creamed with the sugar and the eggs are incorporated one at a time. The flour mixture and milk are added alternately, beginning and ending with the flour.

Folding

Some cakes require whipped egg whites or whipped cream to be folded into the batter creating light and airy texture. Folding is not the same as stirring.

To properly fold whipped egg whites into a batter, you need a large spatula and a large bowl. Place the batter in the large bowl. Add about 1/4 of the whipped egg whites to the batter and stir it in. This helps aerate the batter. Fold the rest of the whipped egg whites into batter by placing the spatula in the center of the batter and pulling it towards you. Do this while turning the bowl in one direction. Repeat folding until the mixture is combined and the whites are incorporated.

Types of Cakes

Flourless cakes

Flourless cakes are not made with gluten flour and are usually made with eggs to produce the release of carbon dioxide, causing the cake to rise.

Shortened Cakes

Shortened cakes use butter or shortening along with chemical leavening agents such as baking soda or baking powder.

Angel Food Cake

Angel food cakes are a type of sponge cake using whipped egg whites. The cake is baked in a tube pan and cooled upside to prevent collapsing

Chiffon Cake

Chiffon cakes are sponge cakes made from whipped egg whites, egg yolks, oil, and chemical leavening agent such as baking powder.

Genoise Cake

Genoise cake is a French sponge cake using both egg whites and egg yolks, but it does not use chemical leavening agents. The yolks are beaten with sugar over a double boiler until thick and pale in yellow and at the "ribbon" stage. The whites are whipped to stiff peaks. The two mixtures are folded together before baking.

Types of Cookies
Shortbread
Shortbread cookies are made with flour, sugar, and flour.

Icebox
Icebox cookies are refrigerated before baking. Usually they are rolled into a cylinder and sliced before baking.

Drop
Drop cookies are "dropped" onto the baking sheet before baking. Chocolate chip cookies are an example of dropped cookies.

Biscotti
Italian cookie that is baked twice producing a crispy, crumbly texture.

Types of Buttercreams
Simple Buttercream
Creaming together butter and powdered sugar to desired consistency. Cream cheese frosting is a type of buttercream.

French Buttercream
A boiling sugar syrup is added to whipped egg yolks creating a light foam. Softened butter is added at the end resulting in a rich icing.

Meringue Buttercream
Whipped egg whites are whipped with softened butter.

Flavoring Buttercreams
- Chocolate: add 3 ounces melted chocolate for each pound of buttercream
- Coffee: Dissolve 1 1/2 tablespoons instant coffee in 1 tablespoon warm water for each pound of buttercream
- Extracts: add according to taste
- Spirits and liqueurs: add according to taste

Types of Meringues
Common Meringue
Egg whites whipped with sugar.

Swiss Meringue
While whipping the egg whites and sugar, they are placed over simmering water. This can be made into a buttercream

Italian Meringue

Hot sugar syrup is added to whipped eggs and flavored with vanilla. It can be made into a buttercream.

Ganache

Ganache is a simple and creamy chocolate topping or filing. It can be used as an icing or whipped into a frosting. It is also the base for chocolate truffles. Ganache is made by adding hot heavy cream to chocolate and whisking until smooth.

To use ganache as a filling, use a 1:1 ratio of chocolate to cream.

To use as a soft icing or pourable glaze, use a 1:2 ratio of chocolate to cream.

EXPERIMENTS

Experiment 1: Chocolate Chip Cookie Variations

Evaluate the effect of different flours, sugars, and fats in a basic chocolate chip cookie recipe.

Basic Chocolate Chip Cookie Recipe

Objective: Test effects of flour, sugar, fat, and chilling dough on basic cookie recipe.

Basic Recipe (control)

- 1 cup + 2 tablespoons AP flour
- 1/2 teaspoon baking soda
- 1/2 teaspoon salt
- 1/2 cup unsalted butter, at room temperature
- 1/3 cup white sugar
- 1/3 cup brown sugar
- 1 large egg, at room temperature
- 1/2 teaspoon vanilla
- 1/2 cup chocolate chips

Preheat oven to 350°F.

In a small bowl, whisk together the flour, baking soda, and salt. Set aside.

In a mixing bowl, cream together the butter, white sugar, and brown sugar until light and fluffy. Add the egg and vanilla. Mix well. Stir in the dry ingredients. Mix well to combine. Stir in the chocolate chips.

Drop by spoonfuls onto a cookie sheet. Bake until golden brown, about 10–12 minutes. Cool on a wire rack.

Variations:

- Replace white sugar with brown sugar (use all brown sugar)
- Replace brown sugar with white sugar (use all white sugar)
- Replace all the sugar (brown and white) with powdered sugar

- Use melted butter in place of softened butter
- Use melted brown butter in place of the softened butter (brown the butter to an amber color)
- Use olive oil in place of butter
- Use cake flour instead of AP flour
- Use whole wheat flour instead of AP flour
- Chill dough for 2 hours before baking

Variation	Flavor	Texture	Appearance
Basic (control)			
All brown sugar			
All white sugar			
Powdered sugar			
Melted butter			
Brown butter			
Olive oil			
Cake flour			
Whole wheat flour			
Chilled dough			

Experiment 2: Cakes and Different Flours

Evaluate the effect of over or under kneading in making yeast bread.

Basic Recipe (Control)

- 1 1/2 cups cake flour
- 2 1/2 teaspoons baking powder
- 1/2 teaspoon salt
- 3/4 cup sugar
- 1/4 cup unsalted butter, at room temperature
- 1 large egg, at room temperature
- 1/2 cup whole milk

Grease and flour an 8-inch cake pan. Set aside. Preheat oven to 350°F.

In a small bowl, whisk together the flour, baking powder, and salt. Set aside.

In a mixing bowl, cream together the sugar, and butter until fluffy. Add the egg and mix well. Add 1/3 of the flour mixture. Mix well. Add 1/2 of the milk to the batter and mix well. Add another 1/3 of the flour mixture to the batter; mix well. Add remaining milk; mix well. Add remaining flour and mix well.

Pour batter into the greased baking pan. Bake for 25–30 minutes. Cool and remove from the pan.

Variations:

- Bread flour
- Whole wheat flour
- Gluten-free AP flour
- Spelt
- Rye flour

Cake	Appearance	Flavor	Texture
Basic (control)			
Bread flour			
Whole wheat flour			
Gluten free			
Spelt			
Rye			

RECIPES

Shortbread Cookies

Yield: 3–4 dozen cookies

- 1 cup unsalted butter, at room temperature
- 1/2 cup powdered sugar
- 1/2 teaspoon vanilla extract
- 2 cups AP flour
- 1/2 teaspoon salt

Preheat oven to 325°F. Line 2 baking sheets with parchment paper. Set aside.

In a large bowl, cream together the butter and powdered sugar. Add the vanilla. Mix well. Add the flour and salt. Mix until well combined. Roll out dough on a floured surface to about 1/4 inch thick.

Using cookie cutters, biscuit cutters, or a pizza slicer, cut out shapes. Place shapes on baking sheets. Pierce with a fork.

Bake 20 minutes or until just lightly browned.

Cool on a wire rack.

Icebox Cookies
Yield: about 4 dozen cookies

- 6 cups AP flour
- 1 1/2 teaspoons baking powder
- 1 teaspoon baking soda
- 1 teaspoon ground nutmeg
- 1 teaspoon ground cinnamon
- 1/2 teaspoon salt
- 2 cups unsalted butter, softened
- 1 cup sugar
- 1 cup packed brown sugar
- 3 large eggs
- 1 teaspoon vanilla extract
- 2 cups chopped walnuts or pecans

Sift together first five ingredients; set aside. In a bowl, cream butter and sugars. Add eggs and vanilla; beat well. Add dry ingredients; mix well. Stir in nuts.

Divide dough into four parts and shape into rolls 11 inches long by 1 and 1/2 inches wide. Wrap in parchment or wax paper and chill overnight.

Slice cookies 3/8-in. thick. Bake on greased baking sheets at 350° for about 10 minutes.

Biscotti
Yield: about 2 dozen biscotti

- 1 1/2 cups all-purpose flour
- 1/2 cup yellow cornmeal
- 1 1/2 teaspoons baking powder
- 1/4 teaspoon salt
- 1 stick (8 tablespoons) unsalted butter, at room temperature
- 1 cup sugar
- 2 large eggs
- 1 1/2 teaspoons almond or vanilla extract
- 3/4 cup sliced almonds

Preheat oven to 350°F. Line a baking sheet with parchment paper.

In a bowl, whisk together the flour, cornmeal, baking powder, and salt.

Working with a stand mixer, preferably fitted with a paddle attachment, or with a hand mixer in a large bowl, beat the butter and sugar together at medium speed for 3 minutes, until very smooth. Add the eggs and continue to beat, scraping down the sides of the bowl, for another 2 minutes, or until the mixture is light, smooth and creamy. Beat in the almond extract. Reduce the mixer speed to low and add the dry ingredients, mixing only until they are incorporated. You will have a soft, stick-to-your-fingers dough that will ball up around the paddle or beaters. Scrape down the paddle and bowl, toss in the almonds and mix just to blend.

Scrape half the dough onto one side of the baking sheet. Form the dough into a log about 12 inches long and 1 1/2 inches wide. The log will be more rectangular than domed. Form a second log with the remaining dough on the other side of the baking sheet.

Bake for 15 minutes, or until the logs are lightly golden but still soft and springy to the touch. Transfer the baking sheet to a rack and cool the logs on the baking sheet for 30 minutes.

Transfer the logs to a cutting board and, with a serrated knife, trim the ends and cut the logs into 3/4-inch-thick slices. Return the slices to the baking sheet—this time standing them up like a marching band—and slide the sheet back into the oven.

Bake the biscotti for another 15 minutes, or until they are golden and firm. Transfer them to racks and cool to room temperature.

Variations

- Dried fruit: add 1/3 cup dried fruit of choice to the dough
- Spices: add spices as desired
  - 1 teaspoon ground cinnamon
  - 1/2 to 1 teaspoon ground ginger
  - 1 teaspoon ground cardamom and 1 tablespoon finely grated orange zest
- Substitute the almonds for walnuts, pecans, or hazelnuts
- Chocolate: replace 1/4 cup of the flour with 1/4 cup cocoa powder

Oatmeal Raisin Cookies
Yield: about 3 dozen cookies

- 3/4 cup whole wheat flour
- 1/2 cup AP flour
- 1 teaspoon baking powder
- 1 teaspoon ground cinnamon
- 1 teaspoon salt
- 1 1/2 cups walnuts
- 1 cup unsalted butter, at room temperature
- 1 cup packed brown sugar
- 1 cup sugar
- 2 large eggs, at room temperature
- 2 teaspoons vanilla extract
- 3 cups rolled oats
- 1 1/2 cups raisins

Preheat oven to 350°F. Line a sheet pan with parchment paper. Set aside.

In a small bowl, whisk together the whole wheat flour, AP flour, baking powder, cinnamon, and salt. Set aside.

In the bowl of an electric mixer fitted with the paddle attachment, cream the butter, brown sugar, and sugar until light and fluffy. Add the eggs, one at a time. Add the vanilla. Add the flour mixture. Mix well. Add the oats, raisins, and chopped nuts. Mix until just combined.

Drop by spoonfuls onto the sheet pan. Bake for 12–15 minutes or until lightly browned. Transfer the cookies to a wire rack and cool completely.

Snickerdoodles
Yield: about 2–3 dozen cookies

Cookie

- 3 3/4 cups AP flour
- 1/2 teaspoon baking soda
- 1/2 teaspoon cream of tartar
- 1/2 teaspoon salt
- 1 cup unsalted butter, at room temperature
- 1 cup sugar
- 1 cup packed brown sugar
- 2 large eggs, at room temperature
- 1/4 cup heavy cream
- 1 teaspoon vanilla

Topping

- 1/2 cup sugar
- 1 teaspoon ground cinnamon

Preheat oven to 350°F. Line a sheet pan with parchment paper. Set aside.

In a small bowl, whisk together the flour, baking soda, cream of tartar, and salt. Set aside.

In the bowl of an electric mixer fitted with the paddle attachment, cream the butter, sugar, and brown sugar until light and fluffy. Add the eggs, one at a time. Add the cream and vanilla. Add the flour mixture. Mix well. The cookie dough should be quite stiff.

In a small bowl, mix together the topping ingredients. Roll the cookie dough into 1-inch balls and roll in the cinnamon sugar mixture. Place on the baking sheet. Bake for 10-12 minutes or until lightly golden brown. Cool completely on a wire rack.

Pistachio Date Cookies

Yield: 1-2 dozen cookies

- 1/2 cup unsalted butter, at room temperature
- 1/2 cup sugar
- 2 large egg yolks
- 1 tablespoon vanilla extract
- 1 teaspoon orange zest
- 1 1/2 cups flour
- 1/2 cup finely chopped dates
- 1/2 cup ground pistachios
- Powdered sugar for dredging

Preheat oven to 400°F. Line baking sheet with parchment paper.

In a mixing bowl, cream together the butter, sugar, egg yolks, vanilla, and orange zest until well combined. Add the flour. Mix well. Add the dates and nuts. Mix well.

Roll 1-2 tablespoons of the cookie dough in your hands. Shape into a crescent. Place on a baking sheet. Bake 10-12 minutes or until the cookies are lightly browned. Remove from pan and place on wire rack. Cool for 10 minutes. Roll in powdered sugar.

Chocolate Cake

Yield: 1 9-inch cake

- 5 ounces dark chocolate (60% or higher)
- 2 tablespoons espresso
- 4 ounces unsalted butter, at room temperature
- 4 ounces sugar
- 4 large eggs, at room temperature
- 3.5 ounces almond flour (meal)
- 1 ounce all-purpose flour
- 1 tablespoon unsweetened cocoa powder
- 1 tablespoon baking powder

Ganache

- 1/2 cup heavy cream
- 4 ounces dark chocolate (60% or higher)

Lightly grease a 9-inch cake pan and line the bottom with parchment paper (grease the paper). Set aside.

Preheat oven to 350°F.

In the top of a double boiler, melt the chocolate. Stir until smooth. Add the amaretto. Set aside.

In the bowl of a stand mixer, cream together the butter and sugar until light and fluffy. Add the eggs one at a time, mixing well after each addition. In a small bowl, stir together the dry ingredients. Add the dry ingredients the egg mixture. Mix well. Pour in the melted chocolate and mix well to combine.

Pour batter into the prepared pan. Bake for 35–40 minutes or until the cake begins to pull away from the sides of the pan. Remove from oven and cool completely. Invert cake onto a plate. Set aside while you make the ganache.

To make the ganache, warm the cream over medium heat until it begins to steam (right before it boils). Remove the cream from the heat and add the chocolate. Stir until melted. Pour the ganache over the cake. Allow to set for 30 minutes before serving.

Marble Cake

Yield: 1 12 × 17-inch cake

- 13 ounces cake flour
- 1 tablespoon baking powder
- 3/4 teaspoon salt
- 6 ounces unsalted butter, at room temperature
- 13 ounces sugar
- 12 fluid ounces whole milk
- 1/2 teaspoon vanilla extract
- 2 ounces dark chocolate, melted
- 1/8 teaspoon baking soda
- 2 teaspoons brewed espresso
- 6 large egg whites
- cocoa fudge frosting (recipe follows)

Preheat oven to 350°F. Lightly grease a 12 × 17-inch sheet pan. Line with parchment paper. In a bowl, whisk together the flour, baking powder, and salt. Set aside.

In a mixing bowl, cream together the butter and sugar until light and fluffy. Add the flour and milk alternately, beginning and ending with the flour. Stir in the vanilla.

Divide the batter into 2 equal portions. Add the melted chocolate, baking soda, and coffee to one portion. Mix well.

Whip the egg whites until stiff peaks form. Divide the whipped egg whites evenly between the 2 batters. Fold the whites into each portion.

Spoon the batters onto the baking sheet alternating the 2 colors. Pull a butter knife through the batters to swirl the colors together.

Bake for 25 minutes. Allow to cool about 15 minutes before frosting.

Cocoa Fudge Frosting

- 1 pound powdered sugar
- 1 ounce cocoa powder
- pinch of salt
- 2 ounces butter, melted
- 1/4 cup whole milk

In a bowl, whisk together the powdered sugar, cocoa, and salt. Add the butter and milk. Mix until smooth.

Angel Food Cake
Yield: 1 cake

- 1 1/2 cups powdered sugar
- 1 cup cake flour
- 1/4 teaspoon salt
- 12 egg whites
- 1 1/2 teaspoons cream of tartar
- 1 cup granulated sugar
- 2 teaspoons vanilla extract

Preheat oven to 375°F.

In a small bowl, whisk together the powdered sugar, flour, and salt. Set aside.

In a mixing bowl, beat the egg whites and cream of tartar until foamy. Gradually beat in the sugar and increase the speed to high. Mix until stiff peaks form. Stir in the vanilla. Do not over beat the eggs.

Sift the flour mixture over the whipped egg whites and fold the flour gently into the whites. Fold until combined. Pour batter in an ungreased angel food tube pan. Run a butter knife though the batter to get rid of any air bubbles.

Bake for 30–35 minutes. The cake will spring back when it's done. Invert pan so that it cools upside down. Cool completely.

Run a knife around the cake edges to release it from the pan. Place on a serving platter and drizzle glaze over the top. Slice with a serrated bread knife.

Vanilla Glaze

- 1/3 cup whole milk
- 2 cups powdered sugar
- 1 teaspoon vanilla extract

Whisk the ingredients together to desired consistency. Add more milk or powdered sugar as necessary.

Flourless Chocolate Cake
Yield: 1 9-inch cake

- 1/2 cup unsalted butter
- 7 ounces dark chocolate
- 5 eggs, separated
- 2 ounces sugar
- Powdered sugar as needed

Preheat the oven to 400°F. Butter a 9-inch cake or spring form pan. Line with parchment paper. Butter the paper. Dust lightly with flour or powdered sugar, tapping out the excess.

Place the butter and chocolate in a double boiler set over simmering water. Stir until melted. Whisk the egg yolks into the melted chocolate. Mix to combine well. Place the chocolate egg mixture into a large bowl. Set aside.

In a mixing bowl, whip the egg whites until foamy and soft peaks have formed. Add the sugar and continue beating until stiff peaks form.

Fold the egg whites into the chocolate mixture. Fold until well incorporated. Pour into the pan. Bake for 10 minutes. Lower the temperature to 350°F and continue baking until done, about 40 minutes.

Cool for 10 minutes in the pan and then remove. Cool completely on a wire rack. Dust with powdered sugar.

Carrot Cake

Yield: 2 9-inch cakes

- 12 ounces AP flour
- 1 teaspoon baking soda
- 1 teaspoon baking powder
- 1/2 teaspoon salt
- 1/2 teaspoon ground cinnamon
- 1/4 teaspoon ground allspice
- 1/4 teaspoon ground nutmeg
- 12 ounces grated carrots
- 10 ounces sugar
- 2 ounces brown sugar
- 3 large eggs, at room temperature
- 6 ounces plain or vanilla yogurt
- 6 fluid ounces canola or olive oil
- 1/2 cup chopped walnuts (optional)

Preheat oven to 350°F. Grease and flour two 9-inch cake pans.* Set aside.

In a bowl, whisk together the flour, baking soda, baking powder, salt, and spices. Add the grated carrot and toss to combine. Set aside.

In another bowl, whisk together the sugar, brown sugar, eggs, yogurt, and oil. Stir in the carrot mixture. Mix well. Fold in the nuts. Pour batter into the prepared pans, dividing as evenly as possible.

Bake for 30-40 minutes or until the cake starts to pull away from the sides of the pan or a toothpick inserted in the center comes out clean. Cool cakes for 10 minutes in the pan. Remove from the pan and cool completely on a wire rack.

Once cool, frost with cream cheese frosting.

*The cake can be made into cupcakes (bake at 350°F for 20-25 minutes) or as a single layer in a 9 or 10 inch springform pan (bake at 350°F for 30 minutes; reduce heat to 325°F and bake for additional 15-20 minutes).

Cream Cheese Frosting

- 8 ounces cream cheese, at room temperature
- 2 ounces unsalted butter, at room temperature
- 9 ounces powdered sugar
- 1 teaspoon vanilla

With a mixer, cream together the cream cheese and butter. Add the powdered sugar and vanilla. Beat until well incorporated. Add more sugar as needed to achieve desired consistency.

Pound Cake
Yield: 1 9 × 5-inch loaf

- 1 cup unsalted butter, at room temperature
- 1 cup sugar
- 4 large eggs, at room temperature
- 2 teaspoons vanilla extract (or 1 tablespoon lemon zest)
- 1/2 teaspoon salt
- 2 cups AP flour

Preheat oven to 350°F. Butter and flour a 9 × 5-inch loaf pan; set aside.

Using an electric mixer on high speed, beat butter and sugar until light and fluffy. Add eggs one at a time, beating well after each addition; add vanilla and salt. With mixer on low, gradually add flour, beating just until combined (do not overmix).

Bake until a toothpick inserted in center of cake comes out clean, about 1 hour (tent with aluminum foil if browning too quickly). Let cool in pan 15 minutes. Invert onto a wire rack, and turn upright to cool completely. Pour glaze over top of cake if desired.

Glaze

- 2 cups powdered sugar
- 2–3 tablespoons whole milk or lemon juice
- 1 teaspoon vanilla extract (if using milk) or 1 teaspoon lemon zest (if using lemon juice)

Mix ingredients together to desired consistency. Pour over the cake.

GF Garbanzo Bean Cake
Yield: 1 9-inch cake

- 8 ounces semi-sweet or bittersweet chocolate chips
- 1 (15-ounce) can chickpeas (garbanzo beans), drained and rinsed
- 4 large eggs
- 3/4 cup sugar
- 1/2 teaspoon baking powder
- 1 teaspoon vanilla extract
- powdered sugar for dusting

Preheat oven to 350°F. Grease a 9-inch cake or spring form pan. Line with parchment paper. Grease the paper. Set aside.

Melt the chocolate in the microwave, being careful not to burn it. Set aside.

Place the chickpeas and eggs in a food processor. Pulse until smooth. Add the sugar, baking powder, and vanilla. Pulse to blend. Pour in the melted chocolate and blend until smooth. Pour the batter into the prepared pan.

Bake for 45 minutes or until a toothpick inserted in the center comes out clean. Cool cake in pan for 10 minutes. Remove from pan and cool completely on a wire rack.

Orange Chiffon Cake
Yield: 1 10-inch cake

- 8 ounces cake flour
- 12 ounces sugar
- 1 tablespoon baking powder
- 1 teaspoon salt
- 4 fluid ounces canola oil
- 6 egg yolks
- 2 fluid ounces water
- 4 fluid ounces orange juice
- 1 tablespoon orange zest
- 1 tablespoon vanilla extract
- 8 ounces (by weight) egg whites

Glaze

- 3 ounces powdered sugar
- 2 tablespoons orange juice
- 2 teaspoons orange zest

Preheat oven to 325°F.

In a large bowl, whisk together the flour, 6 ounces sugar, baking powder, and salt. In a separate bowl, whisk together the oil, egg yolks, water, juice, zest, and vanilla. Add the oil mixture to the flour mixture. Stir to combine well.

In a mixing bowl, beat the egg whites until foamy. Slowly beat in the remaining 6 ounces sugar. Whip until stiff peaks form.

Stir 1/4 of the egg whites into the oil and flour mixture. Fold in the remaining egg whites until well incorporated. Pour batter into an ungreased 10-inch angel food cake pan.

Bake for 1 hour. Invert cake so that it can cool upside down. Cool completely. Remove from pan.

In a small bowl, stir the glaze ingredients together until smooth. Drizzle over the cake. Serve.

Tomato Basil Cake with Goat Cheese Frosting
Yield: 1 9 × 13-inch cake

Cake

- 2 cups AP flour
- 1 tablespoon baking powder
- 1 teaspoon baking soda
- 1/2 teaspoon salt
- 1/2 teaspoon pepper
- 1 cup packed fresh basil leaves
- 3/4 cup sugar
- 2 medium tomatoes, seeded
- 2 tablespoons tomato paste
- 3 large eggs, at room temperature
- 6 tablespoons extra virgin olive oil
- 1/4 cup sun-dried tomatoes in oil, chopped

Goat Cheese Frosting

- 8 ounces goat cheese, at room temperature
- 4 ounces cream cheese (or mascarpone cheese), at room temperature
- 1–2 tablespoons cream
- 2–3 tablespoons chopped fresh basil
- salt and pepper, to taste

Preheat oven 350°F. Grease and flour a 9 × 13 cake pan (or a 1/2 sheet pan). Set aside.

In a bowl, whisk together the flour, baking powder, baking soda, salt, and pepper. Set aside.

In a food processor, combine the basil and sugar. Pulse for 5 seconds. Scrape down the sides of the bowl and add the tomatoes, tomato paste, eggs, and olive oil. Pulse several times to mix together. Pour mixture into the flour mixture. Stir to combine. Fold in the sun-dried tomatoes. Be careful not to overmix the batter.

Pour batter into prepared pan. Bake for 30–40 minutes or until a toothpick inserted in the center comes out clean. Cool on a wire rack.

Frosting: Mix together the goat cheese, cream cheese, and 1 tablespoon cream. Whip until thick and combined well. Add additional cream as necessary to achieve desired consistency. Mix in the basil, salt, and pepper.

Spread frosting over the top of the cake.

Beet Cake

Yield: 2 9-inch cakes

- 1 (15-ounce) can diced beets, drained
- 1 cup unsalted butter, at room temperature
- 1 3/4 cup packed brown sugar
- 3 large eggs, at room temperature
- 1 teaspoon vanilla extract
- 1/2 cup cocoa powder
- 1 1/2 cups whole wheat pastry flour
- 2 teaspoons baking soda
- 1/2 teaspoon salt
- 1/2 cup walnuts, chopped
- white chocolate buttercream frosting (recipe below)

Preheat oven to 350°F. Grease two 9-inch cake pans. Line with parchment paper. Grease the paper. Dust with flour, tapping out the excess. Set aside.

Place the beets in a food processor. Pulse until smooth.

In a large bowl, cream together the butter and sugar until light and fluffy. Add eggs one at a time, beating well after each addition. Stir in the vanilla and the beet puree.

In a separate bowl, whisk together the cocoa powder, flour, baking soda, and salt. Stir flour mixture into the butter mixture. Mix until well combined. Stir in the walnuts. Pour batter into the prepared pans, dividing evenly between the two.

Bake for 35–45 minutes or until a toothpick inserted in the center comes out clean. Cool for 10 minutes in the pans. Remove from pans and cool completely on a wire rack.

White Chocolate Buttercream Frosting

- 1 cup unsalted butter, at room temperature
- 4 ounces white chocolate, melted
- 4 cups powdered sugar
- 2 tablespoons cream

Mix together the butter and chocolate. Place the powdered sugar in a mixing bowl. Add the butter mixture and beat until smooth. Add the cream as needed to get desired frosting consistency.

Coffee Cake
Yield: 1 9 × 13-inch cake

Topping/Filling

- 1/2 cup sugar
- 1/2 cup chopped pecans or walnuts
- 1 teaspoon cinnamon

Cake

- 2 1/2 cups AP flour
- 1/4 cup buttermilk powder
- 1 tablespoon baking powder
- 1/4 teaspoon salt
- 1 1/4 cups sugar
- 1 cup sour cream (or plain yogurt)
- 1/2 cup canola oil
- 4 large eggs
- 1 teaspoon vanilla extract
- 1/2 cup shredded coconut, finely chopped

Preheat oven to 350°F. Generously butter a 9 × 13-inch baking pan.[i]

Make the topping: Combine sugar, nuts, and cinnamon in a small bowl and mix well. Set aside.

In a medium bowl, whisk together the flour, buttermilk powder, baking powder, and salt. Set aside.

In a mixing bowl, fitted with the paddle attachment, mix together the sugar, sour cream, and oil. Add eggs one at a time, beating well after each addition. Add the vanilla.

With the mixer on low speed, add the flour mixture into the egg mixture. Mix well. Fold in in the coconut. Pour half of the batter into prepared baking pan. Sprinkle with half of the nut topping mixture. Pour remaining batter over the nut mixture. Spread to edges of the pan. Sprinkle with remaining nut mixture.

Bake for 45 minutes, or until a cake tester comes out clean. Cool before serving.

---

i   The cake can also be baked in a Bundt pan.

Spice Cake

Yield: 1 Bundt cake

Cake

- 2 1/2 cups AP flour
- 1 teaspoon baking soda
- 1 teaspoon ground cinnamon
- 1/2 teaspoon ground nutmeg
- 1/2 teaspoon ground cloves
- 1/4 teaspoon ground allspice
- 1/2 teaspoon salt
- 1/2 cup unsalted butter, at room temperature
- 1 1/2 cups brown sugar
- 1/2 cup white sugar
- 3 large eggs, at room temperature
- 1 cup buttermilk, at room temperature

Glaze

- 2 tablespoons fresh orange juice
- 2 tablespoons unsalted butter, melted
- 1–2 cups powdered sugar

Preheat the oven to 350°F. Generously grease and flour a Bundt pan. Set aside.

In a small bowl, whisk together the flour, baking soda, cinnamon, nutmeg, cloves, allspice, and salt. Set aside.

In a mixing bowl, cream together the butter, brown sugar, and white sugar until light and fluffy. Add the in the eggs, one at a time, mixing well after each addition. Add the buttermilk. Mix well. Stir in the dry ingredients to the butter mixture and mix to combine well. Pour batter into the prepared pan. Bake for 1 hour and 15 minutes or until a toothpick inserted in the center comes out clean.

Cool the cake for 10 minutes in the pan. Invert the pan to remove the cake. Allow it to cool completely on a wire rack.

Make the glaze:

In a small bowl, stir together the orange juice and butter. Add enough powdered sugar to make a thick glaze (not too thick and not too thin). Pour glaze over the cake.

Serve.

Simple Buttercream

Yield: 2 cups

- 1 cup unsalted butter, at room temperature
- 4 cups powdered sugar, sifted
- 1/4 cup whole milk or heavy cream
- 2 teaspoons vanilla extract

Whip the butter with the paddle attachment of a stand mixer. Add 3 cups of powdered sugar. Add the milk and vanilla. Add remaining powdered sugar as needed to achieve desired consistency.

French Buttercream

Yield: 2 cups

- 1/2 cup sugar
- 3 tablespoons water
- 4 large egg yolks
- 1 cup unsalted butter, cubed, at room temperature
- 1/2 teaspoon vanilla extract
- pinch of kosher salt

Heat the sugar and water in a small saucepan over low heat to dissolve the sugar. When sugar is dissolved, increase heat to medium high and bring to a boil.

As the sugar is boiling, place the yolks in a mixing bowl. Beat until thick and pale yellow.

Cook the sugar syrup to a temperature of 235°F.[ii] Remove from heat. As you whip the yolks, slowly drizzle in the hot syrup. Whip until the mixing bowl feels cool to the touch and the yolks have cooled to room temperature.

Whip in the butter, one cube at a time, beating well after each addition. Add the vanilla and salt. Mix well. If mixture starts to separate, continue beating until it is creamy and smooth.

Use immediately or refrigerate for up to two weeks. If refrigerated, bring to room temperature before using. Beat until smooth and spreadable again.

Italian Meringue Buttercream

Yield: 2 cups

- 1 1/4 cups sugar
- 2/3 cup water
- 5 large egg whites
- 1/4 teaspoon cream of tartar
- 1 pound unsalted butter, cubed
- 1 teaspoon vanilla extract

---

ii   Adjust for high altitudes as discussed in unit 14.

Bring the sugar and water to a boil in a small saucepan over medium heat. Boil the mixture until it reaches 238°F.[iii]

While the sugar is boiling, whip the egg whites in a mixing bowl until foamy. Add the cream of tartar and beat on high until stiff peaks form. Do not overbeat.

With the mixer running, add the hot syrup into the whites. Beat on high speed until it stops steaming, 3–5 minutes. Add the butter, one cube at a time. Beat until it is a spreadable consistency, about 5 minutes. If mixture separates, continue beating until smooth.

Swiss Meringue Buttercream
Yield: 2 cups

- 9 large egg whites, at room temperature
- 1 1/2 cups sugar
- 1 1/2 pounds unsalted butter, cubed, at room temperature

Place the egg whites and sugar in a metal bowl set over simmering water. Whisk until the sugar melts and the mixture becomes thin and warm.

Remove bowl from the water and whip on high speed until stiff peaks form, about 5 minutes. Continue beating on low speed until the mixture cools, about 5 minutes. Beat in the butter, one cube at a time, beating well after each addition. If mixtures starts to separate, continue beating until it is creamy and smooth.

Unit 12 Questions

1. In experiment 1, note the differences between the types of chocolate chip cookies made. Answer the following questions.
   a. Which cookie had the best overall flavor? Worst flavor?
   b. Which cookie had the best texture? Which one was most crumbly?
   c. Which cookie was most greasy? Why was this?
   d. What were the effects of chilling the dough prior to baking?
   e. What were the effects of the different flours used: AP, cake, whole wheat?
   f. What were the effects of the sugars on the end result: both, all white, all brown? Why was this?
2. In experiment 2, note the differences in texture and flavor among the cakes baked with different flours. Were any drier that others? Why would this be? Were any denser? Explain.
3. Why is it important for the ingredients (eggs, milk, butter) to be at room temperature prior to mixing cakes or cookies?
4. Why is flour or powdered sugar sifted before adding to the batter?

---

iii   Adjust for high altitudes as discussed in unit 14.

5. Explain why butter and sugar are creamed together before adding the egg(s) in some recipes?
6. In making cakes, the flour and milk are added alternately. Why is this?
7. Why is cake flour optimal for baking cakes?
8. What is the function of the eggs in the flourless chocolate cake and the garbanzo beans in the GF garbanzo bean cake?

NOTES

1. "History of Cookies," What's Cooking America, accessed May 14, 2019, https://whatscookingamerica.net/History/CookieHistory.htm.
2. "History of Pound Cake," What's Cooking America, accessed May 14, 2019, https://whatscookingamerica.net/History/Cakes/PoundCake.htm.

BIBLIOGRAPHY

What's Cooking America. "History of Cookies." Accessed May 14, 2019. https://whatscookingamerica.net/History/CookieHistory.htm.

What's Cooking America. "History of Pound Cake." Accessed May 14, 2019. https://whatscookingamerica.net/History/Cakes/PoundCake.htm.

Pastries

- Explain different pastries and pastry doughs
- Evaluate different fats in pie pastries
- Use basic cooking techniques to prepare recipes

PASTRIES[1]

The term pastry encompasses many products made from stiff dough comprised of flour and butter. Types of pastries include pies, tarts, and puff pastry. When made properly, these products turn into tender and flaky baked goods. When making pie crust or puff pastry, the butter used needs to stay cold in order to create steam and force the pastry to rise during baking. Pastries can be sweet or savory and can be served at any course. Some pastries are best served as appetizers or as a side dish to an entrée while others will be found at the breakfast table or as a dessert. Pastries are very versatile and are good for many occasions.

Pie Pastry

Pie pastry is made by cutting butter into flour and adding cold water. The dough requires refrigeration for at least one hour prior to baking. This ensures the butter stays cold, resulting in a tender, flaky pie crust.

Tart Pastry

Similar to pie pastry, tart pastry can be made with the same ingredients. However, some recipes call for either eggs or oil added to create a "mealy" crust, as opposed to a flaky crust. A mealy crust will hold its shape better than a pie pastry. Tarts are usually baked in a pan with removable bottoms.

Puff Pastry

Puff pastry is made through a process of layering butter and dough, creating a very flaky, delicate, and tender pastry. When baked, the pastry puffs up due to amount of cold butter folding into layers in the dough.

Phyllo Dough (or Filo)

Phyllo dough is a very thin dough from Greece and other parts of the Mediterranean used to make baklava and other flaky pastries. Because it is not made with much fat and the sheets are stretched paper thin, the phyllo is brushed with melted butter or oil and stacked on each other to create flaky layers when baked.

Strudel Dough

Strudel dough is similar to phyllo dough in that it is a very thin dough made of flour, water, and a small amount of fat.

Galette

Galettes are a type of free-form pie using either a pie or tart pastry.

Pate a Choux

Pate a choux (or choux paste) is a stiff batter used to make profiteroles and eclairs. Choux paste is made by cooking water, butter, and flour together and adding eggs to form a thick paste-like batter. The batter is piped into shapes and baked. The center of the profiterole or eclair creates and air pocket than can be filled with a soft cheese mixture or pastry cream.

BAKING PIE CRUSTS

Blind baking refers to partially or fully baking the pie crust prior to filling it. Some pie crusts are partially baked prior to filling to decrease the chance of creating a soggy crust. Due to its wet filling, pumpkin pie pastry is partially baked prior to filling.

Other times, the crust needs to be fully baked because the filling will not need additional cooking or require a short time in the oven.

Partial Blind Baked Crust

1. Preheat oven.
2. Roll out pastry and fit it into a pie plate (or tart pan) and decoratively crimp the edges.
3. Prick the bottom of the pie with a fork. Line the pastry with foil. Fill with pie weights or dried beans.
4. Bake for 10 minutes.
5. Remove from oven and remove foil and pie weights.
6. Pour in filling. Bake according to recipe instructions.

Fully Blind Baked Crust

1. Preheat oven.
2. Roll out pastry and fit it into a pie plate (or tart pan) and decoratively crimp the edges.
3. Prick the bottom of the pie with a fork. Line the pastry with foil. Fill with pie weights or dried beans.
4. Bake for 10 minutes.
5. Remove from oven and remove foil and pie weights
6. Return pan to the oven. Bake for an additional 10–15 minutes or until golden brown.
7. Remove from oven and proceed with recipe instructions.

EXPERIMENTS

Experiment 1: Pie Pastry Variations

Evaluate the differences between pie pastries made with different fats.

Basic Pie Pastry

- 1/2 cup AP flour
- 1/4 teaspoon salt
- 1/4 teaspoon sugar
- 2 tablespoons cold butter
- 1 1/2 tablespoons cold water

Mix together the flour, salt, and sugar. With a pastry blender, cut the butter into the flour mixture until it resembles coarse meal. Add the cold water and mix until the dough starts to come together, adding more water as necessary if the dough is too dry. Form into a ball and wrap in plastic. Refrigerate for 1 hour.

Preheat oven to 425°F. Line baking sheet with parchment paper.

Roll pastry out on a floured surface. Cut into rectangles or squares. Place on a baking sheet. Bake for 10 minutes or until golden brown. Cool before serving.

Variations:

- Replace the butter with:
  - shortening
  - lard
  - solid coconut oil
- Roll out a store bought pie pastry and bake as described above.

Variation	Flavor	Texture	Appearance
Basic (control)			
Shortening			
Lard			
Coconut oil			
Store bought			

Experiment 2: Pie Pastry and Effects of Softened or Melted Fats

Evaluate the effect of room temperature or melted fats in pie pastry.

Basic Pie Pastry

- 1/2 cup AP flour
- 1/4 teaspoon salt
- 1/4 teaspoon sugar
- 2 tablespoons cold butter
- 1 1/2 tablespoons cold water

Mix together the flour, salt, and sugar. With a pastry blender, cut the butter into the flour mixture until it resembles coarse meal. Add the cold water and mix until the dough starts to come together, adding more water as necessary if the dough is too dry. Form into a ball and wrap in plastic. Refrigerate for 1 hour.

Preheat oven to 425°F. Line baking sheet with parchment paper.

Roll pastry out on a floured surface. Cut into rectangles or squares. Place on a baking sheet. Bake for 10 minutes or until golden brown. Cool before serving.

Variations:

- Replace the cold butter and water with:
  - melted butter and warm water
  - room temperature butter (softened) and lukewarm water

Variation	Appearance	Flavor	Texture
Basic (control)			
Melted butter			
Room temperature butter			

RECIPES

Double Pie Pastry

- 2 1/4 cups AP flour
- 1 tablespoon sugar
- 1 teaspoon salt
- 1 cup cold unsalted butter, cut into cubes
- 1/2 cup cold water

Place flour, sugar, and salt in a food processor. Pulse for 10 seconds to combine. Add the butter; pulse several times until the mixture resembles coarse meal.

With the processor running, slowly pour in the cold water. Pulse until the mixture starts to come together and form a dough.

Divide dough in half. Flatten each one slightly. Wrap each half in plastic. Refrigerate for at least 1 hour. Dough can be kept refrigerated for up to 2 days or frozen up to 2 months.

Single Pie Pastry

- 1 1/2 cups AP flour
- 1 1/2 teaspoons sugar
- 1/2 teaspoon salt
- 1/2 cup cold unsalted butter, cut into cubes
- 1/4 cup cold water

Place flour, sugar, and salt in a food processor. Pulse for 5–10 seconds to combine. Add the butter; pulse several times until the mixture resembles coarse meal.

With the processor running, slowly pour in the cold water. Pulse until the mixture starts to come together and form a dough.

Bring dough together into a ball and flatten slightly. Wrap in plastic. Refrigerate for at least 1 hour. Dough can be kept refrigerated for up to 2 days or frozen up to 2 months.

Tart Dough

- 1 cup AP Flour
- 1 tablespoon sugar
- 1/2 teaspoon salt
- 6 tablespoons chilled unsalted butter, cut into pieces
- 1 large egg, beaten to blend
- 1–2 tablespoons water, if needed

In a bowl, whisk together the flour, sugar, and salt. Add the butter. Using a pastry blender, cut the butter into the flour until mixture resembles coarse meal with a few pea-size pieces remaining. Drizzle egg over butter mixture and mix gently with a fork until dough just comes together. Add water if the mixture is too dry and crumbly.

Turn out dough onto a lightly floured surface and knead until smooth (a few dry spots are okay). Form dough into a disk. Wrap in plastic and chill until firm, at least 2 hours.

Tarte Tatin

- 6 to 8 large, firm-fleshed apples, such as braeburn or golden delicious
- 6 tablespoons salted butter, at room temperature
- 2/3 cup granulated or light brown sugar
- 1 sheet puff pastry, about 8 ounces

At least one day before you plan to cook the tart, prepare the apples: Slice off the bottom of each apple so it has a flat base. Peel and quarter the apples. Use a small sharp knife to trim the hard cores and seeds from the center of each quarter; don't worry about being too neat. Transfer to a bowl and refrigerate, lightly covered, for at least one day or up to three days.

When ready to cook, heat oven to 375°F. Spread the butter in a thick coat on the bottom of a 10-inch cast iron pan. Sprinkle sugar evenly over the top.

Cut one piece of apple into a thick round disk and place in the center of the skillet to serve as the "button." Arrange the remaining apple pieces, each one standing on its flat end, in concentric circles around the button. Keep the pieces close together so that they support one another, standing upright. It should look like the petals of a flower.

On a floured surface, roll out the puff pastry to about 1/8-inch thick. Place an upside-down bowl or pan with the same diameter as your pan on the pastry. Using the tip of a sharp knife, cut out a circle. Lift out the circle and drape gently over the apples. Use your hands to tuck the pastry around the apple pieces, hugging them together firmly.

Place the skillet on the stovetop over medium heat until golden-brown juice begins to bubble around the edges, about 3 minutes. If necessary, raise the heat so that the juices are at a boil. Keep cooking until the juices are turning darker brown and smell caramelized, no longer than 10 minutes longer.

Transfer skillet to the oven and bake for 45 to 50 minutes, until puff pastry is golden brown.

Allow to cool 5 minutes, then carefully invert onto a round serving plate. If any apples remain stuck in the pan, gently use your fingers or a spatula to retrieve them and rearrange on the pastry shell. Cut in wedges and serve warm with sweetened whipped cream or vanilla ice cream.

Lemon Bars
Yield: 8 squares (8- or 9-inch pan)

Crust

- 1/2 cup unsalted butter, melted
- 1/4 cup sugar
- 1 teaspoon vanilla extract or 1/2 teaspoon almond extract
- 1/4 teaspoon salt
- 1 cup AP flour

Lemon Filling

- 1 cup sugar
- 3 tablespoons AP flour
- 3 large eggs
- 1/2 cup fresh lemon juice[i]

Preheat the oven to 325°F. Line the bottom and sides of an 8- or 9-inch square baking pan, preferably glass or ceramic (not metal) with parchment paper, leaving an overhang on the sides. Set aside.

Mix the butter, sugar, vanilla extract, and salt together in a medium bowl. Add the flour and stir to completely combine. The dough will be thick. Press firmly into prepared pan, making sure the layer of crust is nice and even. Bake for 18–20 minutes or until the edges are lightly browned.

In a medium bowl, whisk together the sugar and flour. Add the eggs and lemon juice; whisk until completely combined.

Pour filling over warm crust. Bake the bars for 20–25 minutes or until the center is set and no longer jiggles. Remove bars from the oven and cool completely at room temperature.

Once cool, lift the parchment paper out of the pan using the overhang on the sides. Dust with confectioners' sugar and cut into squares before serving. Cover and store leftover lemon bars in the refrigerator for up to one week.

Gluten-Free Lemon Bars
Yield: 8 squares (8- or 9-inch pan)

Crust

- 1/3 cup GF oat flour
- 1/3 cup coconut flour
- 1/3 cup almond flour/meal
- 1/3 cup GF all-purpose flour
- 1/4 cup sugar
- 1/4 teaspoon salt
- 1/8 teaspoon baking soda
- 1/4 cup unsalted butter, cold, cut into cubes
- 1 ounce cream cheese, cold, cut into cubes
- 1 large egg
- 1/2 teaspoon vanilla extract

---

i Any citrus can be substitute for the lemon juice: blood oranges, oranges, limes, and meyer lemons.

Filling

- 2 large eggs
- 1 cup sugar
- 1/3 cup lemon juice
- 2 tablespoons cornstarch
- 1/4 teaspoon salt

Preheat the oven to 325°F. Line the bottom and sides of an 8- or 9-inch square baking pan, preferably glass or ceramic (not metal) with parchment paper, leaving an overhang on the sides. Set aside.

In a food processor, combine the oat flour, coconut flour, almond flour, GF flour, sugar, salt, and baking soda. Pulse until combined. Add the butter and cream cheese. Pulse several times until mixture resembles coarse meal. In a small bowl, whisk together the egg and vanilla. With motor running, pour in the egg mixture. Pulse just until the mixture starts to clump together.

Press the dough firmly into prepared pan, making sure the layer of crust is nice and even. Allow the crust to rest at room temperature for 15 minutes. Bake for 12–15 minutes or until the edges are lightly browned.

In a medium bowl, whisk together the filling ingredients. Set aside.

Remove the crust from the oven and pour the filling over the hot crust. Return the squares to the oven and bake for 15 to 18 minutes, or until the filling appears set. Remove the squares from the oven and allow to cool in the pan before cutting into 2-inch pieces. Cover the squares and refrigerate until ready to serve.

Chocolate Tart
Yield: 1 9-inch tart

Tart Pastry

- 1 3/4 cups AP flour, plus more for dusting
- 1/4 cup almond meal
- 3 tablespoons sugar
- 1/4 teaspoon salt
- 3/4 cup unsalted butter, cold and cut into small chunks
- 1 large egg, separated
- 2 tablespoons ice water, plus more if needed

Filling

- 1 cup heavy cream
- 1/2 cup whole milk
- 10 ounces bittersweet chocolate, chopped
- 1–2 tablespoons orange flavored liqueur or Amaretto
- 2 tablespoons sugar
- 1/4 teaspoon salt
- 2 large eggs, at room temperature
- 1 tablespoon orange zest

To make the pastry: combine the flour, almond meal, sugar, and salt in a food processor. Add the butter and pulse several times or until it resembles coarse crumbs. Combine the egg yolk with the ice water in a small bowl, whisking to blend. With the motor running, pour the water mixture through the feed tube. Pulse until the pastry holds together without being too wet or sticky. Squeeze a small amount together, if it is too crumbly, add more ice water, 1 tablespoon at a time. Form the dough into a disk and wrap in plastic; refrigerate for at least 30 minutes.

Roll out the pastry on a lightly floured surface into a 12-inch circle about 1/4-inch thick. Transfer pastry to a 9-inch tart pan with a removable bottom. Press the dough into the pan so it fits tightly. Cut off the excess hanging dough with a knife. Put the tart in the refrigerator for 15 minutes.

Preheat the oven to 350°F.

Place the tart pan on a sheet pan. Line the tart shell with aluminum foil and fill with pie weights or dried beans pushing the beans/weights to the sides of the shell. Bake for 25 minutes. Remove from oven and remove the foil and weights. Using a pastry brush, lightly coat the crust with a beaten egg white. Return to the oven and continue to bake for another 10 minutes or until the tart is lightly golden brown. Set aside to cool. Lower the oven temperature to 325°F.

To make the filling: Heat the cream and milk in a pot over medium-low flame, until it simmers slightly around the edges. Remove from the heat; add the chopped chocolate and orange liqueur; stir until melted smooth. Add the sugar and salt and whisk until well incorporated. Whisk the eggs and orange zest in a small bowl and add to the chocolate mixture, stirring until incorporated. Pour the filling into the cooled tart shell and bake at 325°F for 15 to 20 minutes or until the filling is set and the surface is glossy. Cool before cutting.

Apple Tart
Yield: 1 9-inch tart

Tart Pastry

- 6 tablespoons unsalted butter, cubed, at room temperature
- 1/4 cup sugar
- 1 large egg yolk
- 1 tablespoon water
- 1 cup AP flour
- pinch of salt

Filling

- 4 medium apples—golden delicious, braeburn, and/or honeycrisp—peeled, cored, and sliced
- 2 large eggs
- 1/2 cup sugar, plus 2 tablespoons granulated or raw cane sugar, for finishing the tart
- 1 teaspoon vanilla extract
- pinch of salt
- 1 cup heavy cream
- 2 1/2 tablespoons calvados (apple brandy), brandy, triple sec, or dark rum

Make the tart dough by creaming together the butter and sugar together in a stand mixer fitted with the flat beater or paddle attachment on medium low speed, until combined, about 1 minute. Add the egg yolk and water; mix on low speed for 30 seconds. Add the flour and salt; mix until the dough comes together. If necessary, add a sprinkle of water if the dough feels too dry or crumbly.

Shape the dough into a disk and place in the center of a 9-inch tart pan with removable bottom. Using the palm of your hand and fingers, press the dough over the bottom and up the sides of the pan, getting it as even as possible. Refrigerate the dough while getting the filling ready.

Preheat oven to 350°F. Arrange the slices in concentric circles in the unbaked tart shell.

In a bowl, whisk together the eggs and 1/2 cup sugar, vanilla, and salt. Whisk in the heavy cream and calvados, until the mixture is smooth.

Pour the filling over the apples. Sprinkle the top with 2 tablespoons of sugar and bake the tart until deep golden brown on top, about 45 to 50 minutes. Remove from oven and let cool on a wire rack.

Peach Tart

- ▣ In the filling:
  - Decrease sugar to 1/4 cup
  - Add 1/4 cup brown sugar
  - Add 1/2 teaspoon cinnamon
  - Replace apples with peaches
  - Use cognac or brandy (no calvados)

Berry Tart

- ▣ In the filling
  - Replace apples with blueberries, raspberries, and/or blackberries (about 4 cups)
  - Omit liqueur
  - Omit vanilla
  - Omit eggs
  - Omit cream
  - Add 3 tablespoons fresh lemon juice
  - Whisk 2 tablespoons cornstarch with the sugar
  - Decrease baking time to 30 minutes

Lemon Meringue Pie

Yield: 1 9-inch pie

Pie

- ▣ 1 single pie pastry
- ▣ 1 1/2 cups sugar
- ▣ 1/4 cup plus 2 tablespoons cornstarch
- ▣ 1/8 teaspoon salt
- ▣ 2 cups water
- ▣ 1/2 cup fresh lemon juice
- ▣ 1 tablespoon lemon zest
- ▣ 4 large egg yolks
- ▣ 2 tablespoons unsalted butter, cut into 1/2-inch pieces

Meringue

- ▣ 4 large egg whites, at room temperature
- ▣ 1/4 teaspoon cream of tartar
- ▣ pinch of salt
- ▣ 1/2 cup sugar
- ▣ 1/2 teaspoon vanilla extract

Preheat oven to 400°F.

Roll the pie crust out on a lightly floured surface. Place in a 9-inch pie plate and carefully tuck it in. Decoratively crimp the edges. Place in the freezer for 15 minutes.

Remove from the freezer and poke the bottom of the crust with a fork. Line the crust with foil. Fill with pie weights or dried beans. Bake for 15 minutes. Remove from oven and remove the foil and pie weights. Reduce oven temperature to 375°F. Bake the crust for an additional 15–17 minutes. Place on a wire rack to cool.

In a saucepan, combine the sugar, cornstarch, and salt. Add the water, lemon juice, and lemon zest. Add the egg yolks, whisking the mixture well. Place over medium heat and cook, while whisking, until the mixture comes to a boil, about 5–7 minutes. Reduce heat to low and cook for an additional 1–2 minutes. Remove from heat and stir in the butter.

Pour filling into the pie crust. Press a piece of plastic wrap on the surface of the filling to prevent skin from forming. Cool on wire rack until cooled to room temperature. Refrigerate until cold and set.

Just before serving, preheat the broiler. In a large mixing bowl, beat the egg whites until they hold soft peaks, Add the cream of tartar and salt. While whipping, gradually add the sugar, 1 tablespoon at a time until the whites are thick and glossy. Add vanilla.

Mound meringue over the pie filling. Spread meringue to the edge. Place under the broiler and brown the meringue. Depending on the broiler, this can take only 30 seconds.

Serve.

Key Lime Pie with Almond Coconut Crust
Yield: 1 9-inch pie

Crust

- 1 package graham crackers
- 1/2 cup sliced almonds
- 1/4 cup shredded coconut
- 2 tablespoons sugar
- 1/2 cup butter, melted

Pie Filling

- 2 (14-ounce) cans sweetened condensed milk
- 2 large eggs
- 1 cup key lime juice
- 1 tablespoon lime zest
- sweetened whipped cream

Preheat oven to 375°F.

In a food processor, grind the crackers, almonds, coconut, and sugar. With the motor running, pour in the butter and pulse until the mixture starts to clump together. Press into a 9-inch pie plate. Bake for 15 minutes. Remove from oven and place on a wire rack.

Lower the oven temperature to 325°F.

In a large bowl, whisk together the condensed milk, eggs, lime juice, and zest. Pour into the pie crust. Bake for 15 minutes. Remove from oven and place on a wire rack to cool. Refrigerate for at least 2 hours to chill and set.

Top with sweetened whipped cream.

Mixed Berry Pie
Yield: 1 10-inch pie

- 1 double pie crust
- 4 pints berries: combination of blueberries, raspberries, and/or blackberries
- 3/4 cup sugar, plus more for sprinkling the top
- 1/2 cup cornstarch
- 1/2 teaspoon salt
- 1 tablespoon orange zest
- 2 tablespoons fresh orange juice
- 2 tablespoons heavy cream

Preheat oven to 400°F.

Place one pie pastry on a lightly floured surface. Roll out to a 12-inch circle. Carefully transfer pastry to a 10-inch pie plate. Gently tuck in the pastry into the plate.

Place the berries in a large mixing bowl. In a small bowl, whisk together the sugar, cornstarch, and salt. Add the sugar mixture to the berries. Stir to coat. Add the orange zest and juice. Toss to mix well. Pour mixture into the pie crust.

Roll the other pie pastry out on a lightly floured surface. Transfer the pastry to the pie and over the berry filling. Trim off excess pastry to make a 1-inch overhang. Fold the crust under to create a seal with the bottom crust. Decoratively crimp the edges. Cut vent holes in the top of the pastry. Brush the top crust with heavy cream and sprinkle with sugar.

Bake for 25 minutes at 400°F. Reduce heat to 350°F and bake for another 25–30 minutes or until the fillings starts bubbling through and the crust is golden brown.

Allow the pie to cool on a wire rack for 1 hour. Refrigerate for about 2 hours before serving. The pie is good warm or cold and best served with vanilla ice cream.

Pumpkin Pie

Yield: 1 9-inch pie

- 1 single pie pastry
- 15 ounces (1 2/3 cup) cooked pumpkin puree
- 3 large eggs
- 1 1/4 cups heavy cream
- 1/2 cup sugar
- 1/4 cup maple syrup
- 1 teaspoon ground cinnamon
- 1 teaspoon ground ginger
- 1/4 teaspoon ground nutmeg
- 1/4 teaspoon salt

Preheat oven to 375°F.

Roll the pie pastry into a 12-inch circle. Transfer the pastry dough to the pie plate. Tuck the pastry into the pie plate and cut off the excess dough hanging over the sides leaving about 1-inch overhang. Roll the top of the crust under to create an edge and crimp decoratively. Prick the bottom of the crust with a fork. Place piece of foil on the crust, making sure it meets the sides of the crust. Fill with dried beans or rice. Bake for 12 minutes. Remove from the oven and remove the foil and beans.

Lower the oven temperature to 350°F.

In a mixing bowl, whisk together the pumpkin puree, eggs, cream, sugar, maple syrup, cinnamon, ginger, nutmeg, and salt. Pour the mixture into the pie pastry. Bake for 50–55 minutes or until the middle of the pie is just set (doesn't wiggle). Cool for 30 minutes on a wire rack. Chill for at least 2 hours in the refrigerator. Serve with sweetened whipped cream.

Apple Pie

Yield: 1 9- or 10-inch pie

- 1 double pie pastry
- 3 pounds apples, peeled, cored, and sliced[ii]
- 2/3 cup sugar
- 1/4 cup cornstarch or AP flour
- 1 tablespoon lemon or orange juice
- 1 teaspoon ground cinnamon
- 1/2 teaspoon salt
- 2 tablespoons unsalted butter, cut into pieces
- 1 tablespoon cream
- sugar for sprinkling

---

ii   For best flavor, use a mix of apples such as McIntosh, Braeburn, Fuji, Gala, or Honeycrisp.

Preheat the oven to 400°F.

In a bowl, combine the sugar and cornstarch. Add the apples, lemon juice, cinnamon, and salt. Mix well and set aside.

On a floured surface, roll out one pie crust to a 12-inch diameter. Tuck the dough into a 9- or 10-inch pie plate. Be careful not to stretch it; tuck it in. Stretching the pastry causes it to shrink. Pour the filling into the pie shell. Dot the filling with the butter.

Roll out the second pie crust and place over the filling. Cut off any excess pie pastry leaving about an inch lip around the pie. Fold the edges under and crimp decoratively around the edge. Mark the top of the pie crust with 4 slits. Brush the crust with the heavy cream and sprinkle with sugar. Place the pie on a baking sheet (in case it boils over).

Bake for 10 minutes and then lower the temperature to 375°F. Bake for 1 hour to 1 hour 15 minutes. Tent the pie if the edges get too brown. Cool to room temperature on a wire rack. Chill for 3–4 hours before serving. Serve a la mode.

Strawberry Chiffon Pie
Yield: 1 9-inch pie

Crust

- 12 graham crackers
- 2 tablespoons sugar
- 1/4 cup unsalted butter, melted

Filling

- 1 cup cold water
- 1 (1/4 ounce) envelope unflavored gelatin
- 1 1/2 cups fresh or frozen strawberries; thaw if frozen
- 3 large eggs, separated
- 2/3 cup sugar
- 1/2 teaspoon salt
- 1 tablespoon fresh lemon juice

Make the crust:

Preheat oven to 375°F.

Place the graham crackers and sugar in a food processor. Pulse until finely ground. Pour in the butter. Pulse until mixture starts to clump together. Pour mixture into a 9-inch pie plate. Press crumb mixture evenly on the bottom and sides of the plate.

Bake for 8–10 minutes or until golden brown. Cool on a wire rack.

Make the filling:

Pour the water into a small bowl. Sprinkle the gelatin over the water. Allow gelatin to "bloom" or soften.

Place the strawberries in blender (or use an immersion blender). Blend until smooth.

In a medium stainless steel bowl, whisk together the egg yolks, 1/3 cup sugar, salt, and lemon juice. Place bowl over a pot of simmering water. The bottom of the bowl should not touch the water. Cook, stirring often, until mixture is thick, about 5 minutes. It should coat the back of a spoon. Remove from heat.

Add the gelatin to the yolk mixture and stir until dissolved. Stir in the strawberry puree. Set aside.

In a mixing bowl, whip the egg whites until soft peaks form. Gradually add the remaining 1/3 cup sugar. Beat until stiff peaks form. Fold whites into the strawberry mixture until well combined.

Pour filling into the pie shell. Refrigerate until firm, about 2 hours. Serve.

Apple Galette
Yield: 1 9-inch galette

- 1 single pie pastry
- 5–6 medium sized apples, peeled, seeded, and sliced thin (about 2 1/2 pounds)
- zest of 1 orange (about 1 teaspoon)
- 1 tablespoon fresh orange juice
- 1 tablespoon honey
- 1/3 cup sugar, plus more for sprinkling
- 1/2 teaspoon cinnamon
- 2 tablespoons cornstarch
- 1 tablespoon unsalted butter, cut into cubes
- 2 tablespoons heavy cream

Preheat oven to 400°F. Line a baking sheet with parchment paper. Set aside.

In a medium-sized bowl combine the apples, honey, orange zest, and orange juice. In a small bowl, mix together the 1/2 cup sugar, cinnamon, and cornstarch. Add to the apple mixture and stir to combine. Set aside.

On a lightly floured surface, roll pie pastry to a 12-inch diameter circle. Transfer pie crust to a baking sheet. Place the apple mixture in the center of the pie crust, leaving a 2-inch border around the edge of the crust. Dot the filling with the butter. Fold in the sides of the crust, overlapping as you go around the circle. Brush the crust with the cream and sprinkle with sugar. Bake for 25–30 minutes or until crust is golden brown and apples are soft.

Serve with ice cream or sweetened whipped cream.

Raspberry Galette
Yield: 1 9-inch galette

- 1 single pie pastry
- 3 1/2 cups fresh raspberries (or any fruit you choose, sliced/cubed if necessary)
- 1/2–3/4 cup sugar (depending on the sweetness of the fruit)
- pinch of salt
- 1 tablespoon fresh lemon juice (or orange juice)
- 1 teaspoon fresh lemon zest (or orange zest)
- 3–4 tablespoons cornstarch[iii]
- 1/2 teaspoon ground cardamom[iv]
- 1 tablespoon cream
- additional sugar for sprinkling

Preheat oven to 400°F. Line a baking sheet with parchment paper. Roll the pie crust into a 12- to 14-inch circle. Transfer to the baking sheet.

In a large bowl, toss together the fruit, sugar, salt, lemon juice, lemon zest, cornstarch, and cardamom.

Mound the fruit mixture in the center of the crust, leaving a 1–2-inch border. Gently fold the pastry over the fruit, pleating it as you move around the crust. Brush pastry with the cream and sprinkle with sugar.

Bake for 35–45 minutes or until the filling is bubbling and crust is golden brown. Cool for 20 minutes before serving. Serve slightly warm or at room temperature.

Ice cream or sweetened whipped cream optional.

Peach Pie
Yield: 1 9- or 10-inch pie

- 1 double pie pastry
- 3 pounds peaches
- 2/3 cup sugar
- 1/4 cup cornstarch
- 1 tablespoon lemon juice
- 1/4 teaspoon ground ginger
- 1/2 teaspoon ground cardamom
- 1/2 teaspoon salt
- 2 tablespoons unsalted butter, cut into pieces
- 1 tablespoon cream
- sugar for sprinkling

---

iii   Three tablespoons cornstarch for berries; four tablespoons for peaches and other stone fruits

iv   The spice (or herb used) will depend on the fruit you choose. Raspberries and cardamom go well together. Lavender and blueberries are a lovely match. Cinnamon goes with many fruits and berries. Or you can just leave the spice out.

Preheat the oven to 400°F.

Peel the peaches by the same blanching method as the tomatoes. Bring a pot of water up to a simmer (near boiling). Mark an "X" in the bottom of each peach and then place the peaches in the hot, simmering water for 30–60 seconds. Remove each peach and place in ice water. The skins should peel off easily, especially if they are ripe. Cut the pit of each peach and slice into pieces.

In a bowl, combine the sugar and cornstarch. Add the sliced peaches, lemon juice, ginger, cardamom, and salt. Mix well and set aside.

On a floured surface, roll out one pie crust to a 12-inch diameter. Tuck the dough into the pie plate. Be careful not to stretch it; tuck it in. Stretching the pastry causes it to shrink. Pour the filling into the pie shell. Dot the filling with the butter.

Roll out the second pie crust and place over the filling. Cut off any excess pie pastry leaving about an inch lip around the pie. Fold the edges under and crimp decoratively around the edge. Mark the top of the pie crust with 4 slits. Brush the crust with the heavy cream and sprinkle with sugar. Place the pie on a baking sheet (in case it boils over).

Bake for 10 minutes and then lower the temperature to 375°F. Bake for 1 hour to 1 hour 15 minutes. Tent the pie if the edges get too brown. Cool to room temperature on a wire rack. Chill for 3–4 hours before serving. Serve a la mode.

Tomato Onion Tart
Yield: 1 9-inch tart

- 1 tart pastry
- 1 sweet yellow onion, sliced thin
- 2 tablespoons olive oil
- 1/4 cup kalamata olives, pitted and chopped
- 8 ounces Fontina cheese, sliced or grated
- 2–4 medium to large fresh tomatoes, preferably heirloom, sliced
- salt and pepper, to taste

Preheat oven to 375°F.

Roll the tart pastry out on a lightly floured surface to a 14-inch round. Transfer the crust to a 9-inch tart pan with a removeable bottom and tuck the dough into the pan. Cut off excess overhang. Place the tart on a baking sheet.

Spread the onions and olives on the bottom of the crust. Drizzle with olive oil and season with salt and pepper. Place the fontina cheese on top of the onions and then layer the tomatoes on top of the chees. Drizzle with olive oil and season lightly with salt and pepper.

Bake for 1 hour or until the pastry is golden brown. Serve warm or at room temperature.

Flan Parisien
Yield: 1 9-inch tart/pie

Filling

- 2 cups whole milk
- 1/2 cup sugar
- 1/2 cup heavy cream
- 1/4 cup cornstarch
- 5 large egg yolks
- 1 teaspoon vanilla extract

Crust

- 1 1/2 cups AP flour
- 1 tablespoon sugar
- 1/4 teaspoon salt
- 6 ounces (12 tablespoons) cold unsalted butter, cubed
- 1/4 cup cold whole milk
- 1 large egg yolk

Prepare the filling by combining the milk and sugar in a medium saucepan set over medium heat. Bring to a boil. Turn off heat.

In a small bowl, whisk together the cream and cornstarch until smooth. Add the egg yolks, whisking until smooth. Stir egg mixture into the milk mixture.

Cook over medium low heat until the mixture begins to boil and thicken, stirring occasionally to prevent burning. Once it has thickened, remove from heat and add the vanilla. Cover the surface with plastic wrap. Cool in either an ice bath or refrigerator.

Prepare the crust by combining the flour, sugar, and salt in a food processor. Add the butter and pulse a few times until the butter is in small pieces. Add the milk and egg yolk. Pulse until the mixture comes together. Shape into a disk.

Lightly grease with butter a 9-inch tart pan or pie plate. Set aside.

Roll pastry out on lightly floured surface to about a 12-inch diameter. Place the dough into the pan and tuck in in the sides. Cut off any extra overhang. Refrigerate the crust until ready to bake.

Preheat the oven to 400°F.

Pour the cooled custard into the crust. Place on a baking sheet and bake for 40–45 minutes or until the custard is slightly jiggly. Remove from oven and allow to cool to room temperature. Refrigerate for 2 hours.

Serve cold with fresh berries on the side.

Fresh Berry Tart with Pastry Cream
Yield: 1 9-inch tart

- 1 tart pastry
- 2 ounces cake flour
- 6 ounces sugar
- 2 cups whole milk
- 6 egg yolks
- 1 teaspoon vanilla
- 2 tablespoons unsalted butter
- 3 pints fresh berries
- apricot preserves (optional)

Preheat oven to 350°F.

Roll the tart pastry out to about 1/4-inch thick. Carefully place the pastry in the tart pan. Cut off the excess crust. Pierce the bottom of the crust with a fork. Line the pastry with foil and fill with pie weights or dried beans. Bake for 10–15 minutes. Remove foil and pie weights. Bake until golden brown, an additional 10–15 minutes. Cool before filling.

In a small bowl, whisk together the flour and sugar. Set aside.

In medium bowl, whisk 1/2 cup milk and the egg yolks. Add the flour mixture. Whisk until smooth. Heat the remaining milk in a saucepan over medium high heat until it just comes to a boil.

Slowly whisk the hot milk into the egg mixture. Pour the egg/milk mixture into the pan and place over medium low heat. Cook until the custard thickens, whisking frequently. Once the mixture starts to boil (will "blop" on the surface), cook for 1 more minute. Turn off the heat and add the vanilla and butter. Stir until smooth. Cool the pastry cream in an ice bath.

Fill the tart with pastry cream. Decoratively arrange the berries on top. Heat the apricot preserves in a small saucepan until it melts. Brush the glaze over the berries.

Apple Strudel
Serves 10–12

Dough

- 2 1/2 cups AP flour
- 1/4 teaspoon salt
- 2 tablespoons plus 1 teaspoon melted unsalted butter
- 3/4 cup plus 1 tablespoon lukewarm water

Filling 1

- 7 tablespoons unsalted butter
- 1 cup plain breadcrumbs
- 1 tablespoon brown sugar

Filling 2

- 1/2 cup walnuts or almonds, chopped
- 6 large apples, peeled, cored, and sliced
- 3/4 cup sugar
- 2 teaspoons orange zest
- 2 tablespoons orange juice
- 2 tablespoons lemon juice
- 1/4 teaspoon ground cinnamon
- 1/2 cup melted butter
- powdered sugar

Make the dough:

Combine the flour and salt in a bowl. Add the water and oil. Stir until the mixture starts to come together. Place dough on a lightly floured surface and knead until smooth and tacky (but not sticky), about 5 minutes. Add more flour as necessary if the dough is too sticky. Form dough into a ball. Place in the mixing bowl and brush with oil. Cover with plastic wrap and let sit for 1 hour.

Make Filling 1:

Melt the butter in a sauté pan until foaming. Add the breadcrumbs. Cook until the breadcrumbs are golden brown. Remove from heat and cool completely.

Place bread crumbs in a bowl and add the sugar. Set aside.

Make Filling 2:

In a large bowl, combine the apples, sugar, orange zest, orange juice, lemon juice, and cinnamon. Set aside.

Preheat oven to 400°F.

On a lightly floured surface, roll and stretch the dough thin enough to see through or as thin as you can get it and is in the shape of a large rectangle. Trim thick edges off the dough. Brush the dough with 1/4 cup of the melted butter. Spread bread crumbs over 2/3 of the rectangle.

Drain excess liquid off the apples. Spread the apples over the last 1/3 of the rectangle. Roll the pastry up starting at the side where the apples are. Place on a baking sheet lined with parchment. Depending on the size of your sheet, you may need to shape it to fit the pan. Brush with remaining butter. Bake for 20 minutes. Reduce oven temperature to 350°F. Bake for another 40–50 minutes or until golden brown.

Cool on a wire rack. Dust with powdered sugar. Serve with sweetened whipped cream.

Spanakopita

Yield: 1–2 dozen

- 2 (10-ounce) packages frozen chopped spinach, thawed and drained well
- 1 teaspoon dried oregano
- 1/4 teaspoon salt
- 1/4 teaspoon pepper
- 1/2 teaspoon garlic powder
- 1 large egg, beaten
- 2 tablespoons olive oil
- 1 tablespoon fresh lemon juice
- 8 ounces crumbled feta cheese
- 24 sheets frozen phyllo dough, thawed
- 1 1/2 cups unsalted butter, melted

Preheat oven to 350°F. Line a baking sheet with parchment paper. Set aside.

Place the spinach in a colander lined with either a clean towel or cheesecloth. Wrap the spinach in the cloth and squeeze out excess moisture.

Put spinach in a medium bowl. Add the oregano, salt, pepper, and garlic powder. Mix well to distribute the spices. Add the egg, olive oil, and lemon juice. Mix well. Add the feta cheese and mix to combine. Set aside.

Lay 1 sheet of phyllo on a large cutting board. Keep the other sheets covered with plastic wrap to prevent them from drying out. Brush the phyllo sheet with melted butter. Place another sheet of phyllo on top and brush with butter. Repeat 2 more times to have a total of 4 sheets of phyllo stacked on each other.

Using a sharp knife, cut the phyllo into 3–4 strips. Place 2 tablespoons of the spinach filling in the bottom corner of each strip. Fold the strip up like a flag to make a triangle. Place each triangle on the baking sheet. Brush with melted butter.

Repeat process with remaining phyllo and spinach filling.

Bake for 15 minutes or until golden brown and heated through. Remove from oven and cool slightly.

Spanakopita can be served warm or at room temperature.

Eclairs

Yield: 10–12 eclairs

- 1/2 cup whole milk
- 1/2 cup water
- 4 ounces (1 stick) unsalted butter
- 1 teaspoon sugar
- 1/2 teaspoon salt
- 1 cup AP flour
- 4 large eggs

Preheat oven to 425°F. Line a baking sheet with parchment. Set aside. Place a pastry bag fitted with a large tip by your work station.

Pour milk, water, butter, sugar, and salt in a saucepan set over medium high heat. Bring to a boil. Remove from heat and add the flour. Vigorously beat the mixture with a wooden spoon by hand. Put back on the stove and continue beating the mixture until the dough starts to look relatively dry and leaves a film on the sides of the pan.

Transfer the dough to a mixing bowl fitted with a paddle attachment. Run the mixer for 1–2 minutes to allow some of the steam to come off of the dough. As the mixer is running, add the eggs, one at a time. The dough will turn into a thick and smooth batter that fall like a ribbon when the beater is lifted. It may not be necessary to add all the eggs.

Scoop a portion of the paste into the pastry bag and pipe into éclair (or profiterole) shapes onto the baking pan.

Bake at 425°F for 10 minutes. Reduce heat to 325°F. Bake for 30 minutes or until golden brown.

Cool and then fill with pastry cream and drizzle with melted chocolate.

Baklava
Yield: 1 9 × 13-inch pan

- 1/2 pound shelled pistachios, coarsely chopped
- 1/2 pound walnuts, coarsely chopped
- 1 teaspoon ground cinnamon
- 1 cup plain bread crumbs
- 1 pound unsalted butter, melted
- 32 sheets phyllo dough, thawed
- 3 cups sugar
- 1 1/2 cups water
- 6 fluid ounces honey
- 1 tablespoon lemon juice

Preheat oven to 350°F. Combine the pistachios, walnuts, cinnamon and bread crumbs in a bowl. Set aside.

Brush a 9 × 13-inch baking pan with butter. Layer 10 sheets of the phyllo in the pan, brushing each sheet with butter before adding the next sheet. Sprinkle a quarter of the nut mixture over the dough. Layer 4 sheets of phyllo over the nut mixture, brushing each sheet with butter before adding the next sheet. Sprinkle with another quarter of the nut mixture. Layer 4 sheets of phyllo over the nut mixture, brushing each sheet with butter before adding the next sheet. Sprinkle with another quarter of the nut mixture. Layer 4 sheets of phyllo over the nut mixture, brushing each sheet with butter before adding the next sheet. Sprinkle with the remaining nut mixture.

Layer the remaining 10 sheets of phyllo over the nuts brushing each sheet with butter before adding the next sheet. Brush the top with butter. Cut the baklava to make strips about 1 1/2 inches wide. Then cut diagonally, about 1 1/2 inches apart to create a diamond pattern. Bake until golden brown, about 1 hour.

Meanwhile, make the syrup by combining the sugar, honey, and water in saucepan set over medium heat. Cook for 10–15 minutes. Add the lemon juice and boil for 2 minutes. Let cool slightly.

Once the baklava is done baking, pour the syrup over the warm baklava. Let soak, uncovered for at least 6 hours. Garnish with chopped nuts.

Puff Pastry
Yield: 2 pounds

- 4 cups AP flour
- 1 1/2 teaspoons salt
- 1 1/4 cups cold water
- 2 cups (16 ounces) unsalted butter, cut into 4–6 pieces

In a bowl, mix together 3 1/2 cups flour and salt. Make a well in the center of the flour and pour in the water. Mix the water into the flour until a dough starts to form. Add additional water as necessary if the dough is too dry. It should hold together.

Place dough on a lightly floured surface. Knead for 2–3 minutes to allow the gluten to develop. Pat the dough into a 9-inch square. Wrap in plastic. Refrigerate for 30 minutes.

Place the cold butter in a mixer fitted with a paddle attachment. Add the remaining 1/2 cup flour. Mix until blended and smooth. This can also be done by hand. Pat butter into an 8-inch square. Place on a lightly floured wax paper. Cover with another sheet of wax paper. Refrigerate for 30 minutes.

Remove dough from the refrigerator. Place on a lightly floured surface. Roll it into a 12-inch square. Place the chilled butter in the center of the square. Fold the edges of the dough over the butter until they meet in the center. Pinch and seal the edges of the dough together.

Turn the dough over. Tap it into a rectangle shape. Roll into a rectangle about 20 × 10-inches. Add additional flour as necessary to keep from sticking.

When the dough is a large rectangle, brush off excess flour. Fold it up like a business letter (bottom third up toward center, top third over the bottom third). Line the edges up as best as you can. Dab the edges with cold water as necessary to help them stick together.

Turn the dough so the spine is on your left. It should look like a book, ready to be opened. Roll the dough into a 20 × 10-inch rectangle again and fold into a business letter. Turn dough to the spine is on your left. Refrigerate for 15 minutes.

Repeat the process of rolling into a 20 × 10 rectangle and folding into a business letter and rolling out again 4 more times, refrigerating it for 15 minutes after 2 turns.

When all 6 turns are finished, place the dough in the refrigerator for up 1 hour.

Roll dough out on a lightly floured surface to a 12 × 18-inch rectangle. Trim off the edges of the dough. Cut dough in half.

Roll each half into a 12 × 18-inch rectangle, about 1/4 to 1/6-inch thick. Cut into desired shapes.

Puff pastry should be baked at 425°F.

Quick Puff Pastry
Yield: 1 pound

- 6 1/4 ounces AP flour
- 1 1/4 ounces cake flour
- 8 ounces unsalted butter, cut into cubes
- 1/2 teaspoon salt
- 1/2 cup cold water

In a bowl, whisk together the flour and cake flour. Add 2 cubes of butter. With your hands, mix in the butter, tossing and squeezing the butter until no visible pieces remain.

Cut the remaining butter into small pieces and add to the flour mixture. Distribute evenly in the mixture but do not cut it in completely.

Dissolve the salt in the water. Make a well in the center of the flour mixture. Pour the water into the well. Mix until moistened. Add additional water as necessary if the mixture is too dry.

Press dough into a cylinder and place on a lightly floured surface. Using a rolling pin, roll into a rectangle about 1/2-inch thick. Fold into thirds. Roll to 1/4-inch thick. Turn the dough 180°. Roll to 1/4-inch thick. Fold into a book fold. Position the "spine" of the book on the left.

Roll the dough to form a 6 × 18-inch rectangle. Fold the dough into quarters: Fold each side of the rectangle to meet in the center and then fold along the center line. Rotate the dough 180°. Repeat this process 2 more times.

Wrap in plastic and place in the refrigerator for 1 hour. Cut into shapes like pinwheels.

Bake at 400°F for 10 minutes. If making pinwheels, finish each one with a tablespoon of jam and dusting of powdered sugar.

Puff Pastry Photos
Folding in butter (for regular puff pastry)

In regular puff pastry, butter can be folded using 2 different methods: placed in the center or placed on one side.

Center Placement

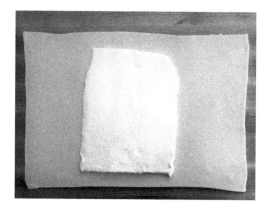

FIGURE 13.1

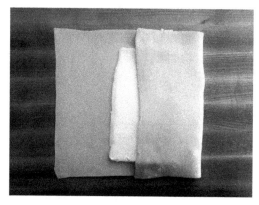

FIGURE 13.2

FIGURE 13.3

Side Placement

FIGURE 13.4

FIGURE 13.5

Folding Puff Pastry

Depending on the instructions, puff pastry can be folded 2 different ways: book fold or envelope fold.

Book Fold

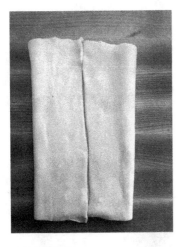

FIGURE 13.6

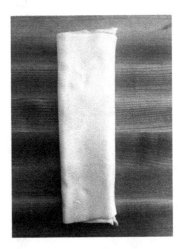

FIGURE 13.7

Envelope Fold

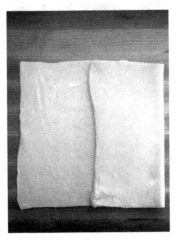

FIGURE 13.8

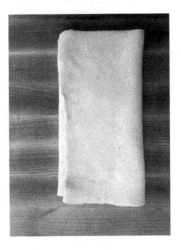

FIGURE 13.9

Pinwheel Design

A simple way to fold puff pastry for baking is to create a pinwheel design that can be filled with cooked fruit or jam after it has baked.

FIGURE 13.10

FIGURE 13.11

FIGURE 13.12

FIGURE 13.13

FIGURE 13.14

Unit 13 Questions

1. In experiment 1, note the differences between the pie pastries made with different types of fat. Which one was the flakiest? Why is this? Which had the best flavor?
2. In experiment 2, note the differences in texture between the pie pastries made with different fats at various temperatures. Which one was the flakiest? Which one had a mealy texture? Explain why this would be.
3. Why are puff pastry and pie pastry chilled before baking?
4. What causes puff pastry to rise or puff up?

NOTE

1. Wayne Gisslen, *Professional Baking*, 2nd ed., (New York: Wiley, 1985), 139–67.

BIBLIOGRAPHY

Gisslen, Wayne. *Professional Baking*, 2nd ed. New York: Wiley, 1985.

Candy and Chocolate

OBJECTIVES

- Describe the molecular structure of sugar
- Explain caramelization of sugar and cooking temperatures
- Describe different types of sugar and sugar substitutes
- Explain effects of high altitudes on candy making
- Demonstrate how to temper chocolate
- Use basic cooking techniques to prepare recipes

INTRODUCTION[1,2]

Honey was the first sweetener used by ancient civilizations about 10,000 years ago. Around 500 BCE, Indians combined sugar with grains to form dessert-like foods. Many years later, around the 12th century, Europeans started perfecting the art of candy making when cane sugar became more popular to use than honey.

Chocolate originated in Central America with the Mayans and Aztecs who used the cacao bean as a beverage for religious ceremonies.

Confectionery foods are rich in sugar and calories but low in nutrients. The category of confections includes many different types of sweets like toffee, taffy, chocolate candies, caramels, hard candy, fudge, among many others.

CANDY

Sugar is a useful molecule in cooking. Sugar and the amino acids of proteins create the maillard reaction or the browning of foods. Sugar also acts as tenderizer in baked goods.

In candy making, sugar is melted and caramelized. The process of heating the sugar breaks its molecules apart. The most common form of sugar used in candy is sucrose or table sugar.

Sugar Molecules

Monosaccharides are single sugar molecules and include glucose, fructose, and galactose.

Disaccharides are sugar molecules containing two simple sugar molecules joined together.

Sucrose (table sugar) = glucose + fructose
Lactose (milk sugar) = glucose + galactose

Candy Temperatures and Caramelization of Sugar[3]

The stages of candy temperatures refers to the how the melted sugar reacts in cold water.

Thread stage: 230–235°F
Soft Ball stage: 235–240°F
Firm Ball stage: 245–250°F
Hard Ball stage: 250–265°F
Soft Crack stage: 270–290°F
Hard Crack stage: 300–310°F

At these stages, all the water has been cooked off and the liquid is 99% sugar. At the brown liquid stage, the sugar begins to cook and turn a brown or amber color. At the burnt liquid stage, the sugar starts to burn, resulting in a bitter aftertaste.

Clear liquid stage: 320°F
Brown liquid stage: 338°F
Burnt liquid stage: 350°F

Types of Sugar[4]

Beet Sugar

Beet sugar is made from pressing and boiling the sugar syrup from the stems of sugar beets. The syrup is crystallized, resulting in table sugar.

Cane Sugar

Cane sugar is made from the stalks of the sugar cane plant. Cane juice is extracted from the plant and boiled down before undergoing crystallization to form table sugar.

Confectioners' Sugar (Powdered Sugar)

Confectioners' sugar is a very fine sugar mixed with cornstarch to prevent caking.

Superfine Sugar

Superfine sugar is a finer form of beet or cane sugar.

Brown Sugar

Brown sugar is cane or beet sugar that has been mixed with molasses.

Molasses

Molasses is a by-product of the cane or beet sugar making process.

Raw Sugar

Raw sugar is minimally processed cane sugar.

Date Sugar

Date sugar is made from dehydrated dates that are ground to resemble sugar.

Coconut Sugar

Coconut sugar is made from the sap of the coconut palm tree; it has been boiled down and crystalized.

Honey

Honey is syrup made from bees after they collect nectar from flowering plants.

Agave

Agave is "honey water" from the core of the blue agave plant, a member of the cactus family grown in Mexico and parts of Central America.

Maple Syrup

Maple syrup is made by boiling the sap of the maple tree.

Light and Dark Corn Syrup

Corn syrup is made from cornstarch. Light corn syrup is the purified version of the syrup whereas caramel and/or molasses has been added to dark corn syrup.

High Fructose Corn Syrup (HFCS)

Created in the 1960s, HFCS is made by adding an enzyme to corn syrup resulting in more fructose molecules to create a sweeter syrup. HFCS is comprised of 53% glucose and 47% fructose.

Artificial Sweeteners

Artificial sweeteners are synthetic forms of sugar that are typically sweeter than table sugar. Below is a list of the most common forms of artificial sweeteners and their manufactured names.

- Sucralose
- Splenda®
- Saccharin
- Sugar Twin®
- Sweet and Low®
- Aspartame
- Equal®
- Nutrasweet®
- Stevia
- Truvia®

- Sugar Alcohols
- Sorbitol
- Xylitol
- Mannitol

High Altitudes and Candy Making[5]

Candy making at high altitudes requires adjustments made to the temperatures to which the candy is cooked. The general guideline is to decrease the temperature for each stage of caramelization (soft ball, hard ball, soft crack, etc.) by 1°F per 500 feet above sea level. This means if you live at 5000 feet above sea level, you need to decrease the temperature to which the candy cooks by 10°F.

TABLE 14.1

High Altitude Candy Temperature Adjustment	
Feet Above Sea Level	**Decrease temperature of caramelization stage by:**
1000 feet	2°F
2000 feet	4°F
3000 feet	6°F
4000 feet	8°F
5000 feet	10°F
6000 feet	12°F
7000 feet	14°F
8000 feet	16°F

Chocolate[6]

Cocoa beans are grown in large pods of cacao trees that are located in Central America and Mexico. The beans are dried in the sun after being removed from the pod. After a few days of being dried in the sun, the beans are roasted. During the roasting process, the beans split open exposing the nib or kernel. Grinding the nibs creates chocolate liquor, the basis for chocolate.

Cocoa powder is created when the chocolate liquor is departed into cocoa butter and cocoa powder. Cocoa powder is an acidic substance. To make it less acidic, some manufacturers make a "Dutched" version where an alkali is added to the cocoa powder. The two should not be used interchangeably in recipes.

Storing Chocolate

Chocolate should be stored in foil or wrapped in parchment paper at room temperature. It should not be stored in plastic, the refrigerator, or the freezer. Doing so creates condensation by holding in moisture and thus damage the chocolate.

Types of Chocolate

White Chocolate

Not technically chocolate because it does not contain any cocoa. It is a mix of cocoa butter, milk solids, and sugar.

Bittersweet Chocolate

Contains cocoa solids, cocoa butter, and sugar. The bitterness is based on the amount of cocoa solids. The higher the percentage (i.e., 70%), the less sweet the chocolate is.

Semi-Sweet Chocolate

Dark chocolate containing 50% sugar and 50% cocoa solids and cocoa butter.

Milk Chocolate

Chocolate containing milk solids. The percentage of milk solids and sugar outweigh the percentage of cocoa solids and cocoa butter.

Unsweetened

Dark chocolate that does not contain any sugar, resulting in a bitter flavor.

Tempering Chocolate

Tempering chocolate gives it a shiny, smooth texture. The process helps control the crystalline structure of the chocolate to the point at which it is most stable.

To control the temperature, chocolate should be melted in a double boiler (a stainless steel or glass bowl set over a pan of simmering water). Before melting, the chocolate should be chopped into small pieces. Chocolate should not be heated above 120°F due to the risk of burning.

There are two methods for tempering chocolate. The first method requires patience and training as it involves many steps to temper chocolate properly. The second method is a quick method and can be used for many recipes.

Quick Method

1. Chop 1 pound of chocolate into small pieces
2. Set aside 1/3 of the chocolate and place the other 2/3 in a bowl set over a pan of simmering water (double boiler)
3. Stir the chocolate until it melts. The temperature of the chocolate should not exceed 120°F. Remove the bowl from over the water.
4. Stir in the remaining 1/3 of the chocolate in 3 batches, making sure that the chocolate is completely melted before adding more.
5. When all the chocolate has been added and stirred in, the chocolate is tempered.

EVALUATION

Evaluation 1: Different Types of Chocolate

Taste and evaluate different types of chocolate

Chocolate Type	Color	Flavor	Degree of Sweetness*
White chocolate			
Milk chocolate			
Semi-sweet chocolate			
Bittersweet chocolate (60–70%)			
Unsweetened chocolate			

degree of sweetness refers to how sweet the chocolate is compared to the others

EXPERIMENTS

Experiment 1: Candy with Different Types of Sugar

Evaluate the different the differences in candy making with sugar

Basic Hard Candy

Yield: 1/4 pound

- 1 cup beet sugar
- 1/2 cup water
- 1/3 cup light corn syrup
- 1/4 teaspoon vanilla extract

Lightly grease a sheet pan. Set aside.

In a heavy-bottomed, 2-quart saucepan, combine the sugar, water, and corn syrup. Cook over medium heat, stirring constantly until the sugar is dissolved. Continue cooking without stirring over medium low heat until the mixture reaches hard crack stage of 300°F.

Remove from heat and add vanilla extract. Pour mixture onto the sheet pan. Allow to cool and break into pieces.

Variations:

- Replace the beet sugar with:
  - 1 cup cane sugar
  - 1 cup raw sugar
  - 1 cup brown sugar
  - 1 cup coconut sugar
  - 1 cup honey
  - 1 cup maple syrup

Variation	Flavor	Texture	Appearance
Basic (control)			
Cane sugar			
Raw sugar			
Brown sugar			
Coconut sugar			
Honey			
Maple syrup			

Experiment 2: Sugar Substitutes in Baking
Test and evaluate the effects of artificial sweeteners in baking

Basic Recipe for Brownies

- 1/3 cup canola oil
- 2 large eggs
- 1 cup sugar
- 1 teaspoon vanilla
- 1/4 cup cocoa powder
- 2/3 cup AP flour
- 1/2 teaspoon salt
- 1/2 teaspoon baking powder

Preheat oven to 350°F. Grease bottom and sides of an 8-inch baking pan.

In a bowl, combine the oil, eggs, sugar, and vanilla. Add the flour, cocoa powder, salt, and baking powder. Mix well. Pour into the pan. Bake for 25 minutes. Cool and serve.

Variations:

- Replace the sugar with:
  - 1 cup sucralose
  - 1 cup aspartame
  - 1 cup stevia

Variation	Appearance	Flavor – note sweetness level	Texture
Basic (control)			
Sucralose			
Aspartame			
Stevia			

RECIPES

For all the recipes below, adjust the temperatures to which the sugar syrup cooks to according to altitude.

Caramel Corn

Yield: 5–6 quarts

- 6 quarts popped popcorn, unpopped kernels removed
- 2 cups brown sugar
- 1 cup unsalted butter
- 1/2 cup light corn syrup
- 1 teaspoon salt
- 1 teaspoon baking soda
- 1 teaspoon vanilla
- 1–2 cups salted peanuts (optional)

Preheat oven to 250°F. Lightly grease 1–2 large baking sheets. Set aside.

Place the popcorn in a large bowl. Set aside.

In a large pot, mix together the brown sugar, butter, and corn syrup. Bring to a boil over medium high heat; boil for 5 minutes. Remove from the heat and stir in the salt, baking soda, and vanilla. The mixture will bubble up.

Pour the mixture over the popcorn and stir gently until evenly coated. Stir in peanuts if desired.

Spread caramel corn onto the baking sheets. Bake for 1 hour, stirring the popcorn every 15 minutes to ensure even cooking and prevent burning. Remove from oven and cool completely.

Chocolate Truffles

Yield: 30 truffles

- 1 1/2 pounds bittersweet chocolate, finely chopped
- 3/4 cup heavy whipping cream
- 3 tablespoons cocoa powder

Place 8 ounces of the bittersweet chocolate in the bowl of a double boiler set over simmering water. Stir until melted. In a small saucepan, heat the cream until boiling. Remove cream from heat and stir in the melted chocolate. Whisk until smooth. Cool to room temperature. Refrigerate for 2–3 hours or until thick.

Line a baking sheet with parchment paper. Fit a large pastry bag with a #5 plain round tip. Fill bag halfway with the truffle cream. Pipe 1-inch mounds onto the baking sheet. Cover with plastic and freeze for 2 hours or refrigerate up to 6 hours.

Dust your hands with cocoa powder and roll each truffle into balls. Place back on the baking sheet. Freeze for 2 hours.

Temper the remaining 1 pound of chocolate. Keep tempered chocolate warm in a double boiler over simmering water. Line another baking sheet with parchment paper. Remove truffles from the freezer. Coat the truffles in the melted chocolate. Place on the baking sheet. Cool to room temperature, about 20–25 minutes. Place in a container using foil or parchment placed between rows. Truffles will keep refrigerated up to 1 month. Truffles are best served at room temperature.

Peanut Clusters

Yield: about 30 clusters

- 6 ounces bittersweet chocolate, chopped
- 1 1/2 cups salted peanuts

Temper the chocolate. Place the melted chocolate in a bowl set over simmering water. Stir in the peanuts.

Line a baking sheet with parchment paper or wax paper. Spoon clusters onto the baking sheet. Let the clusters sit at room temperature for 15–30 minutes. Place in the refrigerator for 30 minutes to set up. Store in a container. Peanut clusters will keep for up to 1 month in the refrigerator.

Peanut Brittle

Yield: 1 pound

- 1 1/2 cups sugar
- 1/2 cup light corn syrup
- 1/4 cup water
- 2 1/4 cups dry roasted salted peanuts
- 2 tablespoons unsalted butter
- 1 teaspoon vanilla extract
- 1 teaspoon baking soda

Lightly grease a baking sheet with non-stick cooking spray. Set aside.

In a heavy 5-quart saucepan with a lid, combine the sugar, corn syrup, and water. Cover pot. Bring to a boil over medium-high heat, about 5 minutes. Stir to dissolve the sugar. Keep lid on until steam beings to escape from the pot. Remove the lid and reduce heat to medium. Insert candy thermometer into the hot syrup. Cook until the temperature reaches 230°F.

Stir in the peanuts and continue stirring until the temperature reaches 300°F and is rich, golden brown in color. This could take 13–18 minutes.

Remove from heat and quickly stir in the butter, vanilla, and baking soda. Stir with a spoon until the butter melts and everything is incorporated. Pour mixture on the greased baking sheet. Spread out with a spatula. Cool for at least 1 hour before breaking into pieces.

Once cooled completely, store in an airtight container for up to 2 weeks.

Caramels
Yield: 60 pieces

- 1 cup heavy cream
- 1 cup plus 2 tablespoons sugar
- 3 tablespoons unsalted butter, cut into cubes
- 2/3 cup light corn syrup
- 1/4 teaspoon salt
- 1/4 teaspoon vanilla extract

Line a square baking pan with parchment and lightly grease the bottom and sides of the parchment with oil. Set aside.

Bring cream, sugar, butter, and corn syrup to a boil in a large saucepan set over high heat. Stir until the sugar dissolves. Reduce heat to medium high and cook, stirring occasionally, until the caramel reaches 245–248°F, about 15 minutes.

Immediately remove caramel from the heat and stir in salt and vanilla. Pour caramel into the baking pan and let stand uncovered at room temperature for at least 8 hours.

Cut into 1-inch pieces. Wrap in waxed paper. Store in airtight container for up to 2 weeks.

English Caramels
Yield: 60 pieces

- 1 cup unsalted butter
- 3 cups sugar
- 1 cup corn syrup
- 1 cup heavy cream
- 1/2 cup sweetened condensed milk
- 1 tablespoon vinegar
- 1 tablespoon vanilla extract

Grease a 9 × 13-inch baking pan. Place near the stove.

In a 3–4 quart saucepan, combine the butter, sugar, corn syrup, cream, condensed milk, and vinegar. Stir over medium heat until the sugar is dissolved. Stir stirring and bring to a boil. Cook until the mixture reaches 245–248°F. Remove from heat and stir in the vanilla.

Cool for 15–20 minutes. Remove from pan and cut into squares. Wrap in wax paper. Keep in airtight container for 1–2 weeks.

Fudge
Yield: 10–15 pieces

- 3 cups sugar
- 2/3 cup cocoa powder
- 1/8 teaspoon salt
- 1 1/2 cups whole milk
- 1/4 cup unsalted butter
- 1 teaspoon vanilla extract
- 1 cup chopped pecans or walnuts

Line 8-inch square pan with foil and grease foil with butter.

In a saucepan, mix together sugar, cocoa, and salt. Add milk bring to a boil over medium heat, stirring constantly. Cook until temperature reaches 230–235°F. Remove from heat. Add butter and vanilla, but do not stir for 10 minutes.

With a wooden spoon stir until the fudge starts to lose its sheen, about 3–5 minutes. Stir in nuts. Spread into prepared pan and let cool. Lift out foil and remove from fudge. Cut into squares.

Peanut Butter Chocolate Fudge
Yield: 10–15 pieces

- 1 cup unsalted butter
- 1 cup creamy peanut butter
- 1 teaspoon vanilla extract
- 1 pound powdered sugar
- 8 ounces semi-sweet chocolate, chopped
- 1/2 cup heavy cream

Line an 8-inch square pan with parchment paper, leaving a 1-inch overhang. Lightly grease the paper. Set aside.

Combine the butter and peanut butter in a 4-quart saucepan. Place over medium heat. Cook, stirring constantly until the butter melts, about 5–7 minutes. Whisk to combine well. Add the vanilla.

With a wooden spoon, stir in the sugar. The mixture will be stiff and hard to stir once the sugar is completely incorporated. Spread into the prepared pan. Smooth the surface. Set aside.

Place the chocolate and cream in a double boiler set over simmering water. Stir until the chocolate is melted. Stir until smooth. Pour the chocolate mixture on top of the peanut butter fudge. Smooth out the top.

Refrigerate for 2 hours before cutting into squares. Fudge will keep in an airtight container for 1 week.

Candied Nuts
Yield: 7 cups

- 3 cups sugar
- 1 1/2 cups water
- 3 tablespoons ground cinnamon (or spices of choice: chili pepper, nutmeg, cardamom, etc.)
- 1/4 teaspoon salt
- 7 cups nuts of choice (almonds, walnuts, pecans, etc.)

Line a baking sheet with parchment paper. Set aside.

Place a large pot on your stovetop set over medium heat and add the sugar, water, spice(s), and salt. Stir occasionally until the sugar dissolves. Continue stirring as the mixture heats up. After 10 minutes, insert the candy thermometer. Cook until the mixture reaches 238°F.

Add the nuts and stir to coat well. Remove from heat and pour onto the baking sheet. Break apart any large pieces. Cool completely.

Peppermint Patties
Yield: 25–30 patties

- 3–4 tablespoons half-n-half
- 1 tablespoon coconut oil melted
- 1 tablespoon light corn syrup
- 1 1/2 teaspoons peppermint extract
- 1 teaspoon lemon juice
- 1/2 teaspoon vanilla
- 3 3/4 cups powdered sugar
- 12 ounces bittersweet chocolate, chopped

In a bowl, mix together 2 tablespoons of half-n-half, coconut oil, corn syrup, peppermint extract, lemon juice, and vanilla. Mix in powdered sugar one cup at a time. Add 1–2 additional tablespoons of half-n-half, if mixture is too crumbly.

Form mixture into a ball and roll out into a circle about 1/4-inch thick. Place mixture on a sheet pan and freeze for 15 minutes until firm.

Using a small circle cookie cutter cut out peppermint patties. Place on a baking sheet. Freeze for 10 minutes.

Temper the chocolate in the bowl of a double boiler.

Using a fork or candy dipper, dip each patty in the chocolate, allowing excess chocolate to drip back into the bowl before transferring it back to the parchment paper line baked sheet.

Set aside and allow the chocolate to set before serving, about 1 hour.

Store in an airtight container, at room temperature, for up to 1 week.

Saltwater Taffy
Yield: 20–30 pieces

- 2 cups sugar
- 2 tablespoons cornstarch
- 1 cup light corn syrup
- 3/4 cup water
- 2 tablespoons butter
- 2 teaspoons food-grade glycerin
- 1 teaspoon salt
- 1/4 to 1 teaspoon flavor extract of choice: strawberry, orange, lemon, vanilla, etc.
- 3 drops food coloring (optional)

Light grease a baking sheet. Set aside.

Mix together the sugar and cornstarch in a heavy saucepan. Stir in the corn syrup, water, butter, glycerin, and salt. Cook over medium heat, stirring until the sugar dissolves. Bring to a boil. Once it boils, stop stirring. Cook until the mixture reaches 250°F.

Remove from heat and add the flavorings and food coloring. Stir to incorporate. Pour onto the greased baking sheet. When cool enough to handle, lightly grease your hands and pull the taffy until it is light in color and has a shiny, glossy appearance, about 10 minutes.

Roll the taffy into a long rope, about half an inch in diameter. Cut into 1-inch pieces. Let pieces sit at room temperature for 30 minutes. Wrap in wax paper. Keep in airtight container for 1–2 weeks.

Maple Candy
Yield: 14–16 pieces

- 1 quart pure maple syrup
- 1/2 teaspoon heavy cream (or 2 tablespoons unsalted butter)

Pour the syrup into a 4-quart heavy saucepan. Over medium heat cook the syrup to 235°F. When it begins to bubble up and come precariously close to the top of the pan, add the cream.

Heat the mixture back to 235°F. Immediately remove it from the heat. Leave the syrup undisturbed until it has cooled to 190°F.

Once cooled to 190°F, stir the syrup with a wooden spoon. It will begin to lose the glossy look. It will start to crystalize. Stir until the crystallization is present throughout the syrup. As you stir, it will turn light and creamy in color. Pour into candy molds.

Cool in the molds for at least 1 hour, then gently release the pieces from the molds. The candy can be stored in an airtight container 1–2 months.

Almond Crunch Toffee
Yield: 1 pound

- 2 cups sliced almonds
- 1 1/4 cups light brown sugar
- 2 tablespoons water
- 1/2 cup unsalted butter
- 1 teaspoon vanilla extract
- 1/4 teaspoon baking soda
- 6 ounces bittersweet or semi-sweet chocolate, chopped

Preheat oven to 350°F.

Place the almonds on a baking sheet. Bake until lightly toasted, about 10 minutes. Cool.

In a food processor, pulse the almonds until finely chopped, but not powdery.

Sprinkle half the almonds on a baking sheet covering approximately 7 × 10-inch area. Set aside.

In a 4-quart saucepan, combine the brown sugar, water, and butter. Stirring occasionally, bring to a boil. Cook until the mixture reaches 285°F. Immediately remove from the heat. Add the vanilla and baking soda. Pour toffee over the nuts. Scatter the chocolate pieces over the hot toffee. After a couple of minutes, spread the chocolate over the toffee. Dust with remaining almonds. Cool and break into pieces.

Keep in airtight container for 1–2 weeks.

Unit 14 Questions

1. In the evaluation, note differences in flavor among the chocolate. Which one was the sweetest? Most bitter? Which was your preference? Why?
2. In experiment 1, were there any textural differences in the candy made? Explain the reasons why some were softer or had different textures than others.
3. In experiment 2, did any of the artificial sweeteners make a good substitute for sugar in the recipe? Why or why not? Note differences in texture and flavor.
4. What is food-grade glycerin and what does it do in candy-making?

5. Why do some recipes say to stop stirring the sugar mixture after the sugar is dissolved?
6. What is the purpose of washing down the sides of the saucepan while making candy?
7. Why is taffy pulled?
8. Why is baking soda added to peanut brittle?
9. What is a benefit of adding corn syrup to candy recipes?

Vaclavik, Vickie A., and Elizabeth W. Christian. *Essentials of Food Science*, 4th ed. New York: Springer, 2014.

NOTES

1. Marissa Fessenden, "Our Ancient Ancestors Probably Loved Honey, Too," accessed 5/14/19, https://www.smithsonianmag.com/smart-news/relationship-between-humans-and-honeybees-goes-back-9000-years-180957245/.
2. Amanda Fiegl, "A Brief History of Chocolate," accessed 5/14/19, https://www.smithsonianmag.com/arts-culture/a-brief-history-of-chocolate-21860917/.
3. Exploratorium, "Candy Making Stages," accessed 5/14/19, https://www.exploratorium.edu/cooking/candy/sugar-stages.html.
4. Vickie A. Vaclavik and Elizabeth W. Christian, *Essentials of Food Science, 4th Edition* (New York: Springer, 2014), 281–82.
5. Vickie A. Vaclavik and Elizabeth W. Christian, *Essentials of Food Science*, 283.
6. Kristina Demichele, "Different Types of Chocolate and How to Use them," accessed 5/14/19, https://www.cooksillustrated.com/articles/1333-all-about-the-different-types-of-chocolate-and-how-to-use-them.

BIBLIOGRAPHY

Demichele, Kristina. "Different Types of Chocolate and How to Use Them." Accessed May 14, 2019. https://www.cooksillustrated.com/articles/1333-all-about-the-different-types-of-chocolate-and-how-to-use-them.

Exploratorium. "Candy Making Stages." Accessed May 14, 2019. https://www.exploratorium.edu/cooking/candy/sugar-stages.html.

Fessenden, Marissa. "Our Ancient Ancestors Probably Loved Honey, Too." Accessed May 14, 2019. https://www.smithsonianmag.com/smart-news/relationship-between-humans-and-honeybees-goes-back-9000-years-180957245/.

Fiegl, Amanda. "A Brief History of Chocolate." Accessed May 14, 2019. https://www.smithsonianmag.com/arts-culture/a-brief-history-of-chocolate-21860917/.

Beverages

- Explain the basics of coffee, tea, beer, and wine
- Demonstrate proper methods for brewing coffee and tea
- Evaluate types of tea and coffee
- Evaluate brewing methods for coffee
- Evaluate types of hot cocoa
- Use basic cooking techniques to prepare recipes

INTRODUCTION

The vast and diverse world of beverages is ever-expanding. Beverages include everything from plain water to sodas, juice, and alcoholic beverages. The most popular beverages in the world are coffee, tea, and water. After water, tea is the most widely consumed beverage on the planet with Turkey, Ireland, United Kingdom, and Russia consuming the most. As for coffee, sixty-four percent of Americans over the age of eighteen drink a daily cup of coffee[1], but Europeans, especially those living in Scandinavian countries, consume even more.[2] In recent years, coffee, tea, and wine have been studied for their antioxidant properties and potential health benefits.

COFFEE

Coffee is thought to have originated in the Ethiopian province of Kaffa when a goat herder noticed his goats were more energetic after eating berries from a certain tree.[3] The berries were from a Coffea shrub, the plant that produces coffee beans.

Yemen and Arabia were cultivating coffee in the fifteenth century, and the Dutch grew coffee in India and Indonesia and are credited with bringing coffee to Europe in the seventeenth century. The first European coffeehouse opened in 1683 in Venice, Italy.

Coffee grows best in tropical regions around the equator with high altitudes.

Brewing Coffee

Brewing coffee extracts the flavors of bean and each growing region and roasting method influence the overall flavor. The coffee grind, either coarse or fine or somewhere in between, determines the strength of the coffee and which brewing method is best. Finely ground coffee is preferred for espresso due to the ratio of coffee grinds to water.

Drip coffee, the method for most standard coffee makers, uses a medium grind of the beans. The ratio for drip coffee is typically 2 tablespoons of coffee per 1 cup water.

The proper temperature at which to brew coffee is 185-195°F. This is the range at which most of the flavor compounds will be extracted from the coffee beans. Boiling coffee at 212°F may result in bitter tasting coffee.

TEA

According to Chinese legend, tea was discovered in 2737 BC by Chinese emperor, Shen-Nung when tea leaves fell into a pot of boiling water.[4] Commercial cultivation of tea began in the eighth century and was eventually imported into Europe through the Dutch East India Trading Company in the seventeenth century. Due to the influx of tea into countries like England, tea became Europe's national beverage in the eighteenth century. The United States contributed to the history of tea through the popularization of iced tea in 1904 at the St. Louis World's Fair[5] and along with the invention of the tea bag.[6]

A native plant to China and southeast Asia, tea is currently grown between the Tropics of Cancer and Capricorn in mountainous regions. Countries producing the most tea are China, Japan, Sri Lanka, India, and Taiwan.

Brewing Tea

Tea is brewed by steeping leaves in a very hot or boiling water for three to five minutes. Steeping tea beyond five minutes may result in a bitter aftertaste. Tea leaves can be purchased loose or packaged in tea bags.

Most common varieties of tea:

Black (Oxidized for four hours)

Black tea accounts for ninety percent of cultivated tea. Assam, Darjeeling, Earl Grey, Lapsang souchong are common types of black tea.

Oolong (Oxidized for two to three hours)

Common types are oolong and jasmine.

Green and White (Not Oxidized)

No oxidation retains the color of the tea leaf.

TABLE 15.1 Brewing Times for Tea[7]

Type of Tea	Brewing Time
Black tea	4 minutes
Green tea	2 minutes
Herbal tea	4 minutes
Oolong tea	3 minutes
White tea	1 minute

WINE[8]

It is believed that the grapes used for making wine were first cultivated in Mesopotamia around 2000 BC. The ancient Greeks brought the grapes to regions along the Mediterranean: Greece, Turkey, and northern Africa around 500 BC. Now wine grapes grow in many different parts of the world.

Grapes prefer growing in temperate climates and most wine regions are located between the thirtieth and fiftieth parallels north and south of the equator. Several countries around the world produce wine: from Italy to South Africa. In Europe, many countries follow strict guidelines and rules for growing grapes and producing wine. For instance, France's appellation d'origine contrôlée enforces strict rules regarding the cultivation of grapes and wine production.

Wine is typically made from a red or white varietal. Common varieties of white wine are chardonnay, sauvignon blanc, riesling, chenin blanc, gewürztraminer, pinot gris, muscat, semillon, and albariño. Common red varietals include cabernet sauvignon, merlot, pinot noir, cabernet franc, sangiovese, tempranillo, syrah, grenache, gamay, and nebbiolo.

In the most basic sense, wine is nothing more than fermented grape juice. One the grapes are ripe, they are harvested and pressed or crushed to extract their juice. In producing white wine, the grape juice is strained from the grape skins prior to fermentation. However, when producing red wine, the grape juice is fermented with the skins for a period of time creating proper pigmentation. In the fermentation process, either national yeasts are used or wine producers add commercial yeast to the juice.

During fermentation, the sugars in the grapes feed off the yeast producing alcohol and carbon dioxide. The carbon dioxide is allowed to escape into the air leaving a final product of alcohol. The time of fermentation varies depending on the grape varietal and which storage methods are used for fermenting, such as oak or stainless steel barrels. Once the fermentation is complete, the wine is sometimes aged for a period of time, allowing it to mature. Not all wines are aged and most are sold within two years of the vintage date.

BEER[9]

The ancient Egyptians were first to brew a beer-like substance containing fermented barley. The beverage traveled to northern Europe where the climate was too cold to grow grapes for wine but was the perfect climate for cultivating grains like barley and wheat. In Germany, monasteries were the first brew masters.

Hops, a flowering plant, was added to delay the spoilage of the fermenting grains.

Beer is a quicker and simpler process to make than wine. It was viewed for many years as the "poor man's beverage." The process takes four steps: mashing, boiling, fermentation, and conditioning. The mashing stage is when the barley malt is soaked in hot water to break down the starch into chains of sugar molecules. In the next stage, boiling, hops are added to the barley mash. Yeast is added in the third stage, fermentation. In this stage, yeast consumes the sugars and produces alcohol. The last step is conditioning where the beer is held to get rid of any off flavors that may have developed and to also increase the amount of carbonation.

Categories of Beer

The main categories of beer are lagers and ales.

Lagers

Lagers include pilsners, pale lagers, and dark lagers.

Ales

Ales include brown ales, porters, stouts, wheat beers, and many others.

EVALUATION

Types of Tea

Evaluate different types of tea.

Brewing Method for Tea

1 cup water

1 tea bag

- Black tea
- Oolong
- White tea
- Green tea

Bring water to just to a boil. Place 1 tea bag in a cup. Pour water over tea. Steep tea according to the chart (Table 15.1). Repeat for each type of tea.

Tea	Color of the liquid	Tea Flavor	Aroma
Black tea			
Oolong			
White tea			
Green tea			

EXPERIMENTS

Experiment 1: Brewing Methods for Coffee

Test and evaluate different brewing methods for coffee.

Method 1: French Press

- 3 tablespoons whole bean coffee, coarsely ground
- 1 cup hot water (190°F)

Place the ground coffee in a French press. Pour the hot water over the grounds and stir to mix. Steep coffee for 5 minutes. Place the lid on the press and plunge the grounds to the bottom. Serve.

Method 2: Drip Coffee Maker

- 6 tablespoons whole bean coffee, ground fine
- 3 cups water

Brew the coffee according to the drip coffee maker instructions. Serve.

Method 3: Italian Moka Pot

- Whole bean coffee, finely ground
- Fill the base chamber with cold water up to the level of the valve. Insert the filter.
- Completely fill the filter with ground coffee, but do not pack it down.
- Make sure the filter and rubber gasket are in place. Screw the two chambers tightly together.
- Place the moka pot on the stove. Warning: keep the heat low.
- Remove pot from heat just when coffee starts to gurgle, before it starts to rise and bubble; you will be sure to extract only the best parts of the coffee.
- Mix the coffee with a spoon before pouring into cups.
- Rinse the coffee maker with hot water and let dry thoroughly before screwing chambers back together.

Variation	Color	Coffee Flavor	Aroma
French press			
Drip coffee			
Italian moka pot			

Experiment 2: Hot Cocoa

Test and evaluate different hot cocoa.

Method 1: Homemade Hot Cocoa

- 1/2 cup sugar
- 1/4 cup cocoa powder
- 1/4 cup water
- pinch of salt
- 4 cups milk (dairy or non-dairy)
- 1/2 teaspoon vanilla extract

Combine the sugar, cocoa, water, and salt in a 2-quart saucepan. Bring to a boil over medium heat; cook for 2–3 minutes. Add the milk. Reduce heat to medium low and simmer until the mixture is heated through, about 10 minutes. Add the vanilla. Serve warm.

Method 2: Commercial Hot Cocoa

- 2 packets of hot cocoa mix
- Hot water

Make hot cocoa according to package directions.

Variation	Color	Flavor	Aroma
Homemade			
Commercial			

RECIPES

Iced Coffee

Yield: 2 1/4 cups

- 2 cups strong, freshly brewed coffee at room temperature
- 1/4 cup half-n-half or whole milk
- 1 tablespoon sugar (optional)
- ice

Combine the coffee, half-n-half, and sugar in a pitcher. Fill two glasses with ice. Pour mixture over the ice. Serve.

Cold Brew Coffee

Yield: 1 1/2 cups

- 1/3 cup medium coarse ground coffee
- 1 1/2 cups cold water
- milk or half-n-half (optional)

In a jar, stir together coffee and water. Cover and let rest at room temperature overnight or 12 hours

Strain twice through a coffee filter, a fine-mesh sieve, or a sieve lined with cheesecloth. In a tall glass filled with ice, mix equal parts coffee concentrate and water, or to taste. If desired, add milk.

Iced Tea (Unsweetened)
Yield: 8 cups

- 8 cups water
- 6 regular-size tea bags
- ice

In a small saucepan, bring 2 1/4 cups water to a gentle boil. Add the tea bags, remove the saucepan from the heat, and cover. Steep for 15 minutes.

Remove the tea bags without squeezing them (which would add bitterness) and pour the steeped tea into a 2-1/2-quart heatproof container (like a large Pyrex liquid measure). Add the remaining 6 cups cold water and mix. Let cool at room temperature and then refrigerate until cold. Serve over ice.

Spiced Iced Tea
Yield: 5 cups

- 4 cups water
- 4 black tea bags[i]
- 3/4 cup sugar
- 2 anise stars or 1 teaspoon anise seed
- 1/2 teaspoon ground cardamom
- 2 whole cloves (or use 1/4 teaspoon ground cloves)
- ice
- 1 cup dairy or non-dairy milk of choice: whole milk, half and half, almond milk, coconut milk, soy milk

In a medium pot, bring water to boil. Add the tea bags, sugar, start anise, cardamom, and cloves. Stir until all the sugar dissolves. Gently boil tea for 4–5 minutes. Remove from heat.

Allow tea to steep for at least 30 minutes at room temperature, allowing it too cool. Remove the tea bags and strain off star anise (or anise seed) and whole cloves, if using.

Fill glasses with ice and pour the tea over the ice, leaving space at the top for the milk. Serve cold.

---

i   For stronger tea, add 1–2 more tea bags.

Strawberry Lemonade
Yield: 4–5 cups

- 1 10-ounce bag frozen strawberries or 1 pint fresh strawberries, cut in half
- 3/4 cup sugar
- 1/4 cup honey
- 3 cups water
- 1 cup fresh lemon juice
- ice

In a saucepan set over medium heat, cook the strawberries until soft and mushy. Mash the strawberries and strain well, reserving the liquid. Pour the strawberry syrup into a small sauce pan and add the sugar. Cook over medium low to dissolve the sugar. Add the honey and remove from the heat. Let the mixture cool. The strawberry syrup can be made up to two days ahead of time.

Combine the strawberry syrup, water, and lemon juice. Serve over ice.

Hot Apple Cider (Wassail)
Yield: 1/2 gallon

- 1/2 gallon (2 quarts) apple cider
- 1/3 cup sugar
- 1 teaspoon whole cloves
- 1 teaspoon whole allspice
- 1 cinnamon stick
- 1 orange, cut into quarters

Heat the cider and spices in a saucepan set over medium heat. Bring to a simmer and cover with a lid. Reduce heat to low and cook for 20 minutes. Strain the liquid and add the oranges to the cider. Serve warm.

Ginger Soda
Yield: 1/2 liter

- 1 cup sugar
- 1/2 cup water
- 2 tablespoons honey
- 1/4 cup finely grated fresh ginger
- 2 tablespoons fresh lemon juice
- 1/2 liter club soda

Bring the sugar, water, and honey to a boil over medium high heat. Stir until the sugar is dissolved. Add the ginger. Remove from heat. Steep for 1 hour. Strain the liquid. Stir in the lemon juice. Chill syrup until ready to serve. To serve, combine with the club soda and serve over ice.

Ginger Ale

Yield: 2 liters

- 1 1/2 cups sugar
- 3 tablespoons honey
- 7 1/2 cups filtered water
- 1/2 cup finely grated fresh ginger
- 1/8 teaspoon instant dry yeast (bakers or brewer's yeast)
- 2 tablespoons fresh lemon juice
- 1 cleaned and emptied 2-liter plastic bottle

Bring the sugar, honey, and 1/2 cup water to a boil over medium high heat. Stir until the sugar is dissolved. Add the ginger. Remove from heat. Steep for 1 hour. Strain the liquid. Stir in the lemon juice. Let mixture cool to room temperature.

Using a funnel, pour the syrup into the 2-liter bottle and add the yeast. Pour in the remaining 7 cups lukewarm water. Place the cap on the bottle and gently shake to combine the ingredients. Leave bottle at room temperature for 48 hours. Burp the bottle 1–2 times to release some of the pressure.

Once you have achieved proper carbonation, refrigerate until ready to serve. Store for up to two weeks under refrigeration, burping once per day to release some pressure.

Mayan Hot Chocolate

Yield: 4 cups

- 1/2 cup raw cacao powder
- 1 teaspoon ground cinnamon
- 1/2 teaspoon ground nutmeg
- 1/2 teaspoon ground chili pepper
- 4 cups milk (dairy or non-dairy)
- 1/4 to 1/2 cup honey

Stir together cacao and spices in a small bowl. Add 1/4 cup milk to make a paste.

In a saucepan, heat remaining milk slowly over medium heat, making sure to remove just before boiling. Slowly add the paste to the saucepan and simmer until slightly thickened. Add honey to taste. Serve.

Mexican Hot Chocolate

Yield: 3–4 cups

- 3 cups whole milk
- 6 ounces bittersweet chocolate, chopped
- 2–3 tablespoons sugar
- 1/4 teaspoon ground cinnamon
- 1/2 teaspoon vanilla extract
- pinch salt
- pinch cayenne pepper

Heat the milk in a saucepan set over medium heat. Heat milk until the small bubbles form around the side of the pan. Add the chocolate and whisk until the chocolate is melted. Remove from heat and add the sugar, spices, and vanilla. Serve warm with sweetened whipped cream.

Pomegranate Ginger Ale

Yield: 6–7 cups

- 3 cups pomegranate juice
- 3 cups ginger ale
- 1/4 cup fresh lime juice
- ice

Stir together the pomegranate juice, ginger ale, and lime juice. Pour over ice. Serve.

Chai

Yield: 6 cups

- 2 teaspoons ground cardamom
- 1 teaspoon whole fennel seeds
- 7 whole cloves
- 1 cinnamon stick
- 4 cups water
- 1-inch piece fresh ginger, peeled and chopped
- 2 cups milk (dairy or non-dairy)
- 2/3 cup sugar
- 8 black tea bags

Add the fennel, cardamom, cloves, and cinnamon to a 4-quart saucepan. Place over medium heat. Cook until the spices are lightly toasted and fragrant, about 2 minutes. Cool slightly. Grind the spices in a spice grinder.

Return the spices to the pan. Add the water and ginger. Bring to a boil. Stir in the milk, sugar, and tea bags. Remove from heat and steep for 6 minutes. Strain into mugs or glasses. Serve hot.

Unit 15 Questions

1. In experiment 1, note the differences between coffee. Which one had the most intense flavor? Why is this?
2. In experiment 2, note the differences between the hot cocoas. Which one had the most intense flavor? Which one was sweetest?
3. When making French press coffee, the instructions say to use coarsely ground coffee. Why is this?
4. Describe the differences between the following coffee drinks: espresso, cappuccino, café au lait, café mocha, and Americano.

NOTES

1. Chris Prentice, "Americans are drinking a daily cup of coffee at the highest level in six years: survey," accessed May 14, 2019, https://www.reuters.com/article/us-coffee-conference-survey/americans-are-drinking-a-daily-cup-of-coffee-at-the-highest-level-in-six-years-survey-idUSKCN1GT0KU.

2. "What is the demand for coffee on the European market?" CBI Ministry of Foreign Affairs, accessed May 14, 2019, https://www.cbi.eu/market-information/coffee/trade-statistics.

3. "The History of Coffee," National Coffee Association, accessed May 14, 2019, http://www.ncausa.org/about-coffee/history-of-coffee.

4. "A History of Tea," Peet's Coffee, accessed May 14, 2019, https://www.peets.com/learn/history-of-tea.

5. "Iced Tea History—Sweet Tea History," What's Cooking America, accessed May 14. 2019, https://whatscookingamerica.net/History/IcedTeaHistory.htm.

6. "The History of the Tea Bag," UK Tea and Infusions Association, accessed May 14, 2019, https://www.tea.co.uk/the-history-of-the-tea-bag.

7. "How to Brew the Perfect Cup of Tea," Twinings USA, Accessed May 14, 2019, https://www.twiningsusa.com/our-expertise/preparing-our-teas/brewing-the-perfect-cup.

8. Harold McGee, *On Food and Cooking: The Science and Lore of the Kitchen* (New York: Scribner, 2004), 722–39.

9. Harold McGee, *On Food and Cooking*, 739–53.

BIBLIOGRAPHY

CBI Ministry of Foreign Affairs. "What is the demand for coffee on the European market?" Accessed May 14, 2019. https://www.cbi.eu/market-information/coffee/trade-statistics.

McGee, Harold. *On Food and Cooking: The Science and Lore of the Kitchen*. New York: Scribner, 2004.

National Coffee Association. "The History of Coffee." Accessed May 14, 2019. http://www.ncausa.org/about-coffee/history-of-coffee.

Peet's Coffee. "A History of Tea." Accessed May 14, 2019. https://www.peets.com/learn/history-of-tea.

Prentice, Chris. "Americans are drinking a daily cup of coffee at the highest level in six years: survey," https://www.reuters.com/article/us-coffee-conference-survey/americans-are-drinking-a-daily-cup-of-coffee-at-the-highest-level-in-six-years-survey-idUSKCN1GT0KU (accessed 5/14/19).

Twinings USA. "How to Brew the Perfect Cup of Tea." Accessed May 14, 2019. https://www.twiningsusa.com/our-expertise/preparing-our-teas/brewing-the-perfect-cup.

What's Cooking America. "Iced Tea History — Sweet Tea History." Accessed May 14, 2019. https://whatscookingamerica.net/History/IcedTeaHistory.htm.

UK Tea and Infusions Association. "The History of the Tea Bag." Accessed May 14, 2019. https://www.tea.co.uk/the-history-of-the-tea-bag.

Fermentation

OBJECTIVES

■ Describe the fermentation process
■ Explain what cultures are and role in fermentation
■ Discuss the nutritional benefits of fermentation
■ Describe the difference between fermentation and pickling
■ Use basic cooking techniques to prepare recipes

FERMENTATION[1]

Humans have been fermenting food for thousands of years as one of the original ways of preserving food. In cold climates, people fermented foods during warmer months for consumption during the winter months. Conversely, people living in warmer climates are able to ferment foods at a faster rate because of the warmer temperatures. Due to the ideal conditions for fermentation, cultures around the equator have many fermented foods in their diets. For instance, the Sudan has roughly eighty fermented foods.

In the most basic sense, fermentation is the transformative action of micro-organisms like bacteria. Nearly every cuisine and culture around the world has some fermented foods. Some of the more popular fermented foods found today include kimchi (Korea), sauerkraut (Germany), miso (Japan), natto (Japan), tempeh (Indonesia), kombucha, olives (Mediterranean), kefir, yogurt, wine, and sourdough bread. However, this list is merely a sampling of the enormous variety of fermented foods found on the market or around the world.

Fermentation requires harnessing bacteria to transform a food product into something else. The byproducts of fermentation are alcohol and acidification.

In acidification, two common acids are produced: lactic acid and acetic acid. Lactic acid is the most common byproduct of fermentation and is the base for many fermented products from sauerkraut to kefir.

Some fermented products require the use of a culture. A culture is a starter set of bacteria used to promote fermentation in foods. For instance, when you make yogurt, a yogurt starter with the bacteria is added to warm milk. The starter contains the particular bacteria needed for fermentation and the warm environment causes the bacteria to multiply and begin ferment the milk.

Nutritional Benefits

As more research is published, fermented foods are currently being touted for their health benefits and improving the status of our gut microflora. Three main nutritional benefits include

Pre-digestion. During fermentation, certain compounds in food are broken down from the digestive action of the bacteria or fungi. For instance, lactic acid bacteria (LAB) convert lactose into lactic acid in milk.

Nutritional Enhancement. Fermentation makes some minerals easier to absorb (i.e., increases bioavailability); increases levels of B-vitamins such as thiamine, riboflavin, and niacin; and increases the availability of essential amino acids such as lysine in grains.

Detoxification. Fermentation also transforms toxic compounds into nutrients. For instance, toxic compounds like anti-nutrients become nutrients. An example of this are phytates that bind minerals. Found in some vegetables, phytates are anti-nutrients. During fermentation, an enzyme phytase releases minerals from the phytate bind, making them available for absorption.

Food Safety Issues

Heeding proper food safety rules is paramount to cooking and making sure food is safe for consumption. However, when it comes to fermenting foods, some contaminating bacteria like salmonella, E.coli, listeria, and Clostridium botulinum have a difficult time surviving highly acidic environments.

Hard cheese, a type of fermented food, is made by inoculating raw milk with certain strands of bacteria. This allows the cheese to cure or age for at least sixty days, giving the good bacteria time to not only create an acidic environment but also create an environment where the bad bacteria (i.e., the foodborne illness-causing bacteria) has to compete for food and survival. However, in soft cheeses where the aging process is less than sixty days, manufacturers should use pasteurized milk to prevent the spread of foodborne illness like listeria.

Improperly Canned Foods

Those with low acidity that were not canned properly have been the greatest source of botulism, not fermented foods like pickles or sauerkraut. When canning low acidic foods like green beans, the jars of beans need to be pressure-cooked where the water temperature meets or exceeds 240°F in order to destroy the botulism toxin.

Ingredients

Even though there are many types of ingredients used to ferment foods, there are two notable ingredients that require special attention: salt and water.

Salt plays a big role in fermentation by affecting the water activity of the foods. It is important to choose an unrefined sea salt instead of iodized salt. Iodine has antimicrobial activity and may interfere with the fermentation process. Kosher and pickling salt can also be used.

Choose water that is filtered and not heavily chlorinated. Chlorine kills off bacteria (good and bad), and water that is heavily chlorinated will greatly affect the fermentation process.

Pickling versus Fermentation

Pickling is not the same as fermentation. Pickling is a method of preserving foods in an acidic solution like vinegar. Vinegar, however, is a fermented byproduct of the wine making process.

RECIPES

Kimchi (Matkimchi)
Recipe from Mijung Kim

Yield: 1–2 quarts

Cabbage

- 2 pounds napa cabbage, chopped
- 1 cup coarse salt

Porridge

- 1 1/2 tablespoons glutinous rice flour (sweet rice flour)
- 3/4 cup water

Seasonings

- 1/2 onion
- 6–7 cloves garlic
- 1-inch fresh ginger
- 1 tablespoon sugar
- 1/4 cup water
- 1–2 tablespoons anchovy sauce
- 1 tablespoon shrimp sauce (optional)
- 1/4 of an apple
- 1/4 cup Asian pear

Vegetables

- 3/4 cup Korean red chili flakes
- 4 ounces green onions, cut into bite-sized pieces
- 1/2 onion, chopped
- 1–2 ounces carrots, chopped
- 1–2 ounces daikon radish, chopped

Pickle the cabbage: Sprinkle the cabbage with salt. Massage cabbage to coat well with the salt. Toss cabbage in the brine every 20 minutes. Pickle the cabbage for 1–2 hours. Rinse and drain the cabbage 3 times. Drain well after the 3rd rinsing.

Make sticky rice porridge by combining the flour and water in a small saucepan. Cook over medium heat until thickened. Set aside to cool.

Place the seasoning ingredients in a blender. Puree.

Combine the porridge, red pepper powder flakes, and pureed seasonings in a large bowl. Add the cabbage and other vegetables. Toss to coat well.

Pack into a mason jar. Refrigerate. The longer it refrigerates, the more it will ferment and change flavor.

Sauerkraut
Yield: 1 quart

- 2- to 3-pound head green cabbage, shredded
- 1 1/2 tablespoons kosher salt
- 2 teaspoons caraway seeds (optional)

Clean and sanitize a mason jar or fermentation crock.

In a medium bowl, combine the cabbage and salt. Massage the salt into the leaves of the cabbage, until it starts to release some moisture, about 5–10 minutes. Add the caraway seeds if using.

Pack the cabbage mixture into a mason jar or crock. Weigh down the top of the cabbage with either a clean plate, bowl, or smaller mason jar (filled with water). Leave the jar/crock in a warm spot, about 70°F. After 24 hours, check to see if the cabbage has produced enough moisture to keep the leaves submerged. If it has not, create a brine of 1 teaspoon salt and 1 cup water, and pour enough over the cabbage to keep it submerged.

Ferment the sauerkraut for 3–10 days. Taste it at 3 days to see if the taste and texture is satisfactory. The warmer the area (around 75°F), the quicker the fermentation, and the cooler the area (60–65°F), the slower the fermentation process.

If mold starts growing on top of the cabbage, remove it immediately. Do not eat any pieces with mold. Skim off any scum that accumulates on the surface.

After the sauerkraut is fermented, remove the weight and transfer to a clean jar. Keep refrigerated for up to 2–3 months.

Kombucha SCOBY
Yield: 1 SCOBY

- 7 cups water
- 1/2 cup white granulated sugar (see Recipe Notes)
- 4 bags black tea
- 1 cup unflavored, unpasteurized, store-bought kombucha

First, make the sweet tea. Bring 4 cups of water to a boil. Turn off the heat and add the sugar; stir to dissolve. Add remaining water and tea; steep until the tea cools to room temperature. Remove and discard the tea.

Combine the sweet tea and kombucha in a glass jar. If you see a blobby "baby SCOBY" in the bottom of your jar of commercial kombucha, make sure this gets transferred. Stir to combine.

Cover the mouth of the jar with coffee filters or paper towels and secure with a rubber band. Place the jar somewhere at average room temperature (70°F), out of direct sunlight, where it can sit undisturbed. This step takes 1–4 weeks.

For the first few days, nothing will happen. Then you will start to see groups of tiny bubbles starting to collect on the surface.

After a few more days, the groups of bubbles will start to connect and form a thin, transparent, jelly-like film across the surface of the tea. You will also see bubbles forming around the edges of the film—a sign of carbon dioxide.

As the SCOBY sits, the film will thicken into a solid, opaque layer. When the SCOBY is about 1/4-inch thick, it is ready to be used to make kombucha tea: Depending on the temperature and conditions in your kitchen, this might take anywhere from 1 to 4 weeks.

The finished SCOBY might look a little rough or weird, which is normal. It will smooth out after a few batches of kombucha.

You can use the liquid used to grow the SCOBY to start your first batch of kombucha.

Kombucha
Yield: 1 gallon

- 3 1/2 quarts water
- 1 cup sugar OR 3/4 cup honey or maple syrup
- 8 bags black tea
- 2 cups starter tea (store-bought: unpasteurized, neutral flavor)
- 1 SCOBY
- stock pot
- 1 gallon glass jar
- cheesecloth or paper towels
- rubber band
- 6 16-oz glass bottles
- small funnel

Bring the water to a boil. Remove from heat and stir in the sugar or maple syrup. Add the tea bags and steep until the water has cooled. To cool this quicker, place in an ice bath and stir until cooled.

Remove the tea bags and add the starter tea. Transfer to the jar and add the SCOBY. Cover with the cheesecloth (or paper towels) and secure with the rubber band. Place in a spot out of direct sunlight at room temperature (70°F). The SCOBY may float at the bottom (this is normal) and you may see fermentation bubbles (again, this is normal). After 7 days, check the kombucha for flavor. It should a balance of sweetness and tartness—your preference. For more tartness, leave for another day or two.

Remove the SCOBY and 2 cups starter tea (for the next batch). Pour the kombucha into the glass bottles. Add fruit, juice, or herbs to flavor it (pureed frozen fruit that has been strained is an excellent choice for flavoring the kombucha). Leave about 1/2-inch headroom at the top of the bottle. Place the bottles at room temperature to allow for carbonation to occur, about 1–3 days. Refrigerate the bottles to stop fermentation. Kombucha will keep for 1 month in the refrigerator.

Teriyaki Tempeh
Serves 2–3

- 1 (8-ounce) package tempeh
- 1 tablespoon oil
- 1/4 cup honey
- 1/4 cup soy sauce
- 1/4 cup rice vinegar
- 1/2 teaspoon crushed red chili flakes
- 2 tablespoons sesame oil
- 3 cloves garlic, minced
- 3/4-inch piece of ginger, minced

Cut up the tempeh into thin strips, then cut in half. Heat up the oil in a large pan and toss in the tempeh. Cook about ten minutes, flipping each slice after a few minutes when the first side is browned. Stir together the sauce ingredients and pour over the tempeh. Continue cooking for about 5 minutes, until the sauce is thickened. Serve with cooked rice.

Chicken Salad with Kimchi
Makes about 4 cups

- 2 cups shredded cooked chicken
- 1/2 cup drained kimchi, chopped
- 1/4 cup diced celery
- 1/4 cup diced apple or pear
- 1/4 cup sliced scallions
- 2 tablespoons sesame seeds
- 1 1/2 tablespoons kimchi liquid
- 1 1/2 tablespoons rice vinegar
- 1 1/2 tablespoons canola or safflower oil
- 1 teaspoon fresh ginger, minced
- 1 teaspoon sesame oil
- salt and pepper, to taste

Toss together the chicken, kimchi, celery, apple, scallions, and sesame seeds. In a small bowl, whisk together the kimchi liquid, vinegar, oil, ginger, sesame oil, salt, and pepper. Add dressing to the chicken mixture. Toss to combine well. Refrigerate until ready to serve.

Mushroom Burgers with Kimchi Mayo and Bulgogi Sauce
Makes 4 burgers

Burgers

- 2 cups mushrooms (crimini, shiitake, or oyster; or a combination of mushrooms), quartered
- 2 large eggs, beaten
- 1/2 cup bread crumbs
- 1/2 cup finely chopped onion
- 1/4 cup flour
- 1/2 teaspoon salt
- 1/2 teaspoon pepper
- 1–2 tablespoons canola oil

Kimchi Mayo

- 1/2 cup mayonnaise
- 1 tablespoon kimchi brine
- 1/4 cup kimchi, drained and finely chopped
- 1 teaspoon sugar
- 2 teaspoons sesame oil
- 1 clove garlic, minced
- 2 scallions, finely chopped

Bulgogi Sauce

- 1/2 cup soy sauce
- 1 1/2 tablespoons red pepper paste
- 3 large cloves garlic, minced
- 1 tablespoon fresh ginger, minced
- 1 tablespoon rice wine vinegar
- 1/4 cup brown sugar
- 2 teaspoons sesame oil

Burger Toppings

- shredded cabbage
- thinly sliced onion
- buns, toasted

Make the Bulgogi sauce: In a small saucepan, mix the soy sauce, chili paste, garlic, ginger, vinegar, and brown sugar. Bring a boil over medium high heat. Cook for 5–7 minutes or until the mixture thickens slightly. Add the sesame oil. Use immediately.

Make the burgers: Finely chop the mushrooms in a food processor. Pour mushrooms into a large bowl. Add eggs, bread crumbs, onion, flour, salt, and pepper. Form into patties. Heat the oil in a large non-stick sauté pan. Cook the patties on both sides, about 3–4 minutes per side.

Make the mayo: Stir together the ingredients for the mayo. Refrigerate until ready to use.

Assemble the burgers: Place the burgers on the buns. Top with the kimchi mayo, bulgogi sauce, shredded cabbage, and onion. Serve.

Sauerkraut Pierogies
Yield: 20 pierogies

Sauerkraut Filling

- 3 cups sauerkraut
- 1 medium onion, finely chopped
- 4 tablespoons butter
- 2 tablespoons sour cream
- Salt and pepper, to taste

Pierogie Dough

- 2 1/2 cups flour
- 1 teaspoon salt
- 1 large egg
- 2 teaspoons oil
- 3/4 cup warm water

Make the filling: Rinse the sauerkraut in water, squeeze dry, and chop finely. Heat 1 tablespoon butter in a sauté pan set over medium heat. Add the onion; sauté for 4–5 minutes. Add the sauerkraut, cream, salt, and pepper. Cook over low heat for 10–15 minutes. Cool completely. Chill until ready to use.

Make the pierogies: Mix the flour and salt in a large bowl. Add the egg, oil, and water. Mix until a soft dough forms. Knead on a lightly floured surface until the dough is smooth. Divide into 2 parts. Cover and let stand at room temperature for 10 minutes.

Roll the dough on a lightly floured surface to about 1/8-inch thin. Cut into rounds. Place a spoonful of filling in the center of the round. Fold the dough over the filling to create a half circle. Pinch the edges together to create a seal.

Bring a pot of water to a boil. Add about 2 teaspoons salt to the water. Boil the pierogies in batches for 3–4 minutes. Remove and drain thoroughly. Place in a dish and toss with a melted butter or oil to prevent from sticking together.

At this point, you can serve the pierogies or you can go one step further and pan fry them in butter or oil until golden brown on each side.

Kimchi Noodle Bowl
Serves 4

- 8–10 ounce soba, udon, or rice noodles
- 2 tablespoons canola or safflower oil
- 2 tablespoons kimchi juice
- 1 tablespoon sambal
- 1 tablespoon low sodium soy sauce
- 1 tablespoon honey
- 1 tablespoon sugar
- 1 tablespoon rice wine vinegar
- 1 tablespoon sesame oil
- 1 cup kimchi sliced or chopped
- 2 large eggs
- 1 cup cucumber, julienned
- 1–2 cups spinach

Cook the noodles in boiling water according to package directions. Drain and rinse in cold water to stop the cooking. Place the noodles in a large bowl. Toss with 1 tablespoon oil to prevent sticking. Set aside.

In a small bowl, combine the kimchi juice, sambal, soy sauce, honey, sugar, vinegar, and sesame oil. Add the kimchi and set aside.

Pour the kimchi sauce over the noodles and toss to mix well.

In a non-stick skillet set over medium heat, add 1 tablespoon oil. Fry the eggs to desired doneness.

To serve, place noodles in serving bowls. Garnish with cucumber, spinach, and fried egg.

Preserved Lemons
Makes 1–2 jars

Preserving time 3–4 weeks

- 9 whole lemons, washed well, quartered
- kosher salt
- 1 teaspoon black peppercorns

Pour a layer of salt on the bottom of the jar. Fit as many lemons as you can in the jar, sprinkling each layer with salt.

Press the lemons down to release their juices. Add peppercorns to the jar.

Close the jar tightly with a lid. Keep at room temperature, shaking the jar every day for 3–4 weeks or until the rinds are tender to the bite. Then place in the refrigerator.

Uses: Remove a piece of lemon and rinse it. (You can add more freshly salted lemons to the brine as you use them). Mince the rind and add to stews or dishes at the end of cooking. The pulp can be added to stews during simmering process.

Chicken and Broccoli with Preserved Lemon Sauce
Serves 4

Chicken and Broccoli

- 4 boneless, skinless chicken breasts
- 3 tablespoons canola oil
- 1 teaspoon garam masala
- 1 teaspoon salt
- 1 teaspoon pepper
- 1 head broccoli, cut into florets
- 1/2 teaspoon crushed red pepper flakes

Lemon Sauce

- 1 cup plain greek yogurt
- 1/4 cup mayonnaise
- 3 cloves garlic, minced
- 1 tablespoon minced preserved lemon rind
- 2 teaspoons fresh lemon juice
- salt and pepper, to taste

Chicken and Broccoli

Preheat oven to 425°F.

Line a sheet pan with foil. Set aside.

In a medium bowl, rub the chicken with 1 tablespoon oil, garam masala, and 1/2 teaspoon salt, and 1/2 teaspoon pepper. Line chicken around the outside of the pan, leaving space in the middle for the broccoli.

In a medium bowl, toss the broccoli florets with the oil and crushed red pepper and season with salt and black pepper. Spread the broccoli in the center of the pan, surrounded by the chicken.

Bake until the internal temperature of the chicken reaches 165°F and the broccoli is tender, about 20–25 minutes.

Sauce

Meanwhile, in a small bowl, mix the yogurt, mayonnaise, garlic, minced lemon rind and lemon juice and season with salt and black pepper.

Serve the chicken and broccoli with the yogurt.

Thousand Island Dressing

Yield: 2 cups

- 1 1/2 cups prepared or homemade mayonnaise
- 1/2 cup ketchup
- 1 teaspoon apple cider vinegar
- 1 1/2 tablespoons finely minced or grated onion
- 3 to 4 tablespoons sweet pickle relish
- 1 teaspoon salt
- 1/2 teaspoon chili powder or freshly ground black pepper
- 1 teaspoon minced pimientos or roasted red pepper, optional
- 1 teaspoon minced fresh chives, optional
- tabasco sauce, to taste

Mix the dressing: In a large mixing bowl, combine the mayonnaise, ketchup, cider vinegar, onion, relish, salt, and chili powder or pepper and mix until well-combined.

Add the egg: Press the egg through a fine-mesh sieve into the bowl and mix well.

Customize the dressing: If you wish, add any combination of optional ingredients (pimientos, chives, and/or hot sauce) and mix well.

Serve: This dressing can be served immediately but tastes even better if refrigerated in a covered container for 12 to 24 hours. It will keep for about 4 days.

Reuben Sandwich
Yield: 1 sandwich

- 2 tablespoons unsalted butter, softened
- 2 slices rye bread
- 1/4 cup Thousand Island Dressing
- 4 slices corned beef
- 3 tablespoons sauerkraut, drained
- 2 slices Swiss cheese

Butter one side of each slice of rye bread and place one slice of the bread buttered side down on a flat surface.

Add ingredients in the following order: 2 tbsp of Thousand Island Dressing, corned beef, sauerkraut (with optional caraway seeds added if desired), Gold Label Swiss cheese, and an additional 2 tbsp of Thousand Island Dressing. Crown the sandwich with the remaining slice of rye, buttered side up.

Preheat sauté pan over medium-high heat, place sandwich in pan, and heat sandwich approximately 3 minutes on each side until the bread is golden brown and the cheese is melted.

Sourdough Chocolate Mocha Cake
Adapted from King Arthur Flour

Yield: 1 9 × 13-inch cake

Cake

- 1 cup sourdough starter
- 1 cup whole milk
- 2 cups AP flour
- 1 1/2 cups sugar
- 1 cup canola or safflower oil
- 2 teaspoons vanilla
- 1 1/2 teaspoons baking soda
- 1 teaspoon salt
- 3/4 cup cocoa powder
- 1 teaspoon espresso powder
- 2 large eggs

Icing

- 1 1/2 tablespoons espresso powder
- 1 tablespoon hot water
- 6 cups powdered sugar
- 3/4 cup butter, melted
- 1/2 cup buttermilk

Drizzle

- 1/2 cup chocolate chips
- 1 tablespoon milk
- 1 tablespoon corn syrup

Combine the starter, milk, and flour in a large mixing bowl. Cover and let rest at room temperature for 2 to 3 hours. It will not necessarily bubble, but it may have expanded a bit.

Preheat the oven to 350°F. Lightly grease a 9 × 13-inch pan.

In a separate bowl, beat together the sugar, oil, vanilla, salt, baking soda, cocoa. and espresso powder. The mixture will be grainy.

Add the eggs one at a time, beating well after each addition. Gently combine the chocolate mixture with the starter-flour-milk mixture, stirring till smooth. This will be a gloppy process at first, but the batter will smooth out as you continue to beat gently.

Pour the batter into the prepared pan. Bake the cake for 30 to 40 minutes, until it springs back when lightly pressed in the center, and a cake tester inserted into the center comes out clean. Remove the cake from the oven and set it on a rack to cool while you make the icing.

Dissolve the espresso powder in hot water. Combine the espresso, butter, and buttermilk in a saucepan. Bring to a boil. Sift the confectioners' sugar into a large mixing bowl.

Immediately pour the simmering liquid over the confectioners' sugar in the bowl and beat until smooth.

Pour the warm frosting over the cake. If you wait too long and the frosting stiffens up, spread it over the cake.

Combine the chocolate chips, milk, and corn syrup in a microwave-safe cup. Microwave until the chips soften, then stir until smooth.

Drizzle/drip the chocolate over the icing. You can do this while the icing is still warm or wait until it has cooled.

Miso and Wild Rice Soup
Serves 4

Soup

- 1 cup dry wild rice
- 2 cups water
- 2 tablespoons canola oil
- 1 cup finely chopped leeks
- 6 ounces fresh shiitake mushrooms, stems removed and caps sliced
- 2 teaspoons minced fresh ginger
- 2 cloves garlic, minced
- 1/4 cup mirin
- 1 teaspoon sesame oil
- 2 tablespoons soy sauce
- 2 cups chopped baby bok choy
- 1/2 cup red miso
- 1 cup firm tofu, cut into cubes
- 1/2 cup scallions, chopped

Broth

- 8 cups water
- 4 scallions, ends trimmed off
- 1/2 cup dried shiitake mushrooms
- 1 1-inch chunk of fresh ginger, sliced
- 2 cloves garlic, smashed
- 1 teaspoon salt

Combine the wild rice and water in small saucepan set over medium high heat. Bring to a boil. Cover and reduce heat to simmer. Cook until the rice opens up and becomes soft, about 45–50 minutes. Drain off excess liquid.

Meanwhile, make the broth by combining the water, scallions, dried shiitake mushrooms, ginger, garlic, and salt. Bring to a boil. Reduce heat to low. Simmer for 20–25 minutes. Strain and set aside.

Heat the oil in a 4-quart saucepot set over medium heat. Add the leeks and shiitake mushrooms. Sauté for 5 minutes or until softened. Add the ginger, garlic, mirin, sesame oil, and soy sauce. Cook for 1–2 minutes. Pour in reserved broth. Cook for 5 minutes.

Add the bok choy and cooked wild rice. Stir in the miso and tofu. Simmer for 5–10 minutes to allow the flavors to develop.

Garnish with chopped scallions.

Tempeh Tacos
Serves 2–3

- 1 (8-ounce) package tempeh
- 1 cup diced tomatoes (canned or fresh)
- 1 chipotle pepper in adobo sauce, chopped
- 2 cloves garlic, minced
- 1 tablespoon fresh lime juice
- 2–3 teaspoons chili powder
- 3 teaspoons cumin
- 1/4 cup soy sauce
- 1/2 red onion, diced
- 1/2 red or green bell pepper, diced
- 1–2 tablespoons canola or safflower oil
- tortillas, toppings for tacos

Crumble the tempeh in a large bowl. Mix in the tomatoes, chipotle, garlic, lime juice, chili powder, cumin, and soy sauce. Toss to mix well. Add the onion and bell pepper.

Heat the oil in a sauté pan set over medium heat. Add the tempeh mixture. Cook, stirring occasionally until the vegetables are soft about 10 minutes.

Serve with tortillas and toppings.

Unit 16 Questions

1. Aside from cabbage, what other vegetables could be fermented?
2. How does air temperature affect fermentation? What is the ideal temperature for fermentation?
3. What is the composition of the average person's microflora in their digestive system? How does consuming fermented foods affect the gut microflora?
4. Do a search on current research (within the last five years) regarding gut microflora, fermented foods, and health/nutrition. What types of research are currently being done? Briefly describe a couple studies and their results.
5. How was your experience with fermentation? Did you experience any issues? If so, what were they?
6. Describe the overall flavors of the food presented during lab. How does fermentation affect the flavor of foods?

NOTE
1. Sandor Ellix Katz, *The Art of Fermentation*, (Vermont: Chelsea Green Publishing, 2012).

BIBLIOGRAPHY
Katz, Sandor Ellix. *The Art of Fermentation*. Vermont: Chelsea Green Publishing, 2012.

CPSIA information can be obtained
at www.ICGtesting.com
Printed in the USA
FSHW021050200121
77808FS

9 781516 598328